Aching

for

Beauty

Published with assistance from the

Margaret S. Harding Memorial Endowment

honoring the first director of the

University of Minnesota Press.

Aching

for

Beauty

FOOTBINDING IN CHINA

Wang Ping

University of Minnesota Press   Minneapolis / London

Frontispiece (on page viii). This lily slipper measures three inches, heel to toe. The heel is covered in green silk, and the upper part of the slipper is covered in pink and red silk. Gold couching is used for the embellished design. The rose fabric originally met at the back and was stitched together; later, the heel lift was installed to accommodate ankle thickness. Although this may have begun as an altar shoe, it was eventually worn, evidenced by wear on the sole. Courtesy of the Historic Costume Collection of the College of Tropical Agriculture and Human Resources (CTAHR), University of Hawaii at Manoa. Photograph by Linda B. Arthur, curator, CTAHR Historic Costume Collection.

Copyright 2000 by Wang Ping

Published by the University of Minnesota Press
111 Third Avenue South, Suite 290
Minneapolis, MN 55401-2520
http://www.upress.umn.edu

Library of Congress Cataloging-in-Publication Data

Wang, Ping, 1957–
    Aching for beauty : footbinding in China / Wang Ping.
        p.   cm.
    Includes bibliographical references and index.
    ISBN 0-8166-3605-2 (hc : alk. paper) — ISBN 0-8166-3606-0
(pbk. : alk. paper)
        1. Footbinding—China—History.   2. Women—China—Social conditions.
    3. Beauty, Personal—China—History.   4. Body image in women—China—
    History.   I. Title.
    GT498.F66 W36 2000
    391.4'1—dc21

                                                                00-009522

Printed in the United States of America on acid-free paper

The University of Minnesota is an equal-opportunity educator and employer.

11 10 09 08 07 06 05 04 03 02 01 00   10 9 8 7 6 5 4 3 2 1

To Ariel and Leonardo,
who accompanied me
throughout the journey

Contents

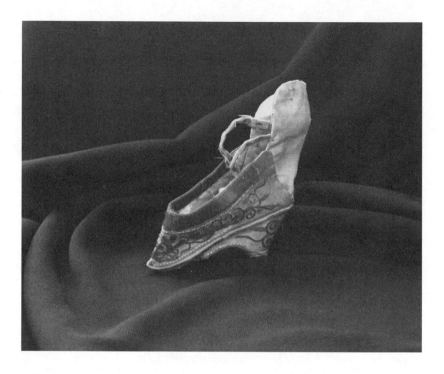

Preface

To be born woman is to know—
Although they do not speak of it at school—
Women must labor to be beautiful.
          —*W. B. Yeats*

Tell me the story
of all these things.
Beginning where you wish, tell even us.
      —*Theresa Hak Kyung Cha,* Dictee

AT THE AGE OF NINE she began to bind her feet on her own. She did not know the elaborate method of the traditional footbinding, which, briefly speaking, was to bend the toes completely under the sole to make a pointed front and to pull the whole front as close as possible to the heel—to arch the foot like a small hook about three inches long. She invented her own method of binding, wrapping her feet tightly with layers of elastic bands to prevent her feet from growing longer and wider. Though she did not bend her toes under her soles or break her bones, it still hurt. Her bandaged feet were on fire day and night. Each step felt as though she were walking on broken glass barefooted. But she bore the pain silently, and with much pride. She was determined to keep her feet from growing. She wanted her mother and sisters to stop mocking her. At the age of nine, her feet had already grown to size six, a pair of "steamboats," a sign, according to the theory of Chinese fortune telling, that she was born to be a maid or a peasant.

That was 1966, the year Mao Zedong launched the Cultural Revolution to fight against the remaining powers of feudalism, capitalism, and revisionism in China. And the practice of footbinding—the symbol of feudal oppression of women in the eyes of revolutionaries—had been eliminated for almost half a century. When I started binding my feet, I had never heard of or seen a real pair of bound feet—golden lotuses—except my paternal grandma's "liberated feet," which she had bound into a size as tiny as a child's, kept in bandages as an adult, then loosened in her forties when Mao took over China in 1949. Deformed and smelly, they symbolized anything but beauty and elegance. It is still a mystery how the urge and determination to bind my feet came to me. Is beauty innate or cultural? Is it socially imposed (since I was tired of being teased as a "peasant" for my big feet)? Why did I think that small feet looked better than naturally big feet and voluntarily suppressed them during a period when anything beautiful, natural or artificial, was considered dangerous and bad and, therefore, outlawed? If the concept of beauty is innate, then why did I choose to work on feet instead of other parts of my body, which were also targets for laughter: my small eyes; my dark, blotchy complexion; and my coarse hands. Whatever it was, my motivation was strong and clear: I would do anything at any cost to have a pair of feet as small and shameful as my mother's and sisters' so that I could be included in the class of the noble, civilized, and fortunate.

In 1986, I saw a pair of lotus shoes in my American friends' apartment in Brooklyn. The size and shape shocked me. I had always thought the "three-inch golden lotus" was merely a metaphor. But the red shoes I saw through the glass cover couldn't have been longer than my palm, and the front was big enough only for a toe. Its delicateness and elegance were beyond my imagination. I turned to my friends. They guessed what I was thinking and swore to me that these were not toys. They had bought the shoes in a market in Yunnan in 1983, and they witnessed a middle-aged woman with bound feet. In fact, her feet were so tiny, they said, she had to be carried on the back of her husband's bike. I gazed at the twin little hooks through the glass, thinking of my grandma's deformed feet, which I had once called "pig feet" behind her back when I was angry. She claimed she used to be known for her tiny feet, which were only three and a half inches long. How could anyone have possibly put her feet into those toy shoes? What did she have to do to her feet to make them so small and pointed? How did she walk? What pain did she have to go through? And for what?

I looked down at my own feet, which had been stunted at size six since I was nine, and recalled the constant burning pain during the six-month binding I had secretly inflicted on myself. The binding did stop the feet from growing for a while; but once the elastic band was lifted, the feet grew wide, leaving my two big toes pointing permanently upward. I held the tiny shoes in my hand and stared at the exquisite patterns of the embroidery. My palm burned with the pain and desire of my female ancestors for the past thousand years, the pain and desire that had been silenced, that had then been sewn stitch by stitch into the three-inch-long and less-than-one-inch-wide space.

Taboo has always been part of the history of footbinding. When the practice reached its peak as a national fashion and cultural fixation in late imperial China, lotus feet became the synonym for femininity, beauty, hierarchy, and eroticism. In other words, feet were the place of honor, identity, and means of livelihood for many women. They guarded their feet fervently, forbidding men other than their husbands or lovers to touch their feet or shoes. After it finally faded out through the national propaganda launched by Chinese intellectuals and Western missionary organizations, and through brutal force and punishments upon the female body, footbinding was rarely talked or written about because it became a symbol of national shame.

But it is high time to lift the taboo, to decipher the mystery of footbinding that had been for a millennium the emblem of femininity, its beauty and eroticism so tightly integrated with pain, violence, and death. And finally it is time to understand this female heritage that was transmitted only through codes of silence, a silence that was only a masquerade. Underneath and behind it was a roaring ocean current of female language and culture that integrated writing and binding with weaving, talking, and female bonding. This was the heritage of my female ancestors, which is now mine.

Although footbinding was unique to females of late imperial China, the concept and practice of enduring violence and pain, mutilation and self-mutilation in the name of beauty can be found in almost every culture and civilization. The study of footbinding, therefore, requires cross-cultural and interdisciplinary perspectives.[1] An examination of the practice in the context of history, literature, linguistics, and psychoanalysis is crucial to a comprehensive understanding of this cultural fetish. In *Aching for Beauty*, I employ poetry, novels, plays, essays, and oral accounts on and related to footbinding by male and female writers from the Ming and Qing dynasties (1368–1911) to the present.[2] I also employ Western linguistic, literary, and psychoanalytic theories as tools and metaphors to enter and examine the ancient Chinese texts. My goal is to build a bridge across the past and present, East and West, history and literature, theory and practice, imagination and reality.

Acknowledgments

MY GRATEFUL ACKNOWLEDGMENTS to Mick Taussig in whose class on taboo and transgression I initiated the research on footbinding; to Tim Reiss, who helped me develop this topic into a dissertation thesis in his methodology class, and whose support and insightful criticism helped me complete the strenuous final stage of the writing; to Jennifer Wicke, who guided me through the project with patience, generosity, insightful critiques, and constructive suggestions; to Paul S. Ropp, who loaned me his priceless materials on Shuangqing and Shi Zhenlin, including his own unpublished and published essays and books on the subject; to Kang-i Sun Chang for her encouragement and instructive comments; to the anonymous reader of my manuscript for her detailed suggestions and sincere critique; and to Joanna Waley-Cohen and Richard Schechner, who served on the dissertation committee.

I also want to thank those whose work paved the path and inspired me in my research and writing: Dorothy Ko, Kang-i Sun Chang, Paul S. Ropp, K. C. Chang, Fred C. Blake, Howard S. Levy, Du Fangqin, Grace Fong, Charlotte Furth, Susan Mann, Cathy Silber, Ann Waltner, Patricia Buckley Ebrey, Marjorie Garber, Pi-Ching Hsu, Ellen Widmer, Wu Hong, Wu Qingyun, and many others.

Special thanks to Lewis Warsh for reading and editing the first draft; to Adam Lerner for his generous help in every possible way; to Mary Jo Wright for reading and editing the first draft; to Ma Yuxin for proofreading the pinyin; to Sandy Lerner for proofreading the dissertation draft; to Zheng Peikan for loaning books to me; to Donna Brodie, director of the Writers' Room, who put a mattress under me when I was kneeling on the floor typing (eight months pregnant and too big to fit into a chair); to Fu Tianyi and Wu Jingshan, whose loving care of my sons allowed me to complete the dissertation with concentration and ease; and to many other individuals who have given me moral and concrete support.

Finally, I want to thank my editor, Jennifer Moore, for her excellent editing of and generous support for the final revision and completion of this project. Thanks also to Douglas Armato of the University of Minnesota Press for his quick response to the manuscript, as well as to others who worked on the production of the book.

PART I

Chinese Eroticism and Female Allure

Three-Inch Golden Lotuses: Achieving Beauty through Violence

The witch tells the Little Mermaid: "Your tail will part and shrink into what humans call nice legs but it will hurt just as if a sharp sword were passing through you. Every step you take will be like treading on a knife sharp enough to cause your blood to flow." When the Little Mermaid finally stands face to face with her beloved prince, her new feet, which she has traded with her lovely voice, bleed. The prince does not notice it, and she does not complain.
— Hans Christian Andersen, "The Little Mermaid"

A pair of tiny feet,
two jugs of tears.
— Chinese ditty

A PAIR OF PERFECTLY BOUND FEET must meet seven qualifications— small, slim, pointed, arched, fragrant, soft, and straight—in order to become a piece of art, an object of erotic desire. Such beauty is created, however, through sheer violence. For about two or three years, little girls go through the inferno of torture: the flesh of her feet, which are tightly bound with layers of bandages day and night, is slowly putrefied, her toes crushed under the soles, and the insteps arched to the degree where the toes and heels meet. Loving mothers suddenly turn into monsters that beat their sobbing girls with sticks or brooms, forcing them to hop around to speed up the rotting of flesh and make sure the bones are broken properly. When the feet are finally shrunk to the size of a baby's—three inches long, half an inch wide in the front—they are completely deformed. Naked, they look like the hoofs of an animal or female genitals. Adorned with shoes, they resemble male genitals, or vegetables like hot peppers and water chestnuts, or things like hooks, bows, writing brushes. The violent mutilation of the feet eliminates boundaries between human and beast, organic and inorganic. It sweeps away barriers that usually divide mortals: wealth, age, sex, and so on. Violence renders the feet sacred. Naked, they become taboo for men. Women guard them as if guarding their lives. It also gives them the power for healing and cursing. All the tears and pus, all the decay and broken bones are hidden under the elaborate adornment of the shoes, which are never taken off, not even in bed. Yet violence is traceable everywhere: the odor of dead flesh seeping through the bandages, the tiny appendages that barely support the frail body. It is the prohibition, the mystery, and the traces of violence that stir up men's desire, a desire derived from fear, pity, and awe. Through the passage of violence, bound feet—a combination of human, beast, vegetable, and object—enter the realm of eroticism and symbolize the ideal of an androgynous body, the body of an immortal or a god.

In this chapter I will explore the links between beauty and violence, mutilation and language, taboo and transgression, the links that characterize footbinding. Bound feet become the emblem of femininity and eroticism through physical and linguistic violence. Sealing decay and death beneath its beautiful surface (wrapping and shoe as masks), footbinding promises immortality; yet at the same time, the odor, shape, and euphemism of the bound foot constantly reminds the fetish lovers of carnality, animality, death, and violence. Footbinding speaks multiple languages. It murmurs about seduction, eroticism, virtue, discipline, and sacrifice. It also teaches little girls about pain, about coming of age, about her place in this world, about her permanent bonding with her mother and female ancestors.

Here are the steps for the initial binding:

1. Place one end of the bandage, about two inches wide and ten feet long, on the inside of the instep and from there carry it over the four small toes and wrap them once.
2. From the inside of the foot, pull the binding toward the front point and turn it tightly around the big toe.
3. Wrap the heel from the outer side of the foot, and pull the binding toward the front point so that the heel and toes are drawn together as closely as possible. Wrap the front except for the big toe.
4. Wrap over the instep, go around the ankle, and return to the instep.
5. Turn toward the heel and wrap the binding from the inner side of the foot to the front point.
6. Wrap from the inner side and over the instep to the outer side. Wrap around the heel and pull the binding back toward the part of the binding cloth on the instep.

7. Repeat the process from the beginning until the entire bandage is used, then sew the end to prevent the binding from coming loose.[1]

Such a binding soon makes the feet inflamed and the flesh deteriorated. Each act of rebinding and washing the feet is accompanied by bleeding and peeling of the rotten flesh. Mothers call this the breaking process, which lasts about two years. The more flesh is deteriorated, the more bones broken, the more slender the feet will become.

In the 1930s, Yao Lingxi, a self-claimed "lotus addict," collected poems, stories, anecdotes, and articles about footbinding, and accounts by women who talked about their pain and sexual enhancement from this practice. He published them in four volumes, titled *Records of Gathering Fragrance (Cai fei lu)*. These works record many accounts of the pain and suffering during the initial binding period, including this oral history:

Born into an old-fashioned family at P'ing-hsi, I was inflicted with the pain of footbinding when I was seven years old. . . . It was in the first lunar month of my seventh year that my ears were pierced and fitted with gold earrings. I was told that a girl had to suffer twice, through ear piercing and footbinding. Binding started in the second lunar month; mother consulted references in order to select an auspicious day for it. I wept and hid in a neighbor's home, but mother found me, scolded me, and dragged me home. She shut the bedroom door, boiled water, and from a box withdrew binding, shoes, knife, needle, and thread. I begged for a one-day postponement, but mother refused: "Today is a lucky day," she said. "If bound today, your feet will never hurt; if bound tomorrow, they will." She washed and placed alum on my feet and cut the toenails. She then bent my toes toward the plantar with a binding cloth ten feet long and two inches wide, doing the right foot first and then the left. She finished binding and ordered me to walk, but when I did the pain proved unbearable.

That night, mother wouldn't let me remove the shoes. My feet felt on fire and I couldn't sleep; mother struck me for crying. On the following days, I tried to hide but was forced to walk. Mother hit me on my hands and feet for resisting. Beatings and curses were my lot for covertly loosening the wrappings. The feet were washed and rebound after three or four days, with alum added. After several months, all toes but the big one were pressed against the inner surface. Whenever I ate fish or freshly killed meat, my feet would swell, and the pus would drip. Mother criticized me for placing pressure on the heel in walking, saying that my feet would never assume a pretty shape. Mother would remove the bindings and wipe the blood and pus which dripped from my feet. She told me that only with

removal of the flesh could my feet become slender. If I mistakenly punc-
tured a sore, the blood gushed like a stream. My somewhat-fleshy big toes
were bound with small pieces of cloth and forced upwards, to assume a
new moon shape.

Every two weeks, I changed to new shoes. Each new pair was one-to-
two-tenths of an inch smaller than the previous one. The shoes were unyielding, and it took pressure to get into them. Though I wanted to sit pas-
sively by the *k'ang*, Mother forced me to move around. After changing more
than ten pairs of shoes, my feet were reduced to a little over four inches. I
had been binding for a month when my younger sister started; when no
one was around, we would weep together. In summer, my feet smelled of-
fensively because of pus and blood; in winter, my feet felt cold because of
lack of circulation and hurt if they got too near the *k'ang* and were struck by
warm air currents. Four of the toes were curled in like so many dead caterpillars; no outsider would ever have believed that they belonged to a human
being. It took two years to achieve the three-inch model. (*Cai fei lu,* vol. 3,
quoted in Levy 1992, 26–28)

Little girls were initiated into the binding between the ages of five and
seven, when their bones were still flexible, their *qi* (primary life force) started flourishing in their bodies,[2] and their minds mature enough *(dongshi)* to
understand the importance of this bodily discipline to undergo a long period of intense physical pain. The trauma radically changed her sense of the
body in space and her sense of being in general. By having to relearn how
to place her reduced feet on the ground and relearn how to walk through a
long period of intense pain, the little girl was forced into a speedy matura-
tion—physically, mentally, and socially. Ironically, it was her reduced feet
that helped her to find a foothold in a male-dominated world: "Through
the bending, twisting, and compressing of the feet, a girl's sense of man-
aging space was radically modified and a mother delivered her daughter
into a world where 'becoming one's body' led to moral and spiritual self-
improvement" (Blake 1994, 681). And it was through pain that she began
to bond with her mother.

In the account above, every movement the narrator makes, every emotional experience she has—be it painful, hateful, or helpless—is related to
her mother, who, through her own earlier experience of similar pain, can
also relate to her daughter's agony. During the two years of the binding
process, the mother has imprinted her secret knowledge of female survival
onto the flesh of her daughter. This secret knowledge is best carried out
by the Chinese character *teng,* which means hurting and loving (caring,

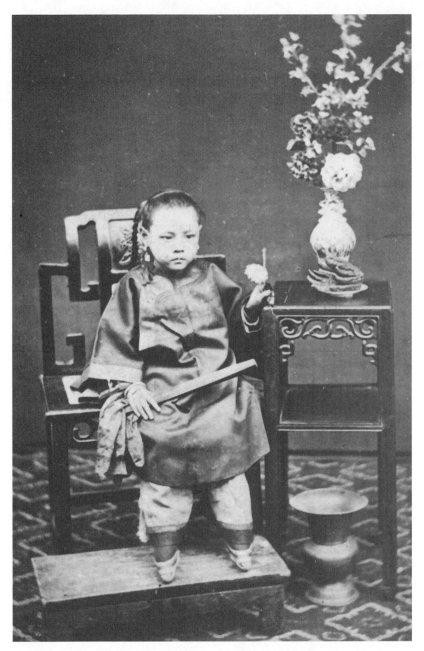

Figure 1. Chinese child with bound feet. Courtesy Peabody Essex Museum, Salem, Massachusetts.

Figure 2. Yao Niang binds her feet. Drawing from *Cai fei lu*.

treasuring) separately or simultaneously. Mother inflicts the horrible pain on her daughter, beats and curses her to keep her walking, washes and changes her binding, makes shoes for her, and cleans the pus and blood off her putrefying feet. *Teng* is embedded in each gesture the mother makes toward the girl. The pain of footbinding, so intense that it is beyond words, forces the little girl to relearn language, a language more preverbal, transmitted from mother to daughter and shared among women. It partly explains why women barely talked about their practice, and why footbinding was mostly recorded by and represented in the male voice. From the few oral accounts of footbound women (recorded by men at the end of the practice), the unanimous description of the pain seems limited to "burning," "on fire," "sleepless," "loss of appetite." Elaine Scarry describes this scarcity of words for such experience: "Whatever pain achieves, it achieves in part through its unsharability, and it ensures this unsharability through its resistance to language" (1985, 4).

The speaker of the above excerpt uses an interesting metaphor about her binding experience: "Four of the toes were curled in like so many dead caterpillars." The process used to make a pair of three-inch feet resemble the different stages of an insect, like the caterpillar spinning thread and wrapping itself in a cocoon, then coming out of it, transformed from a crawling creature into a butterfly, or like a cicada shedding its skin from time to time to grow. The difference is that in the case of the insects the goal is to grow bigger while the aim of footbinding is to reduce feet to the degree that they almost disappear. When the foot is forced to arch like a bow, it gives the illusion of being part of the leg. Thus, with the help of high-heeled lotus shoes, what remains of the original foot becomes the extension of the erect leg. It is quite similar to the effect created by high-heeled shoes. Those stilt-like shoes and boots with heels as high as five to seven inches raise the body dramatically, creating the illusion of lengthened and thinned legs as well as shortened feet. More important, the raised heel alters the sudden break of the line of the leg, making the body appear taller and straighter, away from the dirt, from gravity.

The illusion of overcoming gravity and flying up to the sky is what the tiny-footed ladies aimed to achieve. When Yao Niang, the legendary first footbinder, dances on the golden lotus, she looks as if she were whirling on a cloud. Floating on clouds or water becomes a clichéd metaphor for describing the walk of bound feet in Chinese literature. Goddesses, female immortals, and girls with special talents in paintings of those periods all show this flying movement and highly aestheticized expression of idealized femininity. Their faces and upper bodies were depicted in detail, whereas

Figure 3. Stiletto-heeled shoes.

their lower bodies, especially their feet, were veiled in clouds or fabrics. Their airy weightlessness, embodied in the darting, floating movement of their bodies on the lotus feet that are both there and not there, is the emblem of a femininity purged of earthly dross and carnality.

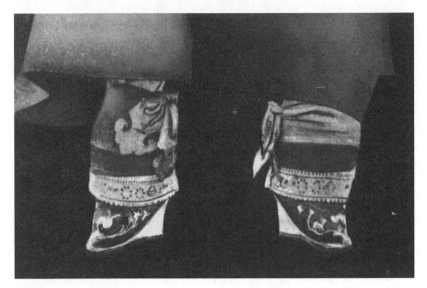

Figure 4. Lotus feet on heels, shoes, and pants embroidered in the patterns of flowers and clouds. Both high heels and lotus shoes have the effect of lifting the feet away from the ground.

However, the opposite also holds in assessing beauty, as Georges Bataille speculates:

> The image of the desirable woman as first imagined would be insipid and unprovocative if it did not at the same time also promise or reveal a mysterious animal aspect, more momentously suggestive. The beauty of the desirable woman suggests her private parts, the hairy ones, to be precise, the animal ones. . . . But above and beyond the sexual instinct, erotic desire has other components. Beauty that denies the animal and awakes desire finishes up by exasperating desire and exalting the animal parts. (1986, 142)

In the eye of the beholder, bound feet represent a true celestial being for the reason that they never have to touch the dirt, being wrapped in bandages and covered with embroidered shoes even during sleep. Yet at the same time, such a foot resembles the hoof of an animal, not the hoof of a cow or a horse, but the foot of a fox or hoof of a deer, which is associated with the myth of footbinding. The *golden lotus*, a euphonious term for bound feet, was originally a special apparatus made of gilded gold in the shape of lotus petals on which palace dancers walked and danced. The tradition was begun by an emperor of the northern Qi, Xiao Baojuan (reign, 498–501), who had his Consort Pan walk on top of the golden lotus blossoms to give the effect of blooming lotuses with each step (*Nan shi* 5:21a).

This invention seemed to have been inspired by an Indian tale of a deer lady (perhaps a mere coincidence) recorded by the Buddhist pilgrim Xuan Zang (596–664). A Rishi was once bathing in a stream when a deer came and gave birth to a girl. She was extremely beautiful, but she had the feet of a deer. The Rishi took her home and brought her up as his own child. When she walked, she left the impressions of lotus flowers on the ground. It was predicted that she would bear a thousand sons, each seated on one petal of a thousand-petaled lotus blossom. And she did (Beal 1906, 2:71–72). What makes the myth extremely interesting is that it underlines all the idealizations of footbinding: the elimination of distinction between creatures, and the assimilation of different things. The girl is the result of the copulation between a man and a deer, a mixture of half-human, half-animal and half-god, half-monster. This monstrous duality, however, makes her a symbol of beauty and fecundity, just as the dual nature of bound feet turn tiny-footed women into the ideal of femininity, the symbol of morality, and the object of desire.

Four centuries later, the fecundity and animal allure of the deer girl tale that had inspired the emperor of the northern Qi and his court were believed to have inspired the imagination of another emperor, Li Yu, reigning in southern China. Not only did he inherit the idea of the golden lotus as a dancing apparatus, but he also invented the binding of the dancer's feet to exhort the allure of the deer-footed beauty. Chinese folklore and mythology tend to represent such a hoof-footed female figure as fox-footed femme fatales. These foxes, such as Da Ji of the Shang dynasty, were often sent by gods to bring down a corrupt dynasty. They could transform themselves into beauties beyond human measure except for their feet, which refused to be metamorphosed. Just as the humans have completely erected themselves from the earth except for the feet that stubbornly remain horizontal, the feet of foxes alone fail to assume a human shape. Yet it is exactly this stubborn animality that gives off the strongest, most irresistible sexual allure, and it is this base animality that has brought down many kingdoms, many civilizations.

How well Chinese women know this secret weapon! When they call one another *xiao tizi*—"little hooves"—whether as a curse or endearment, they are fully aware of the power of this animality, in the disguise of high civilization, morality, and divinity. When the girl from P'ing-hsi tells us that her feet, after the binding, no longer "belong to a human being," the tone is, of course, filled with remorse, but at the same time it is tinged with a sense of great achievement through sheer will and endurance. A tiny-footed beauty appears to be restricted (as well as restricting: the feet, once bound, become taboo for the male gaze and touch) and celestial, away from the muddy, decaying, and excremental quality of sexuality. Yet she provokes more erotic desires by promising a mysterious animal aspect and turning her body into prohibition, taboo. In other words, the lotus foot exasperates and exalts desire for flesh by diminishing and covering the flesh. The tension of such a flux from the animal to the celestial, and from the celestial to the animal, is the key to the erotic attraction of bound feet in the eye of a lotus lover.

The Chinese were not alone in knowing, worshiping, and fearing this power. Pan, the pastoral god of fertility, was originally an Arcadian deity, later associated with the Greek Dionysus and the Roman Faunus, both fertility gods. He is depicted as a merry, ugly man with the horns, ears, legs, and hooves of a goat. All the myths about him deal with his amorous affairs. He invented the panpipe, a musical instrument made of reeds, for the beautiful nymph he loved. The nymph fled, leaving him nothing but a lonely sighing of the wind. The mysterious fear that comes from no known cause is called a *panic* fear. And fear is one of the indispensable ingredients in the working of eroticism: the fear of chaos and violence, of blood and rotting, of death, and the fear of female sexual power yet at the same time the longing for it.

And the sphinx, the fearful monster, is a veritable conglomerate of differences, with its woman's head, lion's body, serpent's tail, and eagle's wings. Perched high outside the city of Thebes, it threatens to destroy the city with a puzzle. No one can answer it except for Oedipus, who passes by the place and solves the riddle. This is the man who, by killing his father, has just transgressed the most fearful taboo and is about to commit an even worse crime—marrying his mother and having children with her, the taboo of incest that ultimately separates man from animals. In other words, Oedipus is himself a mixture of human and beast, and the physical evidence is his clubfeet, the deformed or half-evolved feet that betray his link to the animal world and its power.

Finally, there is the mermaid, the classical half-fish, half-human figure of women's seduction, of fatal voices and the lure of sexuality, immortalized by Homer, then by Hans Christian Andersen. In "The Little Mermaid," she is willing to give up her most precious gift (also her most enchanting attractor)—her voice; she is willing to endure the pain of treading on knives in order to have human legs. In the tale, her metamorphosis is successful, although she fails to win the prince's love after all the sacrifice and suffering. But it is her original form, not her transformed human figure, that prevails, as the statue at the port of Copenhagen, as the icon image in movies, toys, picture books, and art. Again, animality prevails.

A lotus foot has the semblance of a penis; such simulated genitals are devices animals often use to attract the opposite sex. For example, male gelada baboons have patterns on their chests that resemble female genitals (Hersey 1996, 12). The deep crease in the middle part of a lotus foot, caused by squeezing the front and heel together, also suggests the female sex organ.[3] So does a lotus shoe, which looks like a lily petal. *Flower* and *flower heart* are common euphemisms for the vagina in Chinese literature and pornography, sometimes even from the mouth of a country woman (see figure 5).

Records of Gathering Fragrance tells several stories of men stealing lotus shoes for masturbation or to humiliate women.[4] Thus, bound feet not only mingle human with animal and celestial, but also mix the male and female features together. Nothing can be more ironic than this. Footbinding began as a measure to stop the blurring and crossing of gender and social hierarchies, and to mark differences, but only ended in producing an even greater combination of all things. Just as the sphinx combines human and animal features in one body, footbinding gathers all the opposites and differences upon the tiny feet: ugly and beautiful, grotesque and erotic, human and beastly, earthly and celestial, male and female.

Bound feet become mappings of human reproductive systems for both sexes, or what George Hersey calls "vectors"—ornamental indicators that point to or frame the primary or secondary sex organs (1996, 12). By reducing, hurting, hiding, and creating a strict taboo, footbinding actually dramatizes the primary reproductive apparatus.[5] By the same token, earrings, bracelets, necklaces, corsets, and tightly laced boots function as sexual vectors through symbolic binding, penetrating, and self-imprisoning. Such devices for sexual display are no less extravagant than the device men use in the competition for sexual selection—the accumulation and squandering of wealth; the brains of an intellectual; the talents of a literati or artist; the muscles of a warrior.

Of all the male devices of "genitalia extravagance," nothing is more direct than the penis enlargement, which is comically and vividly presented in the erotic novel *The Carnal Prayer Mat* by Li Yu. The main character, Weiyang Sheng, has everything a Chinese male needs to attract women: he is intelligent and good-looking, and he knows how to please women. Although the Chinese have fixed attractors for male and female, such as *lang cai nu mao* or *caizi jiaren* (man's talent and woman's look or talent and

Figure 5. Lotus shoes that resemble lily petals. Drawings from *Cai fei lu*.

beauty), a man's appearance, at least in romance literature, is as important as his talent. If he is not described as being as handsome as the legendary male beauty Pan An, he is at least a *baimian shusheng*—a fair-skinned scholar (fair skin is a most important sign of beauty). Weiyang's ambition is to sleep with all the beautiful women in China. When he asks his thief friend to help him fulfill this dream, his friend examines the size of Weiyang Sheng's "capital"—his penis. Seeing Weiyang's tiny member, the thief ridicules him, then tells him to go home and forget about his sexual adventures. With a sex organ that small, not only will he fail to fulfill his ambition, but he will cause himself endless disasters. In his deep humiliation and desperation, Weiyang Sheng comes across a doctor, a specialist in enlarging male genitals. He implants a dog's sex organ into Weiyang's penis and turns it into an enormous, powerful weapon.

The success of the operation gives Weiyang the same power that a woman gains through footbinding: the appearance of high civilization—a fair-skinned scholar with a primary reproductive apparatus empowered by a dog penis. The first sexual attractor is powerful enough if Weiyang were satisfied with sex within bounds, that is, with his wife and concubine maids. But if he wants to fulfill his ambition of sleeping with all the beautiful women in China—in other words, to transgress his marriage vows—he needs a sex organ that is not only large in size but that also assimilates the shape and power of a beast. Thus Weiyang turns himself into something quite monstrous—a half-human, half-animal creature, a scholar with a dog penis.

Such obsession with sex organs reflects the general anxiety among the literati over gender and hierarchy confusion. Ming and Qing erotic prints show how little difference there is between the naked bodies of scholarly men and women. Both have smooth skin and feminine, slender body lines (see figure 6). The only male figures with muscles, beards, and body hair who seem to be filled with virile power are the Mongols. These horsemen warriors were considered barbarians, closer to animals than civilized Chinese were thought to be. No wonder the fair-skinned scholar Weiyang needs to borrow a dog penis, which grows big, hot, and alive once inside a woman's body. And women love this half-human, half-animal phallus just as much as men love women's half-human, half-hoof lotus foot.

So through much violence inflicted on the foot—the tight binding, bending, bleeding, breaking of the bones, rotting of the flesh, beating, and cursing—the foot is transformed into something that is suggestive of the genitals of both sexes, the hoof of an animal. It has a shimmering, gleaming surface; the shoe and bandage cover the low, degrading nature of the

Figure 6. *South Village,* print from *Erotic Art of China.* In most of the erotic paintings of late imperial China, the only obvious bodily feature that marks the difference between naked men and women is their feet.

human foot, the only organ that keeps humans stuck in the mud, whereas the rest of the body, the head especially, is elevated to the sun, the sky, and other heavenly things. Not only is it considered the filthiest part of the body; the foot is also "psychologically analogous to the brutal fall of a man—in other words, to death" (Bataille 1991, 22). A folk song from Henan Province mocks how a woman's clumsy, grossly big feet threaten the order of the cosmic, her unrestrained/undisciplined body (her big strides and urine) suggesting ruin, pollution, and death, which are brought about by natural disasters such as earthquakes and floods (Liu Xiang 1988, 205–7). Such a body must be tamed, purified, and mediated through human effort—through footbinding. Like the mummy that seals death beneath layers of cloth, the lotus foot, once formed, seals all the degrading qualities associated with the foot inside the bandages. It shields off human follies, their defenselessness against aging, decaying, and dying, and their threat to cosmic harmony.

Mianzi (reputation or prestige) comes directly from the word *mian* (face, surface, outside, outer part). It plays a crucial role in every part of Chinese culture. No Chinese can escape the fear of losing face or the urgent need to keep or save face. *Diu mianzi* (the literal translation is to lose surface or an outer part as well as face) is such a shameful thing that it often leads to violent death. Thus to avoid losing face, women of respectable upbringing were taught to guard their shoes as if guarding their lives. If their feet or shoes were touched, played with, or stolen by men, it was as serious as losing their virginity or chastity. *Records of Gathering Fragrance* contains numerous accounts of women whose feet were played with or whose shoes were stolen by vulgar or rustic men at village theaters. The mortification caused by shame often led to suicide (*Cai fei lu* 1:271–72). While concealment of the foot becomes a canon of proper behavior and moral training for women, it further mystifies the tiny foot and increases the craving of lotus lovers.[6]

When mothers bind feet for their daughters, one thing they do to make their children endure the pain is to threaten that they may lose face on their wedding day, when every visitor is licensed to touch and play with the bride's feet. This is the custom of *nao fang*—disrupting the wedding chamber—that has been popular in almost every part of China for thousands of years. *Yue nao yue fa* means the more jesting, the more prosperity.[7] Hence, relatives, friends, and neighbors gathered in the bridal chamber on the wedding night, taunting the bride (the bridegroom is left alone) with all sorts of vicious dirty jokes and games. All taboos were lifted: "For three days there's no hierarchy" (Huang Huajie 1991, 163). The bride's body (sometimes several bridesmaids were hired as a replacement) was laid defenselessly open to public ridicule and pranks. Even the feet, the most prohibited part of the body, were not exempt from the ritual. Visitors lifted the bride's skirt, measuring her foot size with the rulers they had brought along, pinching and kneading her feet while commenting on the shape and the embroidery, and inventing games to torture the bride, such as making her cross a bridge of upside-down wine glasses. In a story from the northern part of Shandong Province, even the bride's mother-in-law became a target: "The crowd surrounded the hostess, took off her shoes and unwrapped her bandages, and paraded her on a cow's back around the village" (Huang Huajie 1991, 164). The bride's lifelong reputation (face) in her new home, as well as that of her old and new families, was formed at this moment. Whether she was perceived as beautiful, persevering, disciplined, and hard-working depended on whether she had a pair of well-made lotus feet. Badly shaped, oversized feet (more than three to four inches long) meant that the bride had no endurance, no patience, and worst of all, was lazy; therefore she couldn't be a good daughter-in-law or a good wife.

Since the feet became the face and the face closed the bride's fate—her lifelong happiness or misery—mothers dared not loosen the bandages a little bit despite their daughters' tears. They would tell their daughters that if a mother truly loved *(teng)* her child, she would not let herself feel empathy *(teng)* for the foot *(teng nu bu teng zu)*. Thus the character *teng*, with its first denotation (pain) and its second (treasure, care, love—from adults, usually female to children, not vice versa), spells out the muted message of footbinding: a truly loving mother must teach her daughters how to endure pain physically, emotionally, and mentally. Such love mixed and reinforced with unspeakable pain and violence is, as I mentioned earlier, the secret language/knowledge transmitted from mother to daughter during the months and years of the initial process of footbinding, a knowledge that teaches the daughter about the mapping and discipline of the female body in a patriarchal environment, and that prepares her for her sexuality, marriage, reproduction, motherhood. The knowledge, muted or blunted by the intense pain of footbinding, is shared between mothers and daughters as unforgettable memories imprinted on the flesh. It excludes men and writing. When unable to explain why they have to inflict such pain on their daughters' bodies, mothers often tell them that they will understand better when they grow up. And they often do, even expressing their gratitude for what their mothers have done for them. We learn this from the interviews and the oral accounts of bound-footed women recorded in *Records of Gathering Fragrance* as well as from novels.

Poet Adrienne Rich, from an American cultural experience and perspective, reached a similar conclusion: "Mothers and daughters have always exchanged with each other—beyond the verbally transmitted lore of female survival—a knowledge that is subliminal, subversive, preverbal: The knowledge flowing between two alike bodies, one of which has spent nine months inside the other" (1976, 220). So powerful is this unwritten, un-speakable knowledge/language/memory that "verbal instructions and di-dactic manuals on how to behave, how to succeed in the real world, simply paled" (Blake 1994, 708). And little girls, once they understood the impor-tance of footbinding, endured the pain like heroic warriors. The following account, told by Jin Suxin, is one of the stories collected in *Records of Gathering Fragrance:*

> When I was a child, I lived in Mentou Village, eighty li away from Pingxi County. At that time, women competed to have the smallest feet. At age six, my mother bound my feet. . . . I was told not to walk on my heels; other-wise my heels would be deformed and villagers would laugh at me. But when I forced myself to walk on the bent toes, I felt the pain intolerable. Walking became a torture. At night, my feet felt feverish as if on fire. I begged my mother to loosen my bandages, but only got scolded severely. . . . When I was nine, I began to bind myself. Every time I made new shoes, the size became a little bit smaller. At eleven, my feet were thin, small, and arched, about four and a half inches long. One day, I went with my mother to my maternal grandma's birthday party. Among the visitors were two girls of my age from the Weiyang family. Their feet were so tiny, smaller than hands, all wrapped in scarlet embroidered shoes. Everybody admired them. My uncle turned to me, laughing, "Look at their feet, so small and straight. How respectful! Look at yours, so big and fat. Who will be willing to be your matchmaker?" All the visitors turned to look at my feet and laughed. I stood there, frozen, as if a pail of icy water had been poured over my head, as if I had been struck by a thunderbolt. I was so ashamed I began to weep. I wished I could cut my feet into a smaller size on the spot. At that mo-ment, I was determined to bind my feet much more tightly no matter how painful it was.
>
> That night, after I unbound my bandages, I tore my handkerchief into strips and sewed them to the bandages to make them longer. I pressed the four small toes as far as possible to the plantar, wrapped them once, then arched my foot by tightening the bandage over the heel and back. After wrapping my foot like this four times, I inserted the end of the bandage into the plantar and put on my shoes. As I laid down in bed, I felt my feet swelling, burning, and hurting me like hell. I tossed about in agony, but I was determined not to loosen the bandages, even if I died of pain. Sometimes it was too much to bear, and I wept. When I finally drifted into sleep, I dreamed about three-inch feet. The next day I had to hold onto the

wall to walk. . . . Ten days later, my shoes became loose. I knew that my feet were getting smaller. That night I made myself a pair of new shoes. I measured them. Three inches and eight! I had lost almost one inch.

Such an achievement within half a month! More than I had expected. I got a longer pair of bandages and made bed slippers. After binding, I put them on so that the binding would remain tight. Five days later, I suddenly felt a sharp pain in my feet. I unbound the wrapping and saw that the fifth toes were broken and infected. I cleaned and cushioned them with cotton balls. The binding was so unbearably painful that my body trembled all over. I told myself that if I was afraid of pain, all the effort and suffering for the past half a month would be thrown away. My courage came back, and I bound my feet more tightly. It was so painful that after a while, my feet grew numb. Gradually, all my small toes were pushed into the sole, flat and tiny like lima beans. The fifth toes almost touched the heels. The crease in the instep also deepened, almost an inch deep. The front was more pointed, the heel straightened, and the back arched nicely. After thirty days of binding, my feet were reduced to two inches and nine. I wobbled a lot while walking because my feet were so small. One day my uncle saw me and said, "I'll cut off your feet so that you don't have to bind your feet anymore." I think he said that because he was worried I would overbind my feet. When I returned home from my grandma's place, people noticed my small feet and thought I was wearing fake performing shoes. When they looked closer and realized they were real, they admired me, in awe. After that, I was able to make new socks and shoes for my newly formed feet, which had become the number-one beauty in the surrounding villages. (*Cai fei lu* 1:259–60 [my translation])

When she started binding, she was still unable to grasp the meaning of pain/love; hence she cried and begged her mother to loosen the binding. And of course, the mother, out of her love, refused. When she got older, and when she saw her cousins at her same age as a mirror for the mapping of her social and sexual body, she finally got the message of footbinding. Her uncle's cruel comment and mocking triggered her sense of shame; in Chinese terms, the humiliation and fear of losing face prompted the nine-year-old girl to endure the inhuman pain of reshaping her feet.

On the one hand, her superhuman will to endure pain prepares her to find a secure foothold in the capricious environment of male discourse (her uncle mocks her in public when her feet are bigger than the three-inch model, then scolds her severely when he sees her obsession in reducing the size of her feet). On the other hand, her shame is what gives birth to eroticism, which is in essence a transgression, springing from the existence of taboos set up to counter liberty in sexual violence: "Shame, real or pretended, is a woman's way of accepting the taboo that makes a human being out of her. The time comes when she must break the taboo, but then she has to signify by being ashamed that the taboo is not forgotten, that the infringement takes place in spite of the taboo, in full consciousness of the taboo" (Bataille 1986, 134). When a Chinese man sees a pair of lotus feet, he feels a tremendous pity for the fragile beauty that has gone through so much pain and suffering; he is in awe of the wonder that comes out of violence. To make it even more enticing, this wonder and beauty form the taboo of the strictest kind. It is not available to his eyes and hands, unless he is the husband or is present during festivals such as weddings and foot competitions. It is the mixed feelings of awe and pity, and the tension of transgression, that bring out his erotic desire, be it love or lust. After destroying parts of their bodies, women become mediators through whom men are able to experience the terrible abyss of violence on a safe ground, without the risk of abandoning themselves entirely to their own violence. The terribly deformed feet, dressed in the most exquisite adornment, permit men to remove themselves from all the pain, blood, decay, and ultimately, death, keeping them at a safe distance, under tight control.

The character *ai* (love) could also be used in ancient Chinese to mean "treasure," "adultery," or something "hidden" or "appearing to be hidden." *Guo ce: qi ce san* (National policies: Policies of the Qi), from the Spring and Autumn Period, records that Meng Chang Jun's wife commits adultery *(ai)* with her husband's consultants. *The Book of Songs,* the first anthology of poetry also from the Spring and Autumn Period more than two thousand years ago, contains the famous love poem describing the anxiousness and eagerness of a young man waiting for his lover who hides herself somewhere: "Ai er bu jian / sao shou chi chu" ([my lover] hidden and invisible / [I] scratch my head in hesitation). What is most interesting is *ai*'s synonyms: *teng* for hurt, treasure, love; and *lian* for pity, sympathy, spoil, and treasure. As a matter of fact, the combinations of these words— *teng ai* (hurt and love), and *lian ai* or *ai lian* (pity and love or love and pity)—are used to describe parental (often maternal) love for children, or a man's love for women. It is also worth noting that in the Chinese language, love rarely appears alone; instead, it is constantly conditioned by other factors. Thus we have *lian ai* (pity and love), *en ai* (gratitude and love), *jing ai* (respect and love), *qing ai* (emotion and love), *lian ai* (attachment/addiction and love). The most revealing combination is perhaps *teng ai,* a love imbedded in preverbal knowledge, accompanied by unspeakable pain, and shared only through the empathy between the two bodies (mother and daughter) alike.

So much pain and violence inflicted on the body—all for the aim (and in the name) of a beautiful, shining surface that is not to be revealed. What does all the wrapping, binding, and embroidery of the lotus foot try to cover? And what is underneath the flat, shining surface of high civilization? Wrapped by the extravagant and exquisite embroidery, the bound foot seems to have conquered decay and death and finally achieved an eternal beauty. A beautiful face may wrinkle, and a slender body may become fat and saggy, whereas a pair of lotus feet keep their charm as long as the woman lives. *Records of Gathering Fragrance* records stories in which men marry women old enough to be their mothers for their perfectly bound feet. Datong of Shanxi Province was known for its annual foot contest on the sixth day of the sixth lunar month, which was believed to have started during the Zhengde period of the Ming dynasty (1506–1521). Women of all ages and classes, ugly or beautiful, were equal competitors. Their feet, the most hidden objects, were now on display. Anyone who came to the contest could touch and judge the tiny feet. There were three prizes. The first became *wang* (king), the second *ba* (lord), and the third *hou* (queen) (*Cai fei lu* 1936c, 203). Such contests were popular in other areas, too, like Taiyuan and Yuncheng (Shanxi Province), Xuanhua (Hebei), Lanzhou (Gansu), and Fengzhen (Inner Mongolia). Foot contests helped spread the name of the local women's feet, and because of their visibility, women from these places became more diligent in binding their feet to live up to such a name (*Cai fei lu di si bian* 38). Often, after two years of the initial binding, the intense pain subsided and the feet became practically "dead and pain-less" (Fielding 1956, 28). In fact, the tiny feet became the symbol of death itself, as Lin Qin'nan laments in his "Tiny-Foot Lady":

> How inconceivable, that in reducing the foot,
> Her flesh and bones are so distressed
> That she loses her appetite for food.
> So much of her fragrant youth
> Spent weeping by the fallen flowers;
> She hears the chirping of the birds,
> But her bowed foot is like a tiny grave.
> (Quoted in Levy 1992, 83)

From the two tiny graves rose eternal youth and beauty.

As ancient Egyptians were promised their immortality if they bound their bodies tightly, Chinese girls and women were promised an eternal beauty if they bound their feet. By binding and wrapping, they hope to cover up the decadence, decay, violence, and finally, the death of the flesh and of civilization. After all the struggle and suffering, all that matters is the surface, and all that is left is the surface, the surface of a mask. No wonder Fang Xun warns the Masters of the Golden Rooms (men with beautiful women as wives and concubines) that they must not remove the bindings to look at her bare foot, but must remain satisfied with its external appearance and enjoy the outward impression. For if one removes the shoes and binding, the aesthetic feeling will be destroyed forever. Indeed, Chinese pornographic prints and paintings freely presented men's and women's naked bodies and genitals, yet they never crossed the boundary of baring a woman's lotus feet. Once the shoe (mask) is on, it has to be kept forever. The removal of the shoe/surface/mask is the end of eroticism.

Yet death seeps through the bandages, strong and odorous, no matter how much perfumed powder a woman sprinkles on her feet. The lotus foot is known for its peculiar odor. It is a smell of the living flesh being discontinued by a deadly bondage, a smell of life and death, of dirt and purity fermenting and brewing in exuberance within a tightly compressed space. Men are either totally repulsed by or addicted to this odor, but no one can ignore it. The interplay between the illusion of immortal beauty on the surface and the constant reminder of violence—decay, pain, and deformity of the naked feet—from underneath brings eroticism into its final sense, that is, death. If eroticism is what Georges Bataille describes as "assenting to life up to the point of death" (1986, 11), footbinding is then its best manifestation, in language and writing. Here, desire and violence cling to each other, each striving desperately to incarnate its irresistible force in the other, each fighting to have the last word. But violence always triumphs. Death devours everything, just as the mutilation of footbinding erases all distinguishing characteristics, all salient features of each individual until differences end in similarity, and the body (foot) embraces the boundaries of sex and class.

Pan Jinlian is the most deadly and licentious female character in the erotic novel *The Golden Lotus (Jin ping mei)*. She got her name Jinlian, Golden Lotus, from her pair of perfectly bound feet. And she certainly lives up to that name and image—as the symbol of eroticism and object of desire. In the story, Jinlian was sold as a child and raised to be someone's concubine. Almost every character in the book, male or female, who is involved in her sexual intrigues and competitions meets a deadly end, including her first lover, her first husband, Wu Da, her maid, and her second husband, Ximen Qing.

Of the six women that the rich playboy Ximen Qing marries, only Jinlian brings him no amount of money, goods, or property as dowry; she also has no social or economic function in the household. While the other five wives bring wealth, children, or domestic skills, Jinlian has no money, working skill, or a powerful family to back her up. Her assets are her body/feet, her skills to enchant (singing, pouting, and her bedchamber art), and her power to destroy. Yet it is to her that Ximen Qing constantly

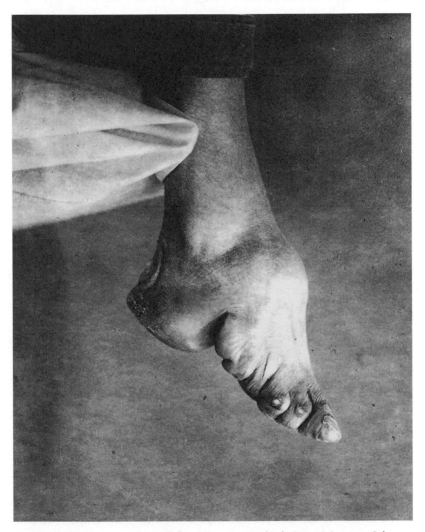

Figure 7. Chinese woman's small foot. Courtesy Peabody Essex Museum, Salem, Massachusetts.

returns, no matter how far he may stray in his search for erotic experiences. Even when he discovers her affair with a servant—the worst crime a woman could commit in a patriarchal system—he only gives her a halfhearted whipping, then immediately engages in sex with her. Together they invent endless sexual games. She understands his erotic needs and is willing to satisfy them. As for her own needs, nothing can stop her from fulfilling them. When she cannot get Ximen Qing, she finds substitutes, servants, a son-in-law as well as a brother-in-law. Her sex drive leaves her totally devoid of conscience or guilt for her crime, be it for murder, incest, or infanticide. In this sense, she is an equal to Ximen Qing, who believes he can get away with raping the Goddess of the Moon or the Goddess of the West because he is rich and powerful as well as destined from his previous life to enjoy all these women. Toward the end of his life, after plunging himself into a sexual frenzy, he staggers back to Jinlian to die in her bed (and body). The following is the scene involving his last sexual encounter with her. Driven wild by her own sexuality, Jinlian, the sex symbol and object of erotic desire manifested through her tiny feet, suddenly turns into a killing machine. She overdoses Ximen Qing with pills and literally "sexes" him to death:

> Golden Lotus had come back from the inner court, but she had not gone to bed. She was lying upon her bed, dressed, waiting for Hsi-men Ch'ing [Ximen Qing]. When he came, she got up at once. She took his clothes and saw that he was drunk, but she asked no questions. Hsi-men put his hands on her shoulders and drew her towards him.
>
> "You little strumpet!" he murmured, "your darling is drunk. Get the bed ready: I want to go to sleep."
>
> She helped him to bed, and as soon as he was on it, he began to snore like thunder. She could do nothing to wake him, so she took off her clothes and went to bed too. She played delicately with his weapon, but it was as limp as cotton-wood and had not the slightest spirit. She tossed about on the bed, consumed with passionate desire, almost beside herself. [She squatted below him and sucked him in many different manners]; it was in vain. This made her wild beyond description. She shook him for a long time and at last he awoke. She asked him where his medicine was. Hsi-men, still very drunk, cursed her.
>
> "You little strumpet!" he cried, "what do you want that for? You would like me to play with you, I suppose, but to-day your darling is far too tired for anything of that sort. The medicine is in the little gold box in my sleeve. Give it to me. You'll be in luck if you are clever enough to make my prick stand up."

Golden Lotus looked for the little gold box and, when she found it, opened it. There were only three or four pills left. She took a wine-pot and poured out two cups of wine. She took one pill herself, leaving three. Then she made the terrible mistake of giving him all three. She was afraid anything less would have no effect. Hsi-men Ch'ing shut his eyes and swallowed them. Before he could have drunk a cup of tea, the medicine began to take effect. Golden Lotus tied the silken ribbon for him and his staff stood up. He was still asleep. She mounted upon his body. [She anointed some medicine on the tip of his penis, then inserted it inside her vagina. As she rubbed herself around it, the penis reached the heart of her flower.] Her body seemed to melt away with delight. Then, with her two hands grasping his legs, she moved up and down about two hundred times. [At first, it was a bit dry; soon her juice came out and it became very slippery.] Hsi-men Ch'ing let her do everything she wished, but himself was perfectly inert. She could bear it no longer. She put her tongue into his mouth. She held his neck and shook it. [She rubbed and kneaded his body with her own. His penis was completely inside her vagina, except for his balls. She rubbed them and felt delightful. Her juice kept running out so fast that soon she had changed five handkerchiefs to wipe herself. She came twice, yet Ximen Qing did not. His penis looked swollen and purple, all the veins exposed, as if it had been burnt by fire. Golden Lotus untied the ribbon, but the penis still looked as swollen as before. She sucked it, lying on top of him, her tongue licked the tip back and forth for the time of a meal. Suddenly, the semen shot out like quicksilver leaking from a glass tube. She rushed to take it with her mouth. It ran out so fast she couldn't swallow it all. In the beginning it was semen, but soon the blood came out.] Hsi-men Ch'ing had fainted and his limbs were stiff outstretched. (*The Golden Lotus* 1955, 84–85)[8]

Sexuality on the loose is like a raging fire that feeds on the very objects intended to smother its flames, absorbing and destroying everything along its path. Jinlian's overflowing sex drive finally brings death—the ultimate form of violence and the most violent consumption—to herself. After Ximen Qing's death, she initiates an incestuous affair with her son-in-law, Chen Jingji, then drowns the infant she has with him. The infanticide leads to the discovery of their secret and Jinlian's expulsion from Ximen Qing's house. When she is put back on the market for sale, Wu Song, the mute brother of Jinlian's first husband whom she murdered, offers to buy her. Jinlian happily follows him home, thinking that he wants her to be his wife. She realizes her mistake when Wu Song pulls out the knife, but it is too late. The door is locked and she is tied up like a chicken. Wu Song tears out her heart and liver and offers them as a sacrifice on her ex-husband's altar.

Wu Song thus completes his revenge for his brother's murder. But it is also his final sexual union with Jinlian, his sister-in-law. As a man who doesn't read or write but takes the value of integrity and tradition with extreme seriousness, he knows not how to transgress the incest taboo, physically or linguistically. (I will further discuss this issue in chapter 3.) The only outlet (or orgasm) for him is through violent rupture—cutting open the body and tearing out the insides of his sexual object. With her body torn from inside out, Jinlian completes her game of sex and desire, completes her reunion with Ximen Qing, who also died of eruption.

Such is the explosive force of expenditure, causing those playing the game of mutilation and self-mutilation, fetishism and eroticism to lose control. Its violence breaks through the surface, revealing the vertigo of the interior. This violence "belongs to humanity as a whole and is speechless" (Bataille 1986, 186).

A Brief History of Footbinding

2

Anointed with fragrance, she takes lotus steps;
Though often sad, she walks with swift lightness.
She dances like the wind,
leaving no physical trace.
Another stealthily tries on this palace style,
but feels such distress when she tries to stand;
So wondrously small they defy description,
Unless placed in the palm.

—Su Shi (1036–1101) (quoted in Levy 1992)

THIS SONG LYRIC ON BOUND FEET in Chinese literature was written by the popular poet Su Shi in the Song dynasty, when footbinding had just started to spread all over the country. Apart from various sayings and a few records scattered here and there in travelogues, no one knows exactly who started the practice of binding, and no one seriously researched its origin until the beginning of the twentieth century, when it was publicly ridiculed, legally forbidden, and about to disappear. In this chapter I summarize the speculations that have been made about the origin of footbinding and examine how this practice spread around the thirteenth century.

According to Yao Lingxi's *Records of Gathering Fragrance*—the first collection totally devoted to footbinding, its history, methods of binding, and the frenzied doting of fanatics on lotus feet—footbinding can be traced back as early as the twenty-first century B.C. Da Yu, the founder of the Xia dynasty (twenty-first to sixteenth centuries B.C.), married a woman who was a fox fairy with tiny feet (*Cai fei lu* 1:28). The last ruler of the Shang dynasty (sixteenth to eleventh centuries B.C.), the king of Zhou, had a concubine named Da Ji. It was said that she was a fox sent from heaven to destroy the corrupt kingdom on earth. She transformed herself into a beautiful woman but was unable to change her feet, so she wrapped them in cloth. When she became the king's favorite, the court women imitated her and started binding their feet, hoping that they, too, could win the king's favor with their tiny feet (Wang Sanping). A few centuries later, during the Spring and Autumn Period (770–476 B.C.) we know of the legendary beauty Xi Shi, who was given to King Wu as a strategy to destroy the kingdom. She soon became the king's favorite concubine and helped bring down the country. She was said to have small pointed feet, and it is believed that she left her tiny footprints on the rock outside a cave in Jiangsu Province. The place became a popular tourist site (*Cai fei lu* 2:169).

Qin Shihuang, the founder of the first feudal dynasty, the Qin dynasty (221–207 B.C.), picked many small-footed women for his court as concubines and maids (Luo Chongqi 1990). In the Han dynasty (206–220 B.C.), Chengdi (reign, 32–6 B.C.E.) was believed to have suffered from impotence and could be aroused only by holding his concubine Zhao Feiyan's feet and rubbing them with his hand. Lotus lovers believe that Zhao's feet must have been extremely tiny and lovely in order to arouse the emperor (*Cai fei lu xu bian* 169). Throughout the Jin dynasty (265–420), court ladies wore pointed shoes made of yellow grass, which resembled the lotus shoes (*Cai fei lu* 4). Donghun Hou of the Qi (the Six Dynasties, 222–80) made gold lotuses and ordered his favorite concubine to walk on them in order to create the spectacle of "each lotus blossom with every step" (Li Yanshou, *Nanshi* 5:21a). The Sui dynasty (581–618) recorded the story of Wu Yueniang. Born from a common family, she was selected, along with hundreds of other girls, to pull the boat for Emperor Sui Yang. She was determined to assassinate the tyrant. She wrapped a knife under her sole and put on a pair of shoes that made lotus footprints on the ground. She knew that the tiny flower prints from her bound feet would catch the emperor's attention, and thus she would have a good opportunity to get closer to him. As she had expected, Emperor Sui Yang summoned her so he could play with her tiny feet. She untied the bandage slowly. In the end, she pulled out the knife but failed to kill him. The emperor gave the order that no woman with bound feet could enter the court (Luo Chongqi 1990, 64).

Yang Guifei (719–756), the most famous imperial concubine of the Tang Emperor Xuan Zong (685–762), was also believed to have tiny feet that measured three inches long. After she hung herself, a local old woman found her three-inch-long socks and became rich by charging viewers an exhibition fee to see them. The emperor wrote a poem for Yang:

> Socks socks,
> Endless dust of fragrance.
> Slender and round,
> Heavenly hook on earth.
> Narrow and bent,
> A new moon in hand.[1]

Zhang Bangji, a twelfth-century commentator, believed that footbinding began in the court of the sovereign poet Li Yu (reign, 961–75), the last emperor of the Later Tang dynasty during the Five Dynasties (907–960). He made a six-foot-high, gold-gilded stage in the shape of a lotus and ordered his favorite concubine, Yao Niang, a talented dancer, to dance on it, her feet bound into the shape of the new moon. When she danced in her white socks, she looked like a whirling cloud rising above the water. All the other court ladies were said to have imitated her.[2]

Books and paintings show that more women started binding their feet from the Northern Song about the end of the eleventh century. Tao Zongyi (1368) records in his *Chuo geng lu* that footbinding was still infrequent between 1068 and 1085. This can be taken as evidence that the practice had already started, although it was still rare. During the rule of Song Huizong (1119–1125), there was apparently a special lotus shoe in vogue in the capital Bian Jing called *cuo dao di,* and it was written about by poet Lu You (1125–1210) in his *Lao xue yan bi ji* (notes from an old schoolhouse). By the Southern Song, the move of the capital to Lin'an (Hangzhou) helped spread footbinding from the northern part of China to the south. In the paintings of the Southern Song, for example, *Sou shan tu* and *Zaju renwu tu* (in the Beijing Gugong Museum), women had small feet. *Yi jian zhi* records the story of Madame San Wang: "When I was alive, I wasted water on washing my hair and feet separately, wasted time and material on the binding and making of shoes. Now in the nether world, I have to drink the five jars of filthy water I used for washing feet in my previous life" (cited in Gao Hongxin 1995, 17).[3] This account is proof that footbinding was already quite popular, though not widely spread throughout the country. By the end of the Song, tiny feet began to be used as a synonym for women.[4]

The Mongols, who founded the Yuan dynasty (1271–1368), loved bound feet. The poem "Song for the Dancing Girl Taking off Her Shoes" was written by Li Jun at the emperor's request.

> The floating white bandage half open,
> Feet so soft and tiny like young bamboo shoots.
> Cloud of three inches long drifts into the hands,

A new moon rising out of the shallow water.
After dancing on the ivory bed, she reclines with such fatigue,
Like the uneven prints of wild geese left on the sand.
The golden lotuses too narrow and tiny to walk,
She stands alone on the jade steps against the eastern wind.

(In Gao Hongxin 1995, 20–21; my translation)

With encouragement from the Mongol rulers, footbinding became more popular in the Yuan dynasty. When it came to describing women in *Yuan qu* and *Yuan za ju* (verse for the singing and poetic drama set to music, both of which flourished in the Yuan period), tiny feet were a must. Not only did they become the measurement for beauty, but they were tools for women to express their feelings. In Wang Shipu's *Xi xiang ji,* the heroine Ying Ying has such lines: "My eyes remain cautious and alert / Only my heels reveal my secrets." When Zhang Sheng peeks at Ying Ying burning incense in the yard, the first thing he notices is her feet: "Each step stirs pity / . . . the fragrant dust / from her shallow footprints" (in Gao Hongxin 1995, 24; my translation). At the end of the Yuan, people began to regard natural feet as something shameful, as Tao Zongyi notes in *Chuo geng lu.*

By the Ming dynasty (1368–1644), footbinding began to spread all over China. Bound feet, apart from being the measurement for beauty, became the symbol for social status. The first Ming emperor, Zhu Yuanzhang, ordered Zhang Shicheng's troops (who fought for the Mongols against Zhu) to be cast into the class of *gai*—beggars. Men from the *gai* households were forbidden to learn how to read and write, whereas women were forbidden to bind their feet. In the areas where the custom was popular, binding became as necessary for a proper woman as learning was for a man. As the old Chinese saying goes, "If you love your son, you don't go easy on his studies. If you love your daughter, you don't go easy on her footbinding" (Shen Defu 1827). For upper-class women, footbinding was the marker of their hierarchy. For girls from the lower class, footbinding gave them an opportunity to move upward in the marriage and service market. For example, Ming Wuzong (reign, 1505–1521) liked to choose young women for his inner court from Datong of Shanxi Province and Xuande of Hebei Province, which were known for tiny feet (Gao Hongxin 1995, 22). Hubei and Sichuan Provinces also had large populations of tiny-footed women. When the rebel Zhang Xianzhong (1606–1646) occupied the two provinces, he had women's feet severed and piled them together to make "the Peak of the Golden Lotuses" (*Cai fei lu* 3:160). By the end of the Ming, footbinding not only seemed to have spread throughout the country, but also from the upper to the lower classes, and it was accepted by society as a symbol for feminine beauty, hierarchy, and morality.

In the Song, the size for tiny feet was about four inches long; there was no requirement for making them arched or pointed. The court ladies of Lizong (reign, 1205–1264) bound their feet into a narrow and pointed shape, but not arched, and named it *quai shang ma* (Gao Hongxin 1991, 19). During the Ming period, however, women aimed for three-inch, curved lotuses through binding to satisfy the aesthetic taste and fashion that required new styles from time to time. The popularity of lotus feet was so ubiquitous that the first empress of the Ming, who was natural-footed, was ridiculed at a lantern festival. A town resident made a lantern depicting a woman with a watermelon in her lap, accompanied by a riddle that alluded to the empress's big feet. In a fit of rage, the emperor had the lantern maker's whole clan, including his most remote relatives, executed (*Cai fei lu* 1:263). This certainly shows the cruel, arbitrary rule of the emperor, but it also reveals how seriously everyone, from the son of heaven to commoners, regarded tiny feet. Palace women had different ways of binding their feet as well as specially designed shoes to please the emperor. The last Ming emperor, Chongzhen (reign, 1628–43), was a lotus lover and favored his concubine Tian for her perfectly formed feet. He once praised Tian's feet to Empress Zhou, whose feet were not as small as Tian's and made her extremely unhappy because she believed he was trying to ridicule her ("Zi zu tan," in *Cai fei lu* 1:34).

Descriptions of feminine beauty in literature began to focus on the tiny feet. Thus we have lines like "Red soft shoes three-inches long" in Wang Hongjian's "Xi lou yue fu," and "A pair of three-inch bow shoes revealed under the curtain" by Zhu Youdun in his "Yuan gong Ci." Even *Xi you ji* (Journey to the West), a novel centered on four male characters, describes women's feet as wearing three-inch arched shoes like a phoenix's beak. As I described in the previous chapter, the erotic novel *Jin ping mei* reveals that lotus feet and shoes play an important role in late-sixteenth-century China. Throughout the book, tiny feet were advertised by matchmakers as a praiseworthy attribute, and lotus shoes were means for flirtation, sexual foreplay, and sentiments. Women took pride in their well-proportioned lotuses, designed and made especially attractive shoes to entice their husbands or lovers.

Footbinding reached its peak in the Qing dynasty (1644–1911), even though the Manchu emperors forbade Manchu girls to bind their feet and throughout their rule gave numerous orders to stop the practice among Han women (the largest population of the ethnicities in China). In 1664,

Emperor Kangxi decreed that if any girl were found binding her feet, her parents would be severely punished. It caused a serious uproar when members of rival families often falsely accused one another of footbinding (mostly for revenge). By 1668, the emperor had to withdraw the regulation. Chinese men regarded this as a victory won by the women since men were forced to cut their hair in the Manchu style—a symbolic surrender to the Manchu rule (Gao Hongxin 1995, 24).

After that time, the lotus foot went beyond eroticism and became the object of fanatic worship as well as the standard for beauty and social status. As the Hangzhou elite Yuan Yuanzi commented in his introduction to Yu Zhiqu's *Notes on Pictures of Footbinding,* a beauty with natural feet was incomplete; whereas bound feet not only enhanced the beauty and made it whole but could also make a girl with an unattractive face beautiful (Yuan Yuanzi 1895). In other words, footbinding was doing what Nature did not. One could create her own beauty instead of relying on nature's caprice. Three inches became the standard measurement for lotus feet, and some women even aimed for less, to the point where they could place their feet on a saucer or had to be carried in order to move around.

It is generally accepted that footbinding began among the court and royal families roughly around the eleventh century, spread gradually to the commoners, flourished in the Ming dynasty, and reached its peak in the Qing. As the binding spread farther throughout the country, bound feet became smaller (from more than four inches to less than three), narrower, and more arched with each dynasty. Footbinding was basically a practice among Han women. Some regions had a much higher rate of women with bound feet, like parts of Guangdong and Fujian Provinces, and Datong, Lanzhou, Yiyang, Chengdu, and others. These places were also known for having the tiniest and most shapely feet (*Cai fei lu* 1:5). Most of the minority ethnicities did not have this custom. And some of the Han women kept their feet unbound. For example, the Hakka women in Guangdong and Fujian Provinces never bound their feet, because many of the Hakka men emigrated and the women had to work in the fields. The Tanka women of the Guangdong Province, who worked and lived on boats all their lives, kept their feet natural, too.

Economic factors and social status, however, are not the only reasons that affected footbinding. In the rich, highly civilized Jiangnan area, women did not seem to bind their feet as zealously as in other regions. In Jiangsu Province, only the women from Yancheng bound their feet into the three-inch model, and the rest were known for their big feet. Even in Suzhou and Yangzhou, where many women were in the entertainment business, women did not bind their feet into a small size; Suzhou women were famous for their facial beauty, and Yangzhou women, although they made their name with their "sea bass" feet *(huangyu jiao),* their feet were still about five to six inches in length. And women from Hangzhou and Jiahu of Zhejiang Province had the biggest-size lotus feet (*Cai fei lu* 1:2–10).

The peak of footbinding also marked its decline. From the eighteenth century on, liberal scholars, writers, and poets joined forces to fight against the evil of footbinding. During the Qianlong era (1736–95), a natural-footed woman poet caused quite a scene with her daring comment on foot-binding. A matchmaker gave her name to a man named Zhao Juntai, who was searching for a concubine. Mr. Zhao was reluctant to accept her because of her unbound feet, even though she was known for her beautiful face and slim figure. The matchmaker reminded him of the girl's talent in poetry. He then asked the girl to write a poem on lotus shoes. She composed:

> Three-inch bowed shoes did not exist in old times,
> And Bodhisattva Guanyin had her feet bare to be adored.
> I don't know when this custom began;
> It must have been invented by a despicable man.
>
> (Jia Shen 1990, 175)

When Yuan Mei (1716–98), the scholar and poet who opposed footbinding in his essays, heard of this incident, he wrote to Zhao, saying that tiny feet alone could not make a woman beautiful. It was the well-proportioned and balanced body and soul that made beauty. In his other essays, he criticized the cultural fixation on bound feet more directly: "What is the good of making a woman's feet so small because every generation is mad about this? I think that to maim your own daughter's limbs to make them prettier is like burning the bones of your parents in order to seek good fortune. How pitiful!" (Yuan Mei 1943, 956). Yuan's contemporary Li Ruzhen voiced his protest through his essays as well as in his novel *Jing hua yuan* (Flowers in the Mirror), for which he is remembered. In the novel, there is a man, a merchant called Lin Zhiyang, who experiences the horror of footbinding in the "Women Country" (1957).

The Qing rulers also banned footbinding as one of the measures to force the Han people to be assimilated into the Manchu culture, just as they forced the Chinese men to cut their hair in the Manchu style and wear Manchu clothing as an ultimate symbol of their overthrow of the Chinese. The ban was also meant to prevent the Manchus from being assimilated by the Han culture. The Qing rulers regarded the Manchu na-tive costumes and fashions as a crucial symbol to identify their origin and superiority, and many of them issued edicts to remind the Manchus of their importance. As Wu Hong points out, "If Qing rulers were willing to borrow anything from Chinese culture (and they indeed borrowed quite a lot), three things—surname, hairstyle, and clothes—must be exceptions" (1997, 354).

Since 1642, royal decrees had been issued from time to time to ban the practice of footbinding among Han women, and heavy penalties were heaped on the male heads of households. Meanwhile, footbinding was strictly forbidden among Manchu women. In 1804, the Jiaqing emperor issued the following edict:

> [Costume] is an important matter related to the tradition of the state and the mind of citizens. I therefore order you, the Commander-in-chiefs and Vice Commander-in-chiefs of both Manchu armies and Han armies in all Eight Banners, to pay great attention, finding out whether there are girls who wear clothes with freely expanded wide sleeves, and whether there are girls who even follow the Chinese costume of having their feet bound. Once you locate such unlawful youths, you must immediately impeach their parents, punishing them according to the legal codes for criminals who disobey government regulations. If after education they still cannot practice the right way and regain their old habit, once I find out this or receive letters of appeal, I will definitely punish them severely, together with the Commander-in-chief and Secretary of their Banner. I will never relent! (Quoted in Wu Hong 1997, 354)

Footbinding apparently went beyond the issue of fashion or costumes, beyond the realm of aesthetics, and was treated as seriously as state affairs. But the Chinese continued binding with greater zeal, and the ban only fanned more desire among the Manchus for tiny feet. Although the Manchus dared not bind their feet as did the Chinese, women wore extremely tight socks and shoes to keep the feet narrow and slender. They even invented a special shoe called *hua pen di* (flower bowl bottom). A small, white support, about two inches high, was affixed to the bottom of the shoe. When the skirt concealed the regular shoe, only the white support was seen. It created the illusion of lotus feet and the effect of lotus steps. Despite all the bans and harsh punishments from the government, footbinding spread more widely until it reached its peak.

Toward the end of the nineteenth century and at the beginning of the twentieth century, however, Chinese intellectuals, led by Kang Youwei and Liang Qichao, launched an antifootbinding propaganda campaign as part of the larger movement for reform, modernization, and feminine equality in China. Their main arguments were that footbinding made China an object of ridicule in the world, prevented the nation from taking its rightful place in international affairs, and weakened the country to a perilous degree by producing weak offspring. Thus, in order to revitalize China, footbinding was one of the first things to go. In the petition he submitted to the throne in 1898, Kang Youwei (1858–1927) stated:

> All countries have international relations, so that if one commits the slightest error the others ridicule and look down on it. Ours is definitely not a time of seclusion. Now China is narrow and crowded, has opium addicts and streets lined with beggars. Foreigners laugh at us or these things and criticize us for being barbarians. There is nothing which makes us objects of ridicule so much as footbinding. . . . With posterity so weakened, how can we engage in battle? I look at Europeans and Americans, so strong and vigorous because their mothers do not bind feet and therefore have strong offspring. Now that we must compete with other nations, to transmit weak offspring is perilous. (Quoted in Levy 1992, 72)

Liang Qichao (1873–1929) regarded footbinding as part of the patriarchal oppression of women throughout the world:

> Over the vast universe and throughout the ages, political edification from the sage and virtuous was diffused like the vast seas, but not a word was said or a deed committed for the sake of woman. Women were treated in one of two ways: they either fulfilled a series of duties or served as playthings. They were reared like horses or dogs to satisfy the first need and adorned like flowers or birds to satisfy the second. These two methods of oppression gave rise to three types of punishment. In Africa and India they pressed a stone against a woman's head to make it level, a punishment like our tattooing; in Europe they wanted the woman to have a slender waist, and to accomplish this they punished her by pressing wood against her waist; in China the woman had to have her feet bound, a punishment like cutting off the lower legs. These three punishments produced imperfect women throughout the world. I don't know when bound feet started, but the originator must have been a corrupt prince, an immoral ruler, a robber of the people, or a despicable husband. (Quoted in Levy 1992, 81)[5]

Once again, the female body was pushed to the front of a political discourse. Only this time, bound feet became a scapegoat for the empire's downfall, a symbol of women's victimization and degeneration, which was extended to symbolize China's peril from Western colonization; natural feet were used as a weapon for women's liberation and China's modernization.

Such a use of the female body for a political cause was not Kang or Liang's invention. Ming scholar Qu Sijiu had once proposed to use tiny-footed women to civilize Mongol barbarians so that they would eventually stop their attacks on China. His proposal may sound like a joke now, and it was not clear whether he was ever taken seriously by the emperor. But China was indeed regarded as the center of civilization for its culture, technology, and economy, and its material abundance during the Song and Ming dynasties, although it was often threatened by Mongol military forces. Footbinding could thus work as a cultural enticement, like food and sex, to assimilate the barbaric invaders into Chinese civilization. At the end of the nineteenth century and the beginning of the twentieth century, however, China's economy had fallen far behind the industrialized West, and its political and cultural status in the world had also sunk low. Footbinding now became an object of international ridicule and evidence of China's barbarity and backwardness. As Chinese intellectuals demanded reforms, which included abolishing old Chinese customs and learning advanced science, technology, even ideology such as democracy from the West, natural feet became part of what China was to adopt from the West. Bound feet thus spiraled down from a symbol of "national treasure" to that of "national shame," from civilization to barbarity, from beautiful to ugly, from high fashion and high class to the backwardness and ignorance of commoners. Meanwhile, natural feet became a sign for a new generation of ideal femininity and beauty. Women with natural feet symbolized health, intelligence, liberation, and equalization; therefore, they carried the hope of China's modernization into the new century.

Kang and Liang's call was answered by thousands of followers. Natural foot societies began to spring up everywhere as part of a mass movement, first in the cities, then branching out gradually to the countryside, where resistance to such propaganda was strong. The movement was enthusiastically joined by Western women who were living in China. In 1895, ten women from different nations founded a natural foot society. They wrote a petition to the Empress Dowager Cixi for her support, signed by "nearly all foreign ladies in the Far East" (Little 1899, 134–63). A Western natural foot society in Shanghai announced its intention in 1897 "to petition the Emperor that Children born after 1897 should not be recognized as of standing unless they had natural feet" (quoted in Levy 1992, 78). Christian missionaries also exerted their influence over the movement. They strongly discouraged footbinding among converts, often making natural or un-bound feet a condition for acceptance into boarding schools, or even for entering the church. By the beginning of the twentieth century, the whole nation—from the masses to the government, from intellectuals' propaganda to law enforcement, from schoolchildren to Westerners in China—joined forces to abolish the thousand-year-old female practice.

To combat the stubborn resistance from women, especially women in the countryside, natural foot societies created many songs and ditties to make the propaganda more accessible. They attacked footbinding aesthetically and ethically, using pictures and X rays of bound feet to prove how ugly and unnatural they were, and quoting Confucius and other Chinese sages as well as religious teaching to condemn footbinding for its brutality and inhumanity. Their most interesting, and perhaps most convincing, argument was that footbinding went against women's personal and economic interests in every possible way. It weakened their bodies, restricted their freedom, prevented them from working efficiently at home or in the fields, and made them easy targets for sexual assaults during wars. Worse, footbinding became an economic burden for the country as so many women, instead of working in the fields and factories, spent most of their time, money, and energy on their feet, bindings, and shoes.

Such an economic argument could appeal to the masses only at the end of the nineteenth century and the beginning of the twentieth century, when China was going through a fundamental change in its social, political, economic, and cultural systems, a change that affected every individual. China was being forced not only to give up its more-than-two-thousand-year-old feudal system and agricultural economy, but also to open the door to capitalist economic ideas and methods as well as to Western ideology more generally. Peasants could no longer follow the norms of the Chinese agricultural tradition, that is, that women stayed home to weave while men worked in the fields.[6] As the changing economy forced more and more peasants into bankruptcy, and as textile factories mushroomed in big cities like Shanghai in the twenties and thirties, women and children, especially young girls from the countryside, were lured or forced by economic need to work in those places as cheap labor. Girls with bound feet would be unable to enter such a market.

In order to entice a wider audience, natural foot societies organized mass meetings where footbound women were persuaded to expose their feet. To make the event more exciting and convincing, the exposure of the bound feet was immediately followed by natural-footed women baring their feet. The intention was to make a contrast between the evils of footbinding and the advantages of natural feet. The female body was thus used in a live performance on the public stage of politics. Side by side on the stage were two camps of women. One was the body of the footbound

Figure 8. Family of literati, leaders in the antifootbinding movement in the west of China.

woman, often middle-aged, old, uneducated (or educated through the old-fashioned, mind-restricting Chinese classics on female virtues), looking fragile and pale from being confined in the inner chamber all her life. She was either a wife of a conservative family, or a concubine, maid, or prostitute. She symbolized the sick, old, feudal China—its weakness, degeneration, backwardness, barbarity, brutality, oppression, and inevitable downfall. The other was the body of the natural-footed, young, healthy, educated woman (often in Christian missionary schools or the newly invented public schools, which taught foreign languages and Western ideologies and science). Embodying a new ideal of femininity, she belonged to a highly respected class (only the open-minded, wealthy, Westernized elite families would and could send their daughters to such schools) and a new generation of women who had the potential of becoming educators, doctors, nurses, revolutionary activists, and wives of modern intellectuals and the new rich. She marked the hope of a new, republic of China—reformed, democratic, scientific, modernized, and Westernized. At the same time, the highly politicized body was also immensely and publicly eroticized. The baring of the feet, be they bound or natural, made the antifootbinding meetings extremely popular. They often attracted thousands of curious and excited spectators, men and women, natural-footed or footbound, as recorded in *Records of Gathering Fragrance* and described in Feng Jicai's *Three-Inch Golden Lotus* (1986, 1994).

The law imposed heavy fines on women who refused to loosen their wrappings or continued binding their children's feet. The government offered rewards for those who could bring in women's binding cloths and lotus shoes. This caused many antifootbinding fanatics and men who had other intentions to break into houses and confiscate wrappings and shoes, or to stop women on the street and force them to take off their shoes and wrappings. Such public humiliation and assault caused a lot of emotional damage, even leading to suicide among some women. Those who were forced to loosen their feet had to suffer more than the initial binding, because without the binding, walking on the shrunken, deformed feet became extremely difficult and painful. Emotionally and psychologically, footbound women suffered even more as they were so publicly ridiculed and attacked on streets. The heaviest punishment inflicted on them was perhaps the loss of economic and social status. A lot of older and middle-aged women were divorced or simply abandoned by their modernized husbands, who often studied or worked in the cities, with the excuse that they could not find love or common language with their footbound wives. Students and young intellectuals only wanted

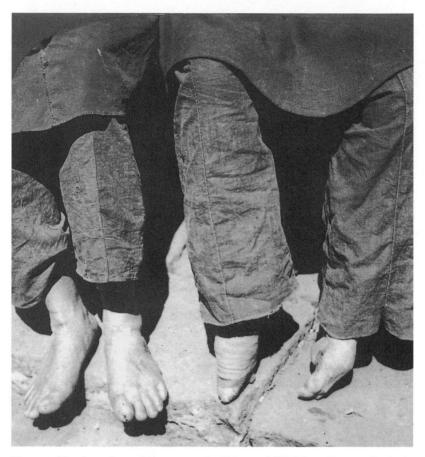

Figure 9. The feet of a working woman in China and "lily" feet. Courtesy Peabody Essex Museum, Salem, Massachusetts.

natural-footed women for their mates. When they were forced into arranged marriages with tiny-footed girls, they often chose to abandon their brides to their hometowns to serve the in-laws, then secretly sought their own ideal women (naturally footed, of course, and educated in modern schools) in the cities. Tiny-footed women thus became "unwanted goods" on the marriage market. Footbinding gradually disappeared during this century, but it ended with as much pain and violence, if not more, as had been inflicted on the body and mind when a little girl was initiated into the practice. Used as a metaphor and a scapegoat for China's collapse as the last empire and its gradual colonization by the West, bound feet, together with natural feet, became a battlefield for the future of China among royalists, nationalists, republicans, communists, and Western imperialists (see Levy 1992).

The ideas of the earlier antifootbinding activists were adopted by the later political and cultural movements from the May Fourth/New Culture Movement (1915–27) to the present. Du Fangqin, a contemporary Chinese scholar on women's studies, emphasizes over and over in her *Nuxing guannian de yanbian* (The Evolution of the Definitions about Womanhood [1988]) that footbinding was one of men's conspiracies to keep women home as slaves physically and mentally, to turn them into sheer objects of men's lust and perversity. Footbinding not only marked women's degradation and humiliation, but also men's moral decadence.

The recent English-language scholarship on Chinese women in late imperial times, however, questions the conventional association of footbinding with the decline in the status of Chinese women around the eleventh century rather than seeing the spread of footbinding as mere functions of Confucian and neo-Confucian thought. These scholars see it as resulting from the complex interplay of social, political, legal, economic, ideological, and cultural forces. Patricia Ebrey points out in her "Women, Marriage, and the Family in Chinese History" (1990) that the rise of footbinding is linked to a redefinition of masculinity in the Song period (960–1279), away from an active Tang (618–907) aristocratic ideal of horseback riding, hunting, polo, and other sports toward the more refined, artistic, sedentary, and contemplative ideal of the Song literati. This is concurrent with the redefinition of femininity away from an active and robust Tang ideal toward a more delicate, frail, and secluded feminine ideal of the late imperial period. Footbinding, Ebrey suggests, may have been part of an effort to differentiate Chinese culture from "loose barbarian" customs (Ropp 1990, 197–223). The practice may also have been part of an effort to protect the sanctity of hierarchical gender relations in an era of rapid social change, as Paul Ropp suggests in "Women in Late Imperial China" (1994, 12).

The blurred lines of gender and hierarchy in particular were caused by the rapid political and economic changes taking place during the Song dynasty. The land reform from Tang's *jun tian* system (in which land was divided equally) to the system of *zu tian* (in which land was rented) forced thousands of peasants off their land and out of their homes into cities, and forced them to sell their children, mostly daughters, as slaves, maids, concubines, and prostitutes. As major cities like Bian Jing and Lin'an became extremely prosperous during a time of fast commercial development, public and private courtesans with high artistic skills (singing, dancing, painting, and writing poetry) flourished in order to meet the demand for sensual pleasures among officials, literati, and merchants. Song rulers encouraged their officials to indulge in material life. The first emperor of the Northern Song, Song Taizu (Zhao Kuangyin; reign, 960–976) urged his ministers and generals to "accumulate gold and buy properties as much as possible to pass down to their children and enjoy the rest of their lives with singing and dancing girls" *(Song shi)*. Song Zhenzong (Zhao Heng; reign, 997–1022) ordered his minister, Wang Dan, known for his honesty and moral integrity, to buy concubines and sent him two maids from his palace. Later, the emperor had twenty beauties trained in singing and dancing and delivered them to Wang's home. In this kind of environment, it was the fashion among officials and literati to keep a large number of maids, concubines, singing and dancing girls, and courtesans at home.

Official and military prostitution also grew rapidly. Entertainment provided by singing and dancing girls was a part of life for literati and officials. Those beautiful and talented in the high arts could rise in social status and become *zhi yin*—bosom friends—with their artist patrons. In fact, the development and spread of the Song lyric songs *(ci)* were deeply intertwined with singing girls. They sang and performed the works of the great poets and politicians like Liu Yong, Su Shi, Xin Qiji, Lu You. Su Shi called himself *fengliu shuai*—ladies' general, a true friend of the female. "I search my past in the green house [brothel] / In order to leave my name in the empty space between flowers" (*Song yan: jin xu,* quoted in Du Fangqin 1988, 96). The great Song prose writer, poet, and historian Ouyang Xiu (1007–1072) devoted his life to restoring the tradition of the prose style before the Qin dynasty (221–207 B.C.), a style of simplicity, straightforwardness, and honesty that appeals to reason and goes against the flowery style of the Song. His essays and poems are full of moral integrity, but his lyric song "Lang tao sha" reflects a totally different side: "Beautiful courtesan with beautiful voice / How can I stop drinking before getting drunk" (*Song yan: ai mu,* in Du Fangqin 1988, 98). Xin Qiji was the great poet of the Southern Song (1140–1207) who was oppressed most of his life by his court enemies for his proposals to fight the Juchen Jin invasion and restore the lost land of China. He even wrote the following song of "Jiu bian er jue": "Which beauty / will fetch a red handkerchief and a green sleeve / to wipe the tears of a hero" (*Song yan: ai mu,* in Du Fangqin 1988, 97). This indulgence in pleasures—drinking, singing, dancing, and women—deepened in the Southern Song. No party, private or official, could be held without courtesans, music, or dance. General Wang Quan was sent to the frontier to fight the Tartars. He wept with his numerous concubines for three days, unable to depart (*Song yan: huo hai,* in Du Fangqin 1988, 97).

Bound feet, singing, and dancing became the most desired feminine qualifications among the royal families and literati. As long as they had "the beautiful music flowing from the singing girl's fingers / the whirling dance on a palm / Who cares if one doesn't know where to go tomorrow," sang Zhao Deling in his "Huan xi sha" (*Song yan: ai mu*, in Du Fangqin 1988, 97). This song, written by Su Shi's royal friend Zhao Deling, reflected the social mentality of the Southern Song: pleasure oneself to death while it is still possible. Even though China was constantly on the verge of being taken over by the Juchen Jin, few people in the court were willing to put up a fight. Threatened by constant invasions from the aggressive, barbaric (masculine) Jin, the passive, sophisticated (feminine) China could only give up land and pay tribute in huge amounts of money and goods in order to get another short period of peace, another period of indulgence in food, drink, sex, music, art, poetry, and other sensual activities before the whole country would be taken over.

This blurring of gender and social hierarchies continued with the further growth of the money-driven economy in the Ming and Qing eras. Providing another example of these blurred lines, James C. Y. Watt describes the merger of arts and crafts, which in turn led to more gender confusion:

> The demand for contemporary works of art reflected both consumer affluence and the success of market forces. Under the stimulus of free competition among independent producers, the quality of many types of decorative art reached a rarely attained level, and certain art forms made their appearance or were popularized for the first time. Hardwood furniture and carvings in wood, bamboo, soapstone, rhinoceros horn, and of course, jade . . . became extremely popular. . . . The result of this boom was blurred demarcation lines between the artist and the craftsman. . . . Late Ming decoration was colorful, and one of the most conscious aspects of fashion at the time was the colorful robes worn by men and women alike. A contemporary writer remarked that "in the districts of southeast, the students and the rich and scholarly families all wore red and purple clothes like women." (1987, 9)

Besides in the realm of fashion, signs of gender confusion were seen everywhere: cross-dressed women, girls raised as boys, women archery experts, male embroidery masters, and so forth. Indeed, the confusion of gender identification went beneath the clothes to the bodies of both males and females. In "Androgynous Males and Deficient Females: Biology and Gender Boundaries in Sixteenth- and Seventeenth-Century China," Charlotte Furth points out that the high incidence of reports from late Ming medical and literary sources on such biological anomalies as hermaphrodites, "natural eunuchs," "stone maidens" (impenetrable hymens), males who became females, females who became males, and finally, transvestites, reflected these gender ambiguities and complexities:

> Bodily ambiguity was translated into social gender according to patterns that identified the female with sexual deficiency and the male with androgynous erotic capabilities. . . . Where individuals were socially powerful and/or had the capacity to act upon the world, their sexual organs and sexual acts could be genderized as male. Female gender, on the other hand, was identified with those powerless persons whose bodies were read as defective and whose sexuality was passive or absent. (1988, 23–24)

The crisis was further complicated by the problems that transvestitism brought out, such as marriages between women, homosexual relationships, young girls and women who lost their virginity and virtue by men masquerading as women, and so on.

The anxieties over the erosion of a clearly defined place for women in family and society also came out through the popularity of stories about shrewish wives and henpecked husbands in seventeenth-century China. Such tales, as Yenna Wu points out, reflect "a male fear of woman's competition for supremacy, anxiety that she may subvert the patriarchal order, and a certain amount of hostility toward her. Men needed women for procreation, support and comfort, yet dreaded their potential power to dominate" (1988, 372). This fear of women, mixed with beliefs in female power and equality, and the anxiety over blurred gender boundaries, greatly affected Chinese men's psyche, emotions, and attitude toward women's bodies and minds as well as their own.

Neo-Confucianism rose in response to this male anxiety along with many other crises: the weakness in state policies that kept giving away land and money to the Juchen Jin for a period of peace; corruption among court and government officials; the successful spread of Buddhism throughout China; cultural decadence; and particularly, social and cultural changes that left gender and class hierarchies shaken. Zhu Xi, the founder of neo-Confucianism, raised the slogan *cunli mieyu*—maintain *li* (reason of cosmos) and eliminate *yu* (human desires). *Li* existed before the sky and earth, the creator of all things, the law of the universe. Zhu Xi believed that the ethical code of *sangang wuchang*—the three cardinal guides (ruler guides subject, father guides son, and husband guides wife) and the five constant virtues (benevolence, righteousness, propriety, wisdom, and fidelity)—is *li*, a law that had always existed before there was any ruler, subject, father, son, husband, or wife: "Before this thing comes into being, there is this 'li.' Just as the li for ruler and subject comes before the existence of ruler and subject, the li for father and son comes before the existence of father and son" (quoted in Du Fangqin 1988, 71; my translation).

For neo-Confucians, selfish human desires *(si yu)* that come from the five senses are the biggest enemies of *li,* therefore they must be eliminated. Men must "cleanse their desires to nurture their hearts, overcome their senses to nurture their spirit" (*Henan Cheng yishu,* in Du Fangqin 1988, 76). To translate this into practice, men must first of all keep away from concubines, beautiful widows, and prostitutes. The Cheng Brothers, the two earlier founders of neo-Confucianism, told a well-known story about their encounters with prostitutes. One day they went to a party and saw two singing girls sitting among the guests. Cheng Yi (1033–1107) left immediately in a rage, whereas his brother, Cheng Hao (1032–1085), stayed drinking with his friends until the party ended. The next morning, the two brothers met again. Yi was still angry. Hao laughed and said, "Yesterday I drank with prostitutes at the party, but they don't exist in my heart. Today my younger brother is sitting at his desk; although there's no prostitute around, he still carries her in his heart" (*Song yan: duan fang,* in Du Fangqin 1988, 99).

Similarly, Zhu Xi has a famous poem called "Self-Warning":

> The body has become light after ten years floating on the sea,
> Yet on the return, one still feels for the dimples on a girl's cheek.
> Nothing is more dangerous than human desire in this world,
> Few have been spared being ruined once they get here!
> (*Song yan: xia hao,* in Du Fangqin 1988, 98; my translation)

Zhu composed this poem to remind himself how dangerous women could be when he heard that the famous minister Hu Quan, on his return from his ten years of exile, wrote a poem to praise the beauty of a prostitute, Li Qian. Such an act, in the eyes of neo-Confucian *junzi* (gentlemen with an unshakable sense of honesty and morality) cost a man his moral integrity.

The neo-Confucian philosophers and literati regarded women, especially the beautiful ones trained for entertaining men, as *huo shui*—disastrous water/flood that if not kept under absolute control could endanger the hierarchies of the state, family, and gender roles. Men should be always on their guard, whereas women from good families *(liang jia fu nu)* must remain chaste and follow the five cardinal guides and five virtues. Girls should protect their virginity, and widows should not remarry. "It's a very small matter to starve to death, but a serious offense to lose one's chastity":

this is the answer the Cheng Brothers gave when they were asked if a widow should marry again out of financial necessity (*Henan Chengshi yishu,* in Du Fangqin 1988, 77).

Footbinding thus became an efficient way to keep women in their place—the inner chamber—physically, mentally, and symbolically. It offered a "means of spreading Chinese culture and teaching the separation of men and women" (Lin Yutang 1995, 165). It was said that Zhu Xi introduced footbinding into Zhanghou, Xiamen Prefecture of Fujian Province, where he served as governor. Seeing that the local women had much sexual freedom before and within marriage, he ordered all women to bind their feet to such an excessive degree that they could get about only by leaning on canes. The term *forest of canes* comes from the fact that when women from Fuzhou and Xiamen gathered for local celebrations or funerals, there were so many canes that they looked like a forest. By hampering women from moving about, Zhu Xi hoped to correct these women's immoral behavior (Jia Shen 1990, 173). Since there is no written document to prove this story, it is very possible that it was attributed to Zhu Xi by later generations.[7] It is not clear whether footbinding really succeeded in keeping women chaste. But one thing is certain: footbinding became the primary mark of class and gender identification. As the sayings reveal, "The tiny-footed is a lady, and the bare-footed [natural] is a maid" (Gao Hongxin 1995, 35), and "Without footbinding, how can one tell the difference between men and women?" (*Cai fei lu* 17).

Whether Zhu Xi's story of forcing women to bind their feet is true or not, the story itself certainly reflects a fundamental contradiction of footbinding. It was designed to keep women chaste to meet the teaching of neo-Confucianism, yet simultaneously it was highly eroticized. Such a contradiction can be seen as diverting erotic energy toward the domestic (Furth 1994). At the same time, it mirrors China's constant oscillation between two extremes: neo-Confucians' moral restraint to eliminate all human desires, and the indulgence in extravagance, expenditure, and sensual pleasures, particularly in food and sex. Morality demanded that women preserve chastity, whereas the fanatic need for pleasures required women to be lewd and lustful. This contradictory nature of Chinese society is manifested in the duality of bound feet—a moral enforcement and erotic object, at once ugly and beautiful, repulsive and enticing, comic and tragic, weak and powerful.

The blurred boundaries of gender and hierarchy also gave rise to a redefinition of femininity, from the Song and throughout the late imperial era in China. As masculinity turned more contemplative, refined, artistic, and sedentary, the ideal of femininity was upheld by the delicate and weak beauty who was also very refined and artistic. Tiny-footed women, especially those talented in poetry, singing, and painting, became the best representatives of such an ideal. By the time of the Song, the sickly, weak, languid, and fragile woman had become more and more the ideal feminine beauty in contrast to the taste for masculine and healthy women in the age of mythology, the ideal of simplicity and serenity during the Spring and Autumn Period, and the full-figured, graceful beauty of the Tang dynasty. Neo-Confucians linked women to *yin*: earth, water, small, weak, curve, passive, silent, and so on; in contrast to the male that is *yang*: the sun, powerful, big, straight, active, and loud. The ideal of feminine beauty reflects this concept: slender, delicate, tender, and quiet. In language, there are metaphors for beauty such as the tiny mouth of a cherry, a face like a pointed seed, a waist of the waving willow. The best natural beauty is "Flower waist and feet of palace style [bound feet]," whereas the sophisticated beauty should "Lean languidly on the railing and yawn." A combination of the two—a languid slender beauty—is of the highest value. A big, tall woman, no matter how beautiful she is, becomes a laughing stock. Su Shi was once invited to a rich merchant's house for a drinking party. The host favored a dancing girl who had a pretty face and a tall figure. When the host asked Su Shi to compose a poem for her, he wrote:

> She waves her sleeves trippingly,
> Like many dragons rolling and thousands of snakes squirming;
> Her voice so sweet,
> Like roaring thunders that turn half of the sky into wind and rain.
> (*Song yan: xi xi,* in Du Fangqin 1988, 121; my translation)

This poem embarrassed the dancing girl so much that she left the party in anger.

Two other important elements of feminine aesthetics were illness and melancholy. *Song ci* (lyric songs), especially those written by female poets, were filled with sick and sad beauties: Li Qingzhao's "I'm thinner than the chrysanthemums" *(Zui hua ying),* "Fearful that the boat from Shuangxi / cannot carry so much sadness *(Wu ling chun),* "How could the word *sad* describe all?" *(Shengsheng man).* In Zhu Shuzhen's *Jian zi hua mu lan,* she wrote "Sad and sick / Still can't enter a dream when the cold lamp dries up." Wu Shuji exclaimed in her *Xiao chong shan: Spring sadness,* "The heart is too small / to hold so much sadness." When we look at the descriptions of women's makeup, fashion, jewelry, and manner, they are mostly based on the aesthetics of melancholy. The Song poet Liu Xueji's lyric song *He xinlang,* a poem praising the well-known prostitute Li Shishi, is a typical example:

> An oriole wakes her up from a nap,
> Cloud of hair hangs slantingly,
> Loose, uncombed,
> A hair pin dangling on the side.
> Suffering from the hangover, cheeks red with last night's rouge,
> The spring hatred flows like water.
> Who can she tell
> About this melancholy?
> When she raises her arms, how slim her waist!
> And how she sighs over the golden bracelets too loose around her wrists.
> This weight on her mind,
> Who can she unload it to?
> . . . .
> Hidden bitterness gathers,
> Between her green eyebrows.
> (*Song yan: xia'ni,* in Du Fangqin 1988, 121; my translation)

It is no surprise that bound feet—so tiny, broken, deformed, delicate, and most important of all, so pitiful—became the symbol of feminine beauty from the Song period on.

Yet the praise for delicate feet and elegant walking predates footbinding. Song Yu, the poet from the Warring States Period (475–221 B.C.), describes different ways the goddess walks and stands in his "Shen nu fu" (Song of Goddess): *yi yi,* the floating movements of clothes as she walks or dances; *po suo,* whirling, dancing; *xu bu,* walks slowly and elegantly. The emphasis mostly falls on the quietness, elegance, and relaxation of the movement. In the Western Han (206 B.C.–24 A.D.), Ban Jieshu wrote about the silk washing girl in her poem "Dao su ge": "Each step makes fragrance." Gradually, the attention moved to shoes and socks. Hence Yang Xiu (53 B.C.–18 A.D.) compares the boots that the goddess wears to lotus blossoms in his "Song of Goddess." Li Po has "The feet in sandals / sockless, white like frost" in his poem "Yue Girl," and "A pair of golden shoes / feet as white as frost" in his "The Washing Girl on the Rock." After Su Shi's first poem about bound feet, more and more poets and playwrights turned their gaze on women's feet to the point that they became the highest symbol of feminine beauty. All the praise and metaphors focus on the lightness, delicateness, and secretiveness of the feet and the lotus steps:

Her silk skirt flows like spring breeze,
Her lotus blossoms so light as if floating on autumn water.
Her shoe tips already hidden under the skirt,
She still looks around in fear that her tiny shoe embroideries be seen.

(Sa'dulla, born 1308)

The first beauty should be golden lotus,
What a pair of phoenix heads;
The peeling petals of new lotus blossoms and the new moon,
Pointed, narrow, and soft, covered with embroidery.
Since our departure, I haven't seen her again,
When will the twin ducks intertwine again?
When will I hold them around my waist, on my shoulders,
And on my back as well as in my hands?

(Tang Yin, 1470–1523)

The silk bandage still warm and fragrant,
Jade lotus hidden under the skirt,
She comes like a floating fairy.
Next to the lifted curtain,
She looks so delicate as if the wind could blow her away;
She walks lightly around the pond, not disturbing the moss.
On the silent path,
Her flowing skirt does not stir any dust.
After a swing,
She leans on her lover's shoulder with a smile,
And takes time to pull off her shoes.

(Liang Qingbiao, early Qing)

In the play *Xi xiang ji* (The Romance of the Western Chamber), Zhang Sheng sits in his room alone, thinking about Ying Ying after their first encounter. His thoughts travel downward, from her delicate eyebrows, her light makeup to her neck powdered with fragrance, then fixing on her tiny golden lotuses under a green skirt. When later he watches her pray before the incense, he pays special attention to her feet. Every step she takes stirs up his pity, including her shallow footprints on the fragrant dust. After they have sex, he notices how touching her tiny feet are as she walks languidly down the steps.

The women presented in these poems and literary works all have the same qualities: they are floating and weightless like a fairy or goddess, fragile and delicate like a child, hidden and mysterious like unreachable treasure. Men cannot help feeling pity for them and falling in love with them. All these are indispensable elements for Chinese eroticism and female allure.

In the Ming and Qing literature, the spectacle of lotus feet extended to their related objects—shoes, socks, binding bandages, *qiku* (embroidered cloth tied around the ankles). Poets and literati gathered together and wrote poems on the golden lotus, from the part to the whole, from the toe to the heel, and from different settings, environments, seasons, and times of the day, comparing it to the most beautiful objects in nature: winter cherries, a rainbow, bamboo shoots. Bound feet became such a powerful erotic object that one look at the golden lotus was enough to stir up a man's desire to the point of frenzy. People believed that since the beginning of history a beauty had to have a pair of slender, tiny feet, that those who loved tiny feet were intellectuals with good taste, and that those who loved money were just vulgar (*Cai fei lu xu bian* 294).

Not only did the bound foot become the object of literary and erotic fixation, but it also entered the everyday language of the common people: folk art, folklore, songs, riddles, sayings, proverbs, and curses. Women with beautiful faces and natural feet were mocked as "half Guanyin," Bodhisattva with only half of the body.[8] *Po xie* (torn shoes) was a term that signified a whore, since a prostitute's shoes wore out easily as she had to put them on and take them off many times a day to do her business. *Xiao tizi* (little hooves) was obviously meant for the tiny hoof-like feet. The proverb "A lazy woman's binding bandage—long and stinky" mocked any long, tedious speech or lecture. There were also sayings like "Those with big heads are gentlemen, and those with big feet are villains" ("Zi zu tan," in *Cai fei lu* 33:36). The bound foot even had a place in the world of death and gods. Female ghosts in stories and goddesses in local temples often had tiny feet. The following folk rhymes (one from Henan Province and the other from Zhejiang), supposedly sung by little boys, show how the concept of tiny-foot beauty had seeped into the consciousness of the Chinese:

> Mother, Mother, it's her I must wed,
> Her flowered high heels are unparalleled.
> While I'm penniless, it's true,
> To have her I'll sell all we've held.

> Her powdered pink face,
> Prettier than a peach;
> Her twin golden lotuses,
> Perfect fit for my hands.
> I'll take you home as my bride,
> In a colored sedan chair.
> (*Cai fei lu* 2:18–19; in Levy 1992, 111)

To be beautiful, or to look beautiful, is an aesthetic impulse as primary, strong, and persistent as the survival instinct. It is quite understandable that when even a little boy desires a tiny-footed girl for his bride, women would do anything to have a perfectly bound pair of feet in order to prepare themselves for the marriage market, which in a patriarchal society provides their livelihood, identity, and social status.

But how do we explain such pain and endurance, such persuasiveness and length of time, such contradictory qualities, and such mad obsession over a pair of tiny feet—for more than a thousand years? If it is true that binding women's feet is part of men's conspiracy to subjugate and control women, then how do we explain the mad obsession on men's part, especially when they are willing to give up all they have for a pair of golden lotuses, even to start binding or compressing their own feet?[9] Isn't it just another kind of subjugation? How does the hunter become the prey, and who has the real control? And all the discipline, the torture and the decay of the flesh, the obsessive ornament and eroticizing of the body part: do they lead to the elimination of the body or the elevation of it, or both, as a means to immortality?

Footbinding and the
Cult of the Exemplary Woman

Erotic thoughts arise after the body is fed and clothed.
—Confucius

Twin red shoes, less than three inches,
With pretty flowers for embroidery.
Wait till I tell the folks at home;
I'll mortgage the house, give up the land,
And wed with tiny feet as planned.
—Hunan ditty (in Levy 1992, 111)

FOOTBINDING HAS MANY DUAL FACES. It shines with beautiful embroidery and irresistible charm on the surface, yet underneath there is only deformity and foul odor. It makes a woman appear celestial and high-bred; when bared, the feet resemble a pair of hooves. Adorned with shoes, bound feet invoke art and magic; under the bandages, however, is the trace of violence. Outside, a bound foot is erect and pointed like a penis; inside, it is creased and curved like a vagina. A pair of bound feet are sacred and dirty, a taboo and an object of desire. Footbinding contaminates and cleanses, curses and heals, masks and displays, seduces and kills. The list can go on indefinitely.

In this chapter I explore how the duality of footbinding reflects the duality of the Chinese feudal system; how this duality and oscillation between moral restriction and great expenditure affected women; and how women, the objects and subjects of the expenditure, affected the economy, culture, as well as language. The rise of footbinding, together with the rise of the cult of the exemplary woman, symbolizes the social, political, and cultural predicaments in the late imperial period. As China faced the threat of foreign invasions, drastic economic and social changes, and the boundary erosion of hierarchy, race, gender, and sex, footbinding and the cult of the exemplary woman were encouraged as ways to deal with these problems. But the result was a total merging of all opposites—battles between masculinity and femininity, reason and flesh, and writing and speech. The dual nature of footbinding and the nation's oscillation between moderation (reason) and indulgence (expenditure) are interlocked with the violent clashes within language.

Throughout the late imperial period, China oscillated between the high moral restriction and purification of neo-Confucianism and the corrupting of the flesh; between the urge to make boundaries for gender and hierarchy, to hold things in their fixed places through language; and the blur of all divisions, the flow of the contents out of their containment, and the destruction of all barriers. Chinese society oscillated between the rapid growth of the economy and commerce that led to a great abundance of wealth, and the urge to spend, a frenzy of squandering resources. From the Song dynasty to the Ming to the Qing, China was often threatened by peasant uprisings and foreign invasions. To deal with these crises, the system tightened the rein on its people: heavy taxes, secret police, strict laws, and appalling punishments. The oppression of women also deepened: the spread of footbinding as a way to confine them to their inner chambers, and the flourishing of exemplary women to keep them chaste. Royalty, officials, and rich merchants, however, turned the race of expenditure into great competitive spectacles, wallowing in sensual pleasures—food, drink, sex, art (poetry, music, dance), craftsmanship, and the construction of grand gardens and monuments. To borrow a term from social theorist Thorstein Veblen, the society was shaped by the law of "conspicuous leisure" as well as "conspicuous consumption" (Veblen 1992, chaps. 3–4). For the noble and rich, mere idleness was not enough: leisure had to be coupled with the obvious waste of valuable resources as a means of putting one's wealth and power on social display and gaining reputability. While women became one of the most valuable human goods in the expenditure spectacle, as active agents of the consumption themselves they began to reshape the definition of womanhood. Talent was now added to virtue and beauty for the new ideal of femininity (Ko 1994, 143). This new definition of womanhood applied not only to gentry women but also to courtesans. Greatly encouraged to cultivate their talents in poetry and art as well as their beauty, women participated both as objects and subjects of the spectacular cultural and economic consumption through footbinding (beauty) and writing/publishing (as well as being written and published about).

The oscillation between these two poles of reason and expenditure is manifested through the rise and spread of footbinding and the cult of the exemplary woman in late imperial China. The effects and affects of footbinding are twofold. On the one hand, it satisfies the demand for reason, morality, and the logic for order, work, and the accumulation of wealth, as well as the need to set boundaries for class and gender. Men used footbinding to straighten out the corrupt morals of the nation. They also tried to use footbinding to corrupt the enemy. The Ming scholar Qu Sijiu proposed to the emperor that they should introduce footbound women to the Juchen invaders as a strategy to stop their vicious attacks on China. He argued that beauty could soften the barbarous nature of these warriors and take away their aggressive manliness. Once they indulged themselves in the sensuality and refinement of tiny feet, they would no longer wish to invade China (Shen Defu, *Wanli yehuo bian,* in Jia Shen 1990, 164–65). In the beginning of the Qing dynasty, footbinding was hailed by Chinese men as a successful resistance against the Qing rule and its oppression. As footbinding spread nationwide, its functions also expanded from a mere aesthetic fashion to the safeguard of morality, the barrier of all divisions, as suggested by Dorothy Ko:

> In this period [the end of the Ming and the beginning of the Qing] of intense anxiety over personal and national survival, loyalty was expressed in gendered terms and sexuality acquired overt political significance. Indeed, footbinding became the terrain on which the ethnic and cultural boundaries between the Han Chinese and the "Other" were being drawn. (1997a, 10)

On the other hand, bound feet serve as the symbol of eroticism, the object of desire. And the realm of eroticism is that of extravagance, expenditure, chaos, transgression, and ruin, set in contrast with the realm of reason: work, accumulation of wealth, respect for taboos, order, and kindness. "Erotic conduct," as Bataille points out,

> is the opposite of normal conduct as spending is the opposite of getting. If we follow the dictates of reason we try to acquire all kinds of goods, we work in order to increase the sum of our possessions or of our knowledge, we use all means to get richer and to possess more. Our status in the social order is based on this sort of behavior. But when the fever of sex seizes us we behave in the opposite way. We recklessly draw on our strength and sometimes in the violence of passion we squander considerable resources to no

real purpose. . . . Our only real pleasure is to squander our resources to no
purpose, just as if a wound were bleeding away inside us; we always want to
be sure of the uselessness or the ruinousness of our extravagance. (1986, 170)

No matter how hard humans work to become rational beings, flesh constantly bursts out of the boundary of logic and rationality. In the case of
footbinding, no matter how men try to gear the practice into usefulness
and the control of women, sexuality overflows the tiny lotus shoes, flood-
ing away the barriers and outer limits, the legal, moral, and cultural restrictions. Once footbinding enters the domain of compulsive consumption of
all resources, including the flesh itself, it takes on a life of its own, recognizing neither reason nor logic, dissolving the boundaries not only between
gods and humans, monsters and animals, dead and living, but also between nature and culture. In the course of this violent squandering and
consumption, the flesh picks up speed toward annihilation, and nothing
can stop it until death swallows everything, be it an individual, a country,
or a dynasty. Death thus turns life into a series of savage consumption
within the general economy of repetition and expenditure.

Of all the expenditures, nothing perhaps is as widespread and consum-
ing as sexual extravagance. And of sexual extravagances, nothing is perhaps
as luxurious as footbinding, with its large scale of participation and long
period of practice, its degree of painful and violent mutilation and auto-
mutilation, and the frenzy that swept most of the areas where the Han
population lived. It is true that footbound women, especially those from
peasant and poor families, were not exempt from working in and outside
the households as equal contributors in the system of economic production. Though women from upper-class and elite families stayed in their
inner chambers, learning needlework and the arts of poetry and painting,
most of them worked as household managers, caretakers of husbands and
in-laws, bearers and educators of children. And women of common background carried out their household duties—such as cooking, cleaning,
sewing, serving their in-laws, and raising children, apart from spinning,
weaving, embroidering, making clothes and shoes for the entire family—as
essential contributors to the grain-based, self-sufficient, labor-intensive
agricultural economy.[1]

Yet footbinding did help to reinforce the division of labor, gender, class
as well as the division of the domestic and public, though such boundaries
were constantly blurred and crossed.[2] Aspired to as a symbol of the leisure
classes and its ideals of femininity, "footbinding simply changed the terms
of that participation such that the labor women contributed was veiled by

mystique of women as sexual and maternal but otherwise worthless" (Blake 1994, 678). By impairing women's feet, footbinding mystified a woman's sexual and reproductive powers, giving her and "those who possessed her a claim on social status" (Blake 1994, 702). With a pair of perfectly bound feet, women of lower rank could have hopes of moving upward socially and economically by entering a more affluent or more educated family, often as a concubine or maid. Despite their low social status, courtesans (especially *mingji*—famous courtesans) were able to excel in art, poetry, dancing, and singing and had great mobility in the public arena dominated by men. In the spectacle of expenditure, footbinding became a mask over women's labor, discipline, morality, adding the veneer of beauty, erotica, leisure, and talent.

To meet the urgent need of the sexual extravagance of late imperial China, prostitution flourished from the Song dynasty onward. *Guan ji* and *ying ji*—prostitutes who were registered with the government and served officials and the army—gradually became commercialized, especially in the capitals Bianjing (during the Northern Song 960–1127) and Lin'an (the Southern Song 1127–1279). The entertainment business, which had been available only to certain classes, was now open to those who were less privileged but well-off enough to afford such amenities—like merchants, traveling traders, and peddlers. In Bianjing, many streets specialized in brothels, plus hundreds of restaurants, wine shops, and tea shops that were frequented by prostitutes. *Dongjing meng hua lu* describes such activities in restaurants:

> All the facades of the wine shops in the capital are decorated with colorful ribbons and flags. When one enters the shop and walks about a hundred steps, there is a yard with small rooms lined along the south and north. In the evening, lights are lit everywhere. Hundreds of prostitutes with heavy makeup stand along the main corridor waiting for the call of customers. They all look like fairies. ("Wine shops," in Meng Yuanlao 1957)

Marco Polo was shocked to see thousands of beautiful prostitutes in the capital of the Southern Song living in such luxury and extravagance. Their art of seduction was so sophisticated it was said that no one could resist their charm.

Prostitution became even more widespread during the Ming and Qing periods. Since both official and private brothels were now open to all classes of society, courtesans were no longer the sole privilege of royalty, officials, and literati. In Beijing, the capital of the early Ming dynasty, "there are more prostitutes than *liangjia*"—women from good families, that is, women

Figure 10. The amah, or serving woman, haggling with a street hawker.

who were not prostitutes ("Di bu yi," in Xie Zhaozhe 1959). The prosperity and fame of the concubine market in Yangzhou (*shou ma*—thin horse) and the prostitute market in Suzhou continued until the end of the last dynasty in China. The Ming government had a policy of selling all female relatives of convicted official families into prostitution. As the dynasty was known for its harsh rule and thousands of unjust verdicts, this policy actually boosted the prostitution business. It is quite shocking and revealing to hear how Emperor Yongle (Ming Chengzu; reign, 1403–1424), known for his wisdom and foresight, responded to an official's question on how to handle a case involving convicted women. According to the procedure, they had all been sold into prostitution. But the official wanted to know what he should do with a three-year-old girl and the female babies that were born and would be born during the trial:

> On the eleventh day of the first month of the third year of Yongle (1406), Yu Youshun from the Education Department presented an oral petition to the emperor at the door: Each of the four women—Qi Tai's older sister and his cousin's wife, as well as Huang Zicheng's sisters—is closely guarded by twenty men every day. Now all the young women are pregnant. [When they are born,] the boys will become servants [according to the rule]. But I need the instruction about a three-year-old girl.
>
> The Emperor replied, "Let her be. Before she grows up, she will already have become a whore!" (*Kui si lei gao: chu yuehu gaihu ji nuyue kao fu gushi,* in Du Fangqin 1988, 264)

Another Ming emperor, Wuzong (1491–1521; reign, 1505–1521), was known for his sexual violence. Unsatisfied with thousands of concubines in his court, he traveled all over the country to rape and plunder women from common families and bring them back to the capital. When he passed by Yangzhou after his battle against Lord Ning, he and his officials pillaged the local residences, raping virgins and widows. His violence plunged the city into such a panic that families grabbed any young men available to marry their daughters. Once, the emperor forced himself into a house and demanded women. He was having so much fun that he forgot to return to his palace, claiming that he was already "at home" (in Du Fangqin 1988, 265). He built a "leopard house" where he and his ministers had orgies day and night with the captive women. He also brought musicians and monks who knew the secrets of bedchamber art into the leopard house to enhance the intensity of the orgies. He finally died there at the age of thirty (in Du Fangqin 1988, 265). In many ways, the story of Ximen Qing from *The Golden Lotus* echoes the deeds of the emperor when Jinlian curses Ximen

Qing: if he had had God's power, there wouldn't be a single woman in the world safe from his hand. "To sleep with all the beautiful women under the blue sky"—this is also the ambition of the protagonist Weiyang Sheng in *The Carnal Prayer Mat.*

With the emperor as their leader, the literati and officialdom competed for varieties and novelties in this grand sexual consumption. The Ming government prohibited officials from visiting brothels, yet "they sat with courtesans on their laps and danced with them all day long" (*Lie zhuan shi ji xiao zhuan,* in Du Fangqin 1988, 294). Some collected historical stories of eccentric literati and imitated their deeds. They rode donkeys, got drunk with courtesans in public while dressed in official uniform, or begged from door to door without shoes or hats (Du Fangqin 1988, 295). Ming literati talked openly about sex, exchanging the secrets of the bedchamber arts. Male bonds and political liaisons were often formed in courtesan houses— *qinglou* (the blue building)—through drinking, game playing, and poetry exchanging. In the late Ming, the "auras of the courtesan and the scholar-official had constructed and reinforced each other" (Ko 1997b, 87). On the one hand, the patronage of the literati elevated the status of the courtesan and helped the blooming of courtesan culture, especially through poetry and its publication. On the other hand, the abundance of the courtesan talents glorified the literati's political power; after all, such highly valued cultural products and producers were men's ultimate prize to claim and served as their "alter egos" (Ko 1997b, 96).

As brothels opened their doors to many socioeconomic classes in the Ming dynasty, spending money on courtesans became more and more popular for commoners, especially merchants, whose social and political status rose rapidly with the development of the economy. Their indulgence was not prohibited by laws, religion, or marriage. They even found teachings from Buddhism and Confucianism to justify their excesses. To seek out courtesans was "to accumulate good deeds and practice great kindness." Affairs between men and women were all predestined, as Ximen Qing pointed out to his wife, who advised him to stop going after whores and start behaving properly for the sake of his son:

> The world is based upon the interaction of the male and female principles and it is natural for men and women to be drawn together. Any irregular little affair that may happen in this present life was predetermined in a former one. It is all written down in the register of marriages. One cannot say that anything we do is out of depravity and evil passion. Besides, they tell me that gold is not despised, even in Paradise, and, in the ten regions of

Hell, money is at a premium. So, if we are generous in almsgiving now, it won't do us any harm if we debauch the angels and run off with the daughters of the Mother of the Gods. (*The Golden Lotus* 3:45)

Since there was no moral, religious, or legal prohibition against men seeking pleasure, adultery held great attraction, because sleeping with other people's wives was the greatest transgression in every sense. People believed that their own wives were not as attractive as concubines, that concubines were not as attractive as prostitutes, that prostitutes were not as attractive as other men's wives, and that those who could be seduced were not as attractive as those who couldn't be. A folk song from this period explains that a woman could burn with desire to such a degree that she was willing to risk the highest punishment for a moment of love:

> I beg my mother and beat my son.
> My heart burns with longing.
> I send a letter to my lover:
> Exile me, take me away from my family,
> Even cut me into a thousand pieces,
> But please, my love, please come to see me,
> Just one more time.
>
> (*Wu ge: gan ren,* in Feng Menglong
> 1986; my translation)

But money is still men's best attractor. In the Ming short story collection *San ke pai an jing qi,* a merchant seduces Tang Guimei's mother-in-law, who then orders her daughter-in-law to sleep with the merchant for more money. Tang refuses and hangs herself so that she won't commit the crime of disobeying her mother-in-law. Throughout the story collection, officials send their wives, sisters, or daughters to sleep with the emperor in order to gain power, and commoners are willing to let their wives sleep with rich merchants for money.

In *The Golden Lotus,* Han Daoguo, an employee in Ximen Qing's herb store, is delighted to see the silver his wife Porphyry gets from Ximen Qing for having sex with him. Instead of feeling jealous, he listens to his wife's story with great interest. Porphyry, Han's wife, tells her husband all about her dealings with Ximen Qing:

"Since you have been away," she says, "he has been here three or four times. He gave me four taels of silver to buy this little girl, and every time he comes, he gives me a tael or two. That younger brother of ours, who does not know the difference between high and low, came piddling around.

Master Hsi-men [Ximen] happened to see him, and he was hailed to the office and well beaten there. Since then he has never dared to show his face again. Our master says this place is not very convenient, and he has promised to buy a house in the main street, and let us go there."

"I see now why he would not take the silver," Han Daoguo says, "but asked me to take it and not to spend it. Now I understand what he was thinking about."

"Well," Porphyry says, "here are fifty taels. We will add a few more, and buy a really fine house. Then we shall have a comfortable life, good eating, and fine clothes. It is obviously worth while my letting him have me."

"To-morrow," Han Daoguo says, "if he should happen to come when I have gone to the shop, pretend that I know nothing about it, and don't treat him unkindly. Do everything he would have you do, for it is no easy matter making money nowadays, and I know no better way than this."

Porphyry laughs. "You rascal. It is easy money for you, but you don't know the sufferings I have to endure." They both laughed heartily. She prepared supper, and they went to bed. (*The Golden Lotus* 2:159–60)

The couple indeed work well as a team in order to extract as much money as possible from Ximen Qing. When Ximen finally dies, they steal a whole boat of merchandise from their deceased master.

This type of sexual extravagance stimulated the need to throw more money and energy into training women in art, poetry, courtship, adornment, and self-presentation. And footbinding was a must for female charm and beauty. In Yangzhou, many families trained girls brought in at young ages to excel in singing, dancing, painting, beautifying, and the art of seduction. Known as "thin horses" (Ko 1994, 261–64) and for their tiny feet, these girls could be sold for a substantial amount of money as prostitutes, concubines, or maids. Each house specializing in such business had four or five girls ready for sale, and more in training. Xie Zhaozhe, author of the compendium of Ming customs and social life *Five Miscellanies* (*Wu za zu* 1959), notes, "The people of Yangzhou have long treated [their beautiful women] as precious merchandise. Merchants bought young girls from everywhere. They dressed up the girls and taught them crafts such as calligraphy, drinking games, zither, and chess, expecting a handsome return" (quoted in Ko 1994, 261). Because of this thriving traffic in women, footbinding became more popular in Yangzhou than in many other areas, as a Qing observer pointed out: "Even coolies, servants, seamstresses, the poor, the old, and the weak have tiny feet and cramped toes" (*Xiang yan cong shu*, quoted in Ko 1994, 263). An early Qing poet Shi Runzhang recorded an old ditty about Yangzhou:

Guangling [Yangzhou] daughters are as numerous as clouds.
They are born not to weave and spin,
But to learn songs and dances.
Powerful men converge in front of their gardens,
Big merchants gather at their gates.
. . . .

At age thirteen or fourteen they are ready,
Who cares if he is old if he has gold.

(*Yangzhou fuzhi, yiwen,* in Ko 1994, 263)

Since tiny feet were the most important object of beauty and eroticism, women of different classes spared neither expense nor time in washing, trimming, massaging, binding, and unbinding their feet, or embroidering shoes. Some went to such an extreme that caring for their feet became an obsession, a compulsive act. Yan Xian, one of the authors from *The Golden Lotus,* told a story of how he witnessed (through a peephole) a woman of leisure pampering her feet when he was a child:

> One day I was staying in my friend's house. There I peeped at a woman who lived next door. She was about thirty or forty years old. She sat near the sunny window, unbinding the bandages. Soon her white feet were all exposed. She looked at them from different directions, then massaged every inch from toe to heel, as if she were playing with some toys. After a while, she rebound her feet very slowly and carefully, then put on a pair of red shoes. Gently, she stepped onto the floor, staring at her feet with full concentration and admiration. I returned to the peep hole half an hour later, and to my surprise, the woman had already unbound her wrapping for the second time and was gazing at her white feet as before. My friend told me that this woman exposed her own feet and stared at them at least ten times a day. He had already gotten used to it. She was originally from An Hui. Her son also married a tiny-footed woman. (*Cai fei lu* 282; my translation)

Fang Xun's *Classification of the Qualities of Fragrant Lotuses (Xiang lian pin zao)* gives detailed advice on how a woman should care for her feet, and how she should present (or hide) them in a manner that would arouse the strongest desire in men, keeping a chaste and proper appearance at the same time. Fang gives a list of the best moments and places to bind and wash feet: on a sunny day, when slightly drunk, after a bath, after a dream, before going to bed, after a trip, before trying on new shoes, in front of flowers, under the moon, under a lamp. According to him, such scenes would greatly enhance a woman's beauty. It is pleasing for men to watch a woman bind, wash, make shoes or try them on, tie shoelaces by the balustrade, or pare down foot calluses with a knife under a lantern. Since these are done in strict privacy, such activities became voyeuristic games.

Bound feet are not only the most erotic objects for the gaze (clandestine as well as open gazing) and display, but also indispensable tools for enhancing pleasure at social events. Fang Xun describes in detail how lotus shoes are used in drinking games at parties:

> Pretty prostitutes spurred on the drinking by playing a game in which small fruits and seeds were tossed into a tiny shoe, delighting both winners and losers. The shoe was first passed around from hand to hand and was widely admired. It was compared to a mythical raft which revolved like the moon and was so referred to in play.
>
> The raft was played according to a fixed set of rules. The prostitute with the prettiest and tiniest feet had both of her shoes removed. A wine cup was placed in one shoe, while the other shoe was placed in a basin. The shoeless prostitute became Recording Secretary. It was her duty to hobble about, basin in hand, before each guest in turn and hold the basin about one and a half feet away. The guests took lotus seeds, red beans, or similar objects from a bamboo box, held them parallel with the basin and tried to throw them into the shoe. The tosses were made by grasping the seeds or beans with the thumb, forefinger, and middle finger. Each person made five tosses and, after all had taken turns, the Secretary prescribed drinking penalties for those who had gotten the fewest throws into the shoe.
>
> The raft might take as long as four to six hours to complete. There were different names for the ways in which throws got into the shoe. A direct throw into the shoe was called a Passing Star, while five successful throws at one turn were called Five Pearls. The most difficult achievement was to have the seed or bean hit the point of the shoe and then go in. If this happened, it was rewarded the same way as were five good throws. If a throw hit the basin first and then entered the shoe, it was counted twice and called a Flying Star Entering the Moon. It was considered an offense to make a throw outside the basin area or cause the shoe to move or turn over; the offender had to take additional drinks, by order of the Recording Secretary. (Quoted in Levy 1992, 121–22)

Such drinking games, together with the so-called Cup of the Golden Lotus, which involved drinking from a wine cup placed in a tiny shoe, originated in the Song, then flourished in the Yuan and later dynasties. In *The Golden Lotus,* Ximen Qing has already played such games with his concubine Jinlian. When they get together for the first time, Ximen takes off Jinlian's lotus shoe in a fit of passion, places his wine cup inside, and drinks from it. As for the throwing game, instead of using her tiny shoe, he throws seeds (replaced with plums in the book) directly into her vagina as Jinlian lies naked on a mat, her feet tied to the grape vines with her foot wrappings:

> "Now," Ximen said, "watch me. I'm going to play 'Flying arrows with a living target.' The game is called 'Striking the Silver Swan with a Golden Ball.' Watch! If I hit the mark at the first shot, I shall treat myself to a cup of wine." He took a plum from the iced bowl, and cast it [at Jinlian's vagina]. He cast three. All of them hit the treasure of the flower. Ximen drank three cups, and ordered Chunmei to pour a cup for Jinlian. Then he placed a plum in her vagina, but would not have sex with her, leaving her trembling with unquenched passion on the mat].[3] (*The Golden Lotus* 1:385)

The story of *The Golden Lotus* is set in the Song dynasty, although the book was written in the Ming dynasty and gives a vivid representation of the culture, politics, economy, and sociology of the epoch in which the author lived.

But if Ximen Qing and the women can be counted only as fictional figures, no matter how authentic they are historically, Hu Xueyan, a rich merchant of the nineteenth century in Hangzhou, is a real figure in history. With a name that means "the living god of wealth," his extravagance with women, especially their feet, even surpasses Ximen Qing. Hu had more than 30 concubines and 130 maids, all of whom lived in separate households in the same compound. Hu wrote their names on ivory chips and drew lots at dusk. Whoever was drawn would spend the night with him. Often he would call four or five concubines overnight, sometimes ten. Most of his concubines came from Suzhou, Hangzhou, Shanghai, Ningbo, and Tianjin. Some came from Dongting, Yiyang, Datong, and Dongwan, all places known for their tiny-footed women.

For Hu, the most important part of women's bodies were the two hooks under their skirts. Whenever he had spare time, he took pleasure in watching his concubines and maids binding and washing their feet. He couldn't sleep unless he held their spring hooks in his hands. The tiniest feet among his concubines were only two inches. Some had feet the size of four to five inches. But all his maids had three-inch lotuses. That was because when he bought his concubines, they were already adults, and it was very difficult to reform their feet. On the other hand, when he bought his maids at ages five or six, he immediately had their feet tightly bound by experts.

Hu had house rules for all the women: those who had feet smaller than three inches could wear scarlet shoes with golden embroidery; those whose feet were larger than three inches could only wear pink shoes; and those who had feet longer than four inches could wear any other color except for red and pink. But if their feet were larger than five inches, only blue cotton shoes were allowed. If a woman was diligent with her binding, she would be rewarded with more monthly allowance. If she was lazy, she would be whipped. These rules were strictly applied to each woman, even to Hu's favorite concubine.

Everyone, whether a concubine or a maid, wore red silk slippers to bed. Those who were chosen to spend the night with the master wore slippers with musk powder. In the summer, they wore slippers with jade soles so that the feet would give a cool sensation when held in the master's hands. The concubines wore silk socks, whereas the maids wore cotton ones. Socks were changed once a day, and shoes every ten days. There were maids in charge of the changing and washing. Each morning, twenty women specialized in binding went from house to house to bind feet for the concubines and maids. Before bedtime, they unbound their own feet and washed them, then rebound them. This was the homework for all the women in Hu's household.

If a new concubine's feet didn't match the standard size, Hu would choose four experts to reshape her feet. Every morning they washed her feet in hot water, bound them, and sewed the wrapping tightly. After that, they helped her walk around to speed up the reforming process. A few hours later, they rebound the feet in case the wrapping got loose. Usually the feet would miraculously become very small within three months. If the woman was not strong, she often got sick. Even so, Hu would not let her loosen the binding.

Hu's concubines were known all over Hangzhou City for the tiny size and delicate shape of their feet. Rich families hired Hu's maids to bind feet for their wives and daughters. When Hu went bankrupt, most of his concubines and maids moved to Liuxia, a town near Hangzhou. Local women imitated their binding, and the town became famous for tiny feet. Even when natural feet became fashionable, Liuxia women still treasured tiny feet and kept the custom alive.[4]

It is not clear if Hu Xueyan went bankrupt because of a political downfall, economic failure, or his extravagant bound-foot consumption. His case adds another chapter to the record of the nation's foot fetish, another page to the Chinese history of sexual extravagance. It shows that when flesh overflows all the boundaries, when a nation sinks into the frenzy of expenditure and sensual pleasure, nothing—neither reason nor moral and legal restrictions—can stop the downward spiral until the flesh exhausts its last resource and ends in annihilation. As the Hunan ditty (sung by children) goes, they will "mortgage the house, give up the land," in order to "wed with the tiny feet as planned."

While footbinding displays the female body through a lifelong, painful reconstruction of the feet, coquettish hiding, and mystification, the cult of the exemplary woman in the Ming and Qing dynasties reached an even grander and more spectacular level through brutal self-mutilation and shocking methods of suicide. They gouged out their eyes; cut off their noses, ears, hair, or arms; bit off their fingers; destroyed their faces—all in order to show their determination not to remarry after the death of their husbands or fiancés. When women were forced to remarry or were raped by bandits and soldiers, they often committed suicide to maintain their chastity. Ming and Qing scholars collected and recorded their gruesome methods of death with even more enthusiasm: hanging; cutting their throats; drowning in wells, lakes, latrine pits; jumping off cliffs or into a fire; holding hunger strikes; swallowing chopsticks, soil, or gold; throwing themselves against trees (Bao Jialin 1991, 226). Local intellectuals collected such self-mutilation and suicide stories with great enthusiasm and helped to spread the cult to wide-reaching areas of China.

The cultural fetishization of the female body through footbinding and the cult of the exemplary woman was not a mere coincidental or isolated phenomenon, but was connected to the political, economic, and social situations of late imperial China. As the cultivation of agriculture, the development of commerce as well as the arts brought great material abundance and artistic richness to China of this era, Chinese culture also faced severe invasions by foreign cultures. From the Song onward, China was under constant siege by the Qidan (Khitan), Nuzhen (Juchen), and Mongols, who established the Liao, Jin, and Yuan dynasties on their own land as well as the Chinese land they invaded. By the thirteenth century, the Mongols had taken over the whole country and established the first foreign monarchy in China. Then the Manchu established the Qing dynasty in the seventeenth century, the last monarchy of China.

The longer China was ruled by foreign emperors, the more urgent was the need to tighten the rein on the female body. Footbinding and the cult of the exemplary woman were encouraged as a way to preserve Chinese culture and tradition, to reinforce the eroded boundaries of hierarchy, gender, and sex, and to rectify language (writing) that was corrupted and feminized by foreign languages. According to *Gujin tushu jicheng*, there were records of only three women martyrs during the 210-year rule under the

Liao dynasty (916–1125).[5] During the Jin (1115–1234), the number rose to thirty. But the Yuan dynasty (1271–1368) recorded 402 women who killed themselves for chastity. This did not include those who mutilated themselves to avoid a second marriage. When China was finally under the Han rule again in 1368, one of the things the first Ming emperor did was to collect the stories of these exemplary women, build arches, and give out honors to the villages and clans that produced such women. Again, the female body was used to cleanse the pollution of the foreign reign and restore Chinese tradition, identity, and hierarchy. With encouragement from the top, the cult of female chastity spread like wildfire. The number of exemplary women recorded in the Ming skyrocketed to 35,829 in comparison to the Yuan's record of 408 (Bao Jialin 1991, 240). This did not include those who were not on the record. Even footbinding underwent such a test. When China was taken over by the Manchurians in 1644, the Chinese people rebeled against the foreign reign in all sorts of ways, including refusing the imperial order to grow hair and braids in the Qing style. All their efforts failed, except for women's resistance to the royal ban on footbinding. Chinese men hailed this as a great achievement in resisting the foreign rule.

However, since women's bodies were the sites for both commercial and sexual consumption, and since this consumption manifested itself in male anguish over identity, hierarchy, gender, and language, the cult of exemplary women soon took on the dual nature of the foot fetish: virtue and vice, innocence and sexual lewdness, purity and pollution, beauty and violence. On the one hand, after many violent physical ordeals, public spectacles, and celebrations, Chinese female bodies had been used quite successfully by men to perform the task often impossible for themselves in crisis—that is, to undergird the idealized Chinese pyramid of loyalty and integrity. Yet on the other side of these public arches, the vivid details of women's physical ordeals, mutilations, and violent deaths as recorded by men actually eroticized the female bodies immensely. The didactic purpose of these tales was to praise those whose bodies were not available for the male gaze or touch and to warn men to keep away; yet the result was a much more publicized, visible, fetishized, and desirable female body, which together with footbinding and prostitution pushed the nation into a further spending frenzy.

Let's turn again to *The Golden Lotus,* to Pan Jinlian and Ximen Qing, whose sexual extravagance drives them to death, bringing many victims along with them on their path. In the earlier chapters, Ximen Qing is a calculating merchant, grabbing and accumulating as much wealth as possible through cheating, robbing, bribing, and marrying rich widows. After he meets the sex/death symbol Jinlian and takes her for his fifth concubine, he slowly loses his control, spirals down into the abyss of sex, and finally dies in Jinlian's bed. All his wealth and his women disperse or die. He bought Jinlian as a plaything, an object of his consumption, and ended up being consumed by the object. "Who can explain this?" the author of *The Golden Lotus* says in the first chapter. "Whoever loves her [Jinlian] loses his life as well as his wealth."

Before Jinlian married Ximen Qing, she was the wife of a poor peddler and had to cook and wash for her husband as part of their shared labor. She was unhappy about it and tormented her husband daily. When she became Ximen's concubine, she was given two chambermaids just to take care of her personal needs, plus numerous common servants and cooks for the household. The only work she did was to make her own shoes. And even that was part of her effort to please Ximen Qing and stir up his desire. Dedicated as she was to erotic games and sexual expenditure, Jinlian cut herself off completely from work. Just as in the folk song about the Yangzhou thin horses, Jinlian was born not to spin and weave but to sing and charm. When Ximen's wife met Jinlian for the first time, she looked at the bride closely:

> The Moon Lady [Yueniang] looked at from her head to her feet; every inch of the exquisite body seemed endowed with the power of fascination. She looked at her from her feet to her head; this extraordinary charm seemed to issue from her as water from a fountain. She was like a translucent pearl lying on a crystal dish, like the early morning moon shining above the topmost branches of a pink apricot tree. The Moon Lady gazed at her without speaking, and she said to herself, "When the boys came home, they used to say, 'How strange that Wu Ta should have so beautiful a wife.' I have never seen anyone so beautiful. No wonder that brave husband of mine fell in love with her." (*The Golden Lotus* 1:123)

With her bound feet and her practiced art of seduction, Jinlian found a home much more luxurious than her old one. In exchange for being a sex object, she is given all sorts of extravagances and things that have nothing to do with the regularity of commerce or production. It all would have worked out fine except for one problem: Jinlian is not a passive object of desire; she is also a subject of this extravagant consumption. Her own sexual exuberance refuses to be reduced to mere things; instead, it burns like fire, destroying everything and everybody around her, including the very man who is her provider, and including herself.

In the beginning the novel presents Ximen Qing as a rational merchant.

The women he marries, as mentioned before, all bring him social or economic benefits. He has been able to follow the dictates of reason—that is, to use all his means to get richer and possess more until the urges of the flesh pass all bounds, and he is seized by the fever of lust, by the frenzy of his genital extravagance triumphing over all kinds of taboos. Instead of marrying more widows to increase his wealth, he runs after endless prostitutes, maids, servants' wives, and singing girls who consume his resources, physical and financial, until he fails and falls and has no firm ground beneath his feet. Although he longs for women of the upper classes, the women who really arouse him are those from the lower classes. Even Jinlian finally dresses herself as a maid, in her effort to stir up Ximen's desire for her again, and she succeeds. In front of these women, he is able to display his sexual extravagance, his penis and money, to the highest level. He often first flaunts his extraordinarily large sexual organ (with the help of tools and medicine) to the woman he seduces, and in the middle of intercourse, he promises her money, jewelry, silk, and other things. His needs for squandering and displaying accelerate at the same speed as his need for violent sex games. In addition to having oral and anal intercourse, he ties women up, burns them with incense, and makes them drink his urine. Toward the end of the novel, his entire being is consumed by drinking, eating, and sex—until death, the most luxurious consumption of energy resources, swallows him up. Even his death takes place in the manner of an excessive eruption. Instead of being drained or impotent from having too much sex (a belief shared by many Chinese doctors and people), he cannot stop having orgasms. His sperm spurts out continuously until blood comes out, and his penis stays erect and swollen in his last remaining days of unconsciousness. When it finally erupts with pus and blood, he dies.

As an erotic novel, the beginning of *The Golden Lotus* is quite peculiar upon the first reading. Instead of introducing the main characters—Ximen Qing (who first appears in the middle of the second chapter), Jinlian, and other women—it starts with a minor character, Wu Song, describing in graphic detail how he beats a tiger to death with his bare fists in a forest. This minor character, who is the mute brother of Jinlian's first husband, whom she murders, disappears very soon from the book and shows up again briefly toward the end of the book (chap. 87). The sole purpose of his return is to kill Jinlian and offer her head, heart, and liver as a sacrifice to his murdered brother. Just as Jinlian is presented as the symbol of femininity and the object of desire, Wu Song is presented as a typical macho hero:

Full seven feet tall is this majestic figure
A hero striking terror into all beholders
With stern and rugged face, and sparkling eyes that blaze like glittering stars
Clenched fists like sledgehammers.
If he raises his foot, the tigers in their mountain lair feel their courage wane.
One blow with that fist, and the great bear trembles in his lonely valley.
He wears a magic cap with silver flowers
And his long-sleeved gown is soaked with his victim's blood.

(*Golden Lotus* 1:22)

Four soldiers carry him on an open sedan to celebrate his heroic deed of killing a tiger with his bare fists, the creature that has been terrorizing the district for a long time. The wild beast was so strong that even when it is dead, four young men can barely carry it.

Wu Song is being displayed as a phallus, his body illuminating nothing but pure yang and manliness. This is hinted at in the name of his birthplace, Yang Gu. The first character is *yang,* the sun, brightness, masculine. His name also implies the same concept: *wu,* as military, fierce; *song,* as pine tree (an important symbol for integrity and masculinity in Chinese culture). Indeed, he lives up to his name: he is skilled in the martial arts, and extremely loyal to his male friends and to the patriarchal system that he serves. After he kills the tiger on the hill of Jingyang, he comes down to Qing He (clear river) County. River is a symbolic place for yin, a body of water that is supposed to be clear because of its name but that is in reality totally polluted by economic exploitation, political corruption, and sexuality that has gone wild. Such symbolic uses of names, and the dramatic contrast between the heroic, masculine Wu Song and the lustful, corrupt, and feminine main characters, imply how language (or writing) is or will be corrupted by reality, femininity, and the vernacular (or speech).

Wu Song comes to Qing He in search of his brother, Wu Da, who is the opposite of what Wu Song represents. Though they come from the same mother, Wu Da is a dwarf and simpleton who makes his living by selling cakes on the street. He is nicknamed Three-Inch Scraggy Bark for his pinched face and deformed body. To make things worse, his wife Jinlian finds out that he is "not much of a man" (*The Golden Lotus* 1:26). Wu Song remains absolutely loyal and respectful to Wu Da because, deformed as he is, he is still his older brother. And since their parents have long been deceased, the older brother also represents the father figure, although from time to time Wu Song has to take care of him as if he were a son. This can be regarded as a subtle analogy to what often takes place in the court, where a weak, incompetent emperor (the father) is served by extremely loyal and capable ministers (the sons). The two brothers also represent two kinds of men analyzed by Keith McMahon in his *Misers, Shrews, and Polygamists*—the henpecked husband and the stiff moralist (the miser and ascetic).[6] Both of their lives are affected and afflicted by Pan Jinlian, the shrew.

Opposite as they are, the two brothers share one common thing: they are both impaired linguistically. Wu Da's disability in language has happened at birth. As the book describes, "The poor man was neither very strong nor very intelligent, so he became a constant butt for the wits of the neighborhood" (*Golden Lotus* 1:24). At home, he is a constant target for Jinlian's anger. She is angry at being a woman, unable to control her own life. Her beauty, intelligence, artistic talents, and ambition have so far only made her life miserable. Before she turns twenty, she has already been sold three times, and each transaction pushes her further to the bottom of society, until she lands in the hands of a dwarf. She takes out all her frustration on him daily: "Never a day passed but she found some quarrel to pick with him" (1:27). But Wu Da swallows it all. Silence is his only means to survive and protect himself in the world of corruption. The couple is a typical case of the shrew and her henpecked husband.

Wu Song's silence is, however, the product of linguistic self-exile[7] and asceticism. He can speak and speak well when he chooses, if the conversation concerns only the communication of daily life and business. In other words, he can handle language very well as long as words do not interact with one another but stay within their own positions and function only at the level of usefulness and logic, exchange of information, communication, and so forth. Once words cross the border of reason and enter the realm of emotion and sexuality, Wu Song immediately withdraws into silence. He is aware of Jinlian's beauty and sexuality from the beginning. As soon as they are introduced, he turns his eyes away to avoid looking directly at her beautiful face. When she stares at him openly with admiration and desire, he just blushes and bends his head. He knows the intention of her enthusiastic service. Her cooking, washing, and caring for him come from her desire to attract him. He accepts them all but refuses to acknowledge her in words or action, shunning her totally. When she flirts with him with wine and words, her hair loose, her breasts half-exposed, all he can do is drink and poke the fire. Frustrated, Jinlian grabs the poker out of his hand and cries, "You don't know how to poke. Let me do it for you. I want it as hot as a bowl of fire" (*Golden Lotus* 1:35). Her metaphoric remarks make Wu Song thoroughly uncomfortable. His awkwardness indicates that he understands Jinlian's language, but he will not or is unable to respond to her. Even when Jinlian tells her husband that Wu Song has tried to seduce and rape her, Wu Song is unable to say a word to defend himself. He just leaves in a silent rage.

He is silent because the language he knows is totally different from Jinlian's language. His is masculine, part of a world that interacts only with men. It is clean, self-contained and containing, and manageable. Wu Song prides himself as a man of honor and integrity and constantly quotes his ancestors' words and sayings to demonstrate his principles, guide his actions, and protect himself from corrupting forces (represented by the shrew Jinlian and the wastrel Ximen Qing) around him. Although in an earlier novel *The Water Margin (Shui hu zhuan),* in which he was originally created as a rebel hero who could not open his mouth without cursing, he barely does so in *The Golden Lotus.* Here, the words he speaks are as formal and highly stylized as what he would write. Here he speaks a language inherited from his male ancestors, a language that keeps him away from human interactions. His linguistic self-exile and asceticism come out through his body as a desexualization, even impotence, just as his brother Wu Da's linguistic impairment transforms him into a henpecked, impotent husband.

When Jinlian asks Wu Song if it is true that he has been keeping a singing girl in his office, Wu Song denies this vehemently, saying he is never this kind of man. "I don't believe you," Jinlian retorts. "Your heart speaks one language and your tongue another." She has said this as a way of teasing and flirting, but she has unconsciously put her finger on the spot: she intuitively senses how Wu Song's linguistic impairment has split his mind and body, how his phallus-like body is not all that different from the body of his dwarf brother. It doesn't take her long to realize that his phallus-like body is just an empty shell, as she tells her husband that his so-called hero brother is "like a yellow quince, good to look at and rotten inside" (1:37).

Jinlian, on the other hand, speaks the language of the shrew, charged with sexuality, femininity, seduction, charm, and power. Compared to Wu Song's language, hers is petty, vulgar, colloquial, and unpredictable; at the same time, it can sound sweet, seductive, smooth, and soothing. No one can charm and seduce as well as Jinlian; and no one has a fouler mouth than she when it comes to cursing and destroying an enemy. Her language does not obey any rules, whether linguistic or moral. Nor does it distinguish between true and false, real and fake, good and bad. As Keith McMahon points out, the literal translation of a shrew—*po fu*—is a "'scattering woman,' one who 'spills' and 'splashes,' *po,* and in general acts in ways that make men lose face" (McMahon 1995, 55). Since a shrew has no financial, social, or political means to back up her actions, her "scattering" or "spilling" is mostly a linguistic maneuver. Jinlian's language not only pollutes but castrates. It is a language "of action" (Lecercle 1990, 199), listening and responding only to the demands of flesh. Among many nicknames Ximen Qing calls her, his favorite is "little oily mouth." This oily mouth, together with her golden lotuses and her pretty face, gives her an invincible sexual prowess and makes her an equal to Ximen Qing.

Jinlian speaks a vernacular that is full of idioms, slang, and the jargon of everyday life. Wu Song also speaks the vernacular, but its high style, syntax, and vocabulary that are borrowed from ancient quotations and sayings equate it more to the written. In its ideographic form, Chinese writing has been regarded as sacred since its creation by Qin Shihuang (259–210 B.C.). The unification of the script has made, and is still making, it possible for Chinese who speak many different dialects to share a written linguistic culture. Because of its relative stability and its representation of the great unification, it came to symbolize origin (since characters were created by gods) and truth, transparency and virility, purity and integrity, stability and tradition, the essence and flower of language. As a vital tool of ideology and bureaucratic administration since the beginning of the Chinese feudal system,[8] it is used to record history and documentary materials, to conduct state affairs and business, and finally, to create the highest form of art—poetry. Writing is thus made to function as an incorruptible force against the constant onslaught of the oral, the colloquial of daily life, and the dialects spoken by the masses in different regions. Unlike writing, the oral language is vulgar, muddy, and overflowing. It contaminates and changes. It does not respect boundaries or conventions but constantly, willfully crosses and destroys them. It is a language that works through sinuosity and ambiguity, through the veil of metaphor and what Jean-Jacques Lecercle calls the "remainder" in *The Violence of Language* (1990). It represents impurity, contamination, and sexuality. Since no one ever speaks *wen yan* (the written), the split between writing and speech, between *wen yan* and the vernacular, was doomed from the very beginning.

When Jinlian besieges Wu Song with her charming appearance and her "oily" words of seduction, all Wu Song can do is defend himself by remaining silent (with clenched fists). He can't save himself from the awkward situation by employing his own or Jinlian's language, because the language he knows and uses does not allow him to cross any border to mingle or interact with the enemy. Nor does it allow him to bend backward like his brother. When Jinlian's language renders him speechless, and when he in his silence can no longer resist her advances, he bursts with violence:

> Wu Sung [Song] felt even more uneasy, but he still said nothing. Golden Lotus [Jinlian] was not in any way put out. She set down the poker and poured out another cup of wine. She drank a mouthful, looked meaningfully at Wu Sung, and said, "If you feel like it,[9] drink what I have left."
>
> This was too much. He snatched the cup from her hand and dashed the wine upon the floor, crying, "Don't be so shameless," and at the same time pushed her so violently that she almost fell. Then he gazed haughtily upon her.
>
> "My feet are steadfast upon the earth and I aspire to reach the heavens. I am a man with teeth in my mouth and hair upon my head. I am a man, I say, not a swine or a cur, that I should pay no heed to the sacred laws of honor or flout the precepts of common decency. You must not behave in this shameless way. If I hear any whisper of your ever doing such a thing again, my eyes may tell me that you are my sister, but my fist will not recognize you." (*Golden Lotus* 1:35–36)

In fact, he always ends up using his fists to solve problems. This is the only way he can interact with the world and deal with sexuality—with periodic ruptures of violence. In the end, Wu Song also squanders. Unlike Ximen Qing and Jinlian's gradual spending of wealth and sexuality that spirals downward into a frenzy, his squandering is a rupture, a violent tearing of things/flesh inside out. His excessive energy is released through the only channel he knows—by killing and destroying, just as Jinlian's exuberance comes out through lust and death.

At first glance, it seems odd that Wu Da, a henpecked dwarf, is paired with Wu Song, a phallic symbol of masculinity. And it seems even odder that these two remain loyal to each other and are inseparable mentally or psychologically. The combination of the two seeming extremes, however, can be seen as a split of a Chinese man, of his body and mind, of his sexuality and integrity. Such a split is manifested in the two brothers' inability to use language. In other words, the split between writing and speaking comes out through their bodies in the two extreme forms—the dwarf and the phallus, both of which are totally desexualized. The two brothers' linguistic and sexual incapability is set in contrast to the highly sexual Ximen Qing, whose verbal skill in flirting and seducing equals that of Pan Jinlian.

The duality of footbinding and the society's oscillations between the need to accumulate and preserve and the instinct to pleasure oneself to death in grand spending is rooted in the duality of language: the relevant and formidable part that can be constructed as syntax, grammar, and so on, and Jean-Jacques Lecercle's "remainder"—the irrelevant, odd, untidy, awkward, and creative part that works as an undercurrent within and through language, nourishing or destructive according to the circumstances. In Chinese, this duality is manifested through the discrepancy between speech and writing, and the violence that constantly erupts from this discrepancy. When Qin Shihuang established the first monarchy of China in 221 B.C., the first thing he did was to standardize writing as a means of unifying numerous dialects (speeches) of different states, and of course, hundreds of political and philosophical schools that flourished during the period. He managed to do that through violence, and through violence only: burning all the books that could not be included in his system and burying alive the scholars who refused to conform to his school. Since then, monarchy and writing have been inseparable from and indispensable to each other's existence and preservation. Writing has drifted so far away from the present, so locked in stability and past, that *wen yan* has little to do with *bai hua*—plain speech, the vernacular—the language that people speak daily. This phenomenon lasted until the last emperor was dethroned in 1911. Eight years later, the May Fourth Movement advocated replacing *wen yan* with *bai hua* in all writing, including poetry. The end of the monarchy was violently and painfully followed by the end of *wen yan* (and, interestingly, by the end of footbinding).

The clash between Wu Song and Jinlian is thus not merely personal. It is an eruption derived from the split within language, a split between a pure, functional language and a contagious, sexualized language that refuses to be contained and constricted. When they meet, violence is inevitable. Thus the battle between Wu Song and Jinlian can be nothing but deadly. Like Wu Song's encounter with the tiger, either he lets her empower him with her wild sexuality or he crushes her completely, not only because violence and destruction are the only language he knows, but also because he is fully aware that Jinlian's sexuality (her language) is as impenetrable and untamable as the tiger's wildness. The only way is to destroy. There is nothing in between.

Edible Beauty:
Food and Foot Fetishes in China

A beauty in a boudoir
Binds her lotus feet.
A handsome lad walks by;
Miss, oh how tiny they are,
Like tender bamboo shoots of winter,
Festival dumplings of May,
But more fragrant and sweeter in every way;
Or like the fruit of June, Buddha's hand,
Only more elegant, better defined.
                    —Jiangxi ditty

If you utter something, that something goes through your mouth; therefore, when you utter "a chariot," a chariot goes though your mouth.
                    —Gilles Deleuze, *Logique du sens*

NEARLY ALL EUPHEMISMS about bound feet have to do with food. And the sexual play is often involved with oral consumption—the mouth that kisses, bites, and licks the tiny feet as well as the language that dotes on them. The connection between food and foot seems only natural and inevitable since food and sex always go hand in hand in the Chinese history of expenditure. Once the lotus foot enters the realm of food, however, it is immediately associated with all the signs, functions, and rituals of food culture in China. As cooking is the symbolic process of transforming nature into culture, savage into civilization, footbinding "cooks" the raw, savage female body into something that can be consumed for pleasure as well as for political and moral purposes; footbinding initiates the wild, uncontrollable female sexuality in erotic games and economic cycles. The obsession of metaphorizing bound feet as food marks two opposite transformations: first, it transcends flesh, the primitive, nature, and death, transforming them into spirit, civilization, culture, and immortality; second, footbinding marks a descent from the most complicated human body to the primal state of being—plants and things—through imitation and euphemization. Both cooking and footbinding involve violence from beginning to end, and their products (food and bound feet) both end up in the mouth, physically and linguistically. Language, through metaphor and euphemism, functions as a medium that allows the link and constant flow between sex and food, foot and mouth, transcendence and descent, nature and culture—a "cooking furnace" where all the opposites dissolve, fuse, and start all over again.

Bound feet are described by many euphemisms: lotus, golden lotus, fragrant lotus, bamboo shoot, water chestnut, dumpling, red beans, and *zongzi*.[1] All suggest the pointed toe and tiny size of the bound foot. *Twin wild ducks* indicates the feet traveling in pairs like mandarin ducks. *New moon, twin hooks,* or *bows* and their variations (*lotus hooks* and *fragrant hooks*) refer to the tiny feet successfully bound into the shape of these objects. Except for those relating to the moon and hooks, the euphemisms are all related to food or plants that are edible. An anonymous author who called himself Lotus Knower wrote an essay that was included in *Records of Gathering Fragrance* describing eighteen positions of sexual intercourse in which tiny feet were the major erotic object as well as the tool for the game. The titles used in his essay bear a striking resemblance to a Chinese restaurant menu:

Titles for Sex Scenes	*Food Menu*
Lotus-Petaled Buddhist Devotee	Buddhist Delight
Encircling Twin Lotuses	Tripe Sautéed with Lotus Root
Bright Flowers, Concealed Willows	Blossom of One Hundred Flowers
Twofold Joy of Bamboo Shoots	Bamboo Shoots with Twin Mushrooms
Jade Claws Touching the Cave	Deer Horn at Wind Cave
Two Dragons Playing with a Pearl	Phoenix Eye Jade Pearl

Apart from being the major and most favored ingredient for digestive and sexual pleasures, lotus serves as a religious symbol in Buddhism, Taoism, and Hinduism, as Buddha saw humanity in the form of lotus flowers, its root buried in the mud yet its flowers rising out of the mud, clean and pure. When the lotus is consumed as food and sexual object, it subtly hints that such a mundane use of the sacred symbol is a way of transcending from mud to purity. Just as the food menu tries to appeal to eaters' appetites through the senses of smell, color, and taste, the sex menu (excerpted below) emphasizes the pleasurable impact of the bound foot on the five senses, especially the senses of smell, taste, and sight:

X. Bright Flowers, Concealed Willows

He grasps the beautiful hook and gets the sensations of its being pointed, slender, soft, and tiny. Twin lotuses, twin delight; *the bright one for visual pleasure, the bared one for playful palm manipulation.*

XI. Lovebird on One Foot

She takes off her left shoe and places the revealed lotus in his left palm. He enfolds her tiny waist with his right arm and raises his head to kiss her as she leans forward. They bite each other's tongues. Their souls are assured a sublimity beyond Heaven, with tongues caressing, one lotus touching earth, looking like a *red pepper,* and the other in his hand like a *spring bamboo shoot.*

XIV. Twofold Joy of Bamboo Shoots

The *jade-like bamboo shoots* are pointed and fine, glossy and flawless. In his palms, they feel warm and as soft as silk, with the *skin as slippery as grease.* Twinfold pleasure is created from either playing with the plantar or from squeezing the entire lotus. How can you describe the delight of lotuses which *overflow with fragrance?*

XV. A Head Inserted in Lotus Petals

She lifts up her bare lotuses and places them on his shoulders in such a way that they tightly press against his cheeks. *They play with his face and touch his nostrils; their fragrance overflows his lips and teeth. And this jade bamboo shoot contemplation so satisfies the five senses that all other flavors of life are obliterated* (*Cai fei lu* 4:225–36, quoted in Levy 1992; emphasis mine)

Such merging of food and foot can also be found in the buying and selling of lotus shoes. There were two shops in old Beijing that specialized in making extremely refined and elaborate shoes for special occasions, such as the initiation of the binding, or bed slippers that had pornographic pictures embroidered inside. Rice was used as a tool of measurement for the purchase. Instead of telling the shop assistant the shoe size, a customer would slide a small bag of rice over the counter. The assistant took the bag inside and poured the rice into a shoe. If the rice filled just to the top, not too much or too little, then the shoe was the right size. A pair of shoes like this cost at least two taels of silver, sometimes six, depending on the style and elaboration of the embroidery (*Cai fei lu* 279).

The same interest in sensual pleasures and display can be seen in the description of food in *Baihua ting,* a thirteenth-century Yuan drama. An actor dressed as a fruit vendor comes on the stage and delivers the following patter:

> Fruits on sticks for sale, fruits on sticks for sale! I've just left the tile districts [pleasure quarters], departed the tea houses to swiftly pass the pleasureland of kingfisher green and worldly red to enter the district of orioles and flowers. . . . This fruit is homegrown, just picked. There are juicy-juicy-sweet, full-full-fragrant, sweet-smelling, red and watery fresh-peeled round-eye lichees from Fu-chou; from P'ing-chiang [Su-chou] some sour-sour-tart, shady-cool, sweet-sweet-luscious, yellow oranges and green tangerines with the leaves still on; there're some supple-supple-soft, quite-quite-white, crystal-sweet, crushed-flat candied persimmons from Sung-yang; from Wu-chou I have snappy-snappy-crisp, juicy-juicy-fresh, glitter-glitter-bright dragon-twined jujubes kneaded in sugar; there are ginger threads from Hsin-chien split fine and dipped in honey sugar as well as Kao-yu water caltrops wrinkled by the sun, dried by the wind and skinned; I have the blackest of black, reddest of red fingertip-size large melon seeds gathered in Wei; from Hsuan-ch'eng some half-sour, half-sweet, half-sweet, half-sour soft peaches skewered just right. I can't exhaust the list, so I'll lay out several kinds before your eyes. Oh, you sweet elegant ladies, beautiful women from fragrant chambers and embroidered kiosks; great and noble gentlemen from high halls and great buildings—I'm not just bragging to make false claims, but try mine and you'll forsake all others. You'll be sure to buy them once you try them. Oh! Sticks of fruit for sale! (Quoted in West 1972, 58–59)

What an extravagant display for the eye, nose, and tongue! Note that the vendor has just left the tile district (a euphemism for the streets where brothels are located) to enter the residential area for officials and commoners. Apparently, he has sold the colorful, mouth-watering fruits first to prostitutes and their customers before he sells the same merchandise (or the leftovers) to those who live in the fragrant chambers and high halls.

Food was an important part of the erotic life for entertaining women as well as commoners, just as lotus feet became the standard of beauty for women of all classes. Lin Yutang points out in *My Country and My People* that the Chinese have developed such a sensitive and sophisticated sense of smell and taste that even their books and studies smell fragrant. Hence *fragrant lotus* is a very appropriate phrase to symbolize the sensuality of the Chinese (Lin Yutang 1995, 156). Indeed, smelling and tasting the lotus foot had become such an erotic part of sexual foreplay that Gu Hongming, a Chinese scholar and lotus lover of the early twentieth century who received a master's degree from Edinburgh University, insisted that the only beautiful lotus feet were those that could be inserted halfway up the nostrils. The pleasure from the odor of bound feet was beyond description, a taste that required sophistication, like eating stinky cheese or fermented bean curd (*Cai fei lu* 2:223).

Yin shi nan nu, ren zhi da yu cun yan: the literal translation for this famous statement from Confucius is "Drink, food, man, and woman, these are where the greatest human desires exist." This observation that Confucius made more than two thousand years ago about the close link between food and sex is deep in every Chinese consciousness and unconsciousness, affecting their living styles and their contemplation of life and death. "Few other cultures are as food oriented as Chinese," K. C. Chang points out in his introduction for *Food in Chinese Cultures* (1977). Throughout Chinese history, the basic needs for food, drink, and sex have been translated into spectacular expenditures. Just as the quantity and quality of women a man can possess mark his social and political positions, what people eat and how they eat reflect what they are socially, politically, and intellectually. Thus, the display of food plays a similar role to the display of sex and women.

The food that goes into a Chinese emperor's dishes often has little to do with his personal interest or taste but, rather, serves as a magnificent show of his power and unlimited resources. Preparation of food for the imperial family was so sizable and complex a business that it required the services of several different offices of government. For instance, more than one thousand cooks were employed to prepare meals for the Song royal kitchen. For a meal, forty boxes were needed to carry the dishes to the emperor's table (Xu Song 1957, 371–75). Zhou Mi's report on the banquet of Song Gaozong (reign, 1127–1162) in the house of the Prince of Qing-ho showed that imperial dining adhered to ritual practices reflecting the emperor's position in the whole order of things. The meal consisted of more than thirty courses with hundreds of dishes, presented and received with clockwork regularity. All the food and drink were served with the finest dishes and utensils of jade and silver. Among the vessels were a *Ding*, an ancient cooking dish, designed in the shape of a dragon, three vessels from the Shang dynasty (1766–1122 B.C.), and four from the Zhou (1122–221 B.C.).

The quantity and variety of dishes served for each eater reflected the gradations of political power and the formal structure of government. High officials who served in the palace enjoyed eleven courses. Officials of the third rank were given seven courses plus one box of sweet deep-fried food and five pitchers of wine. Those of the fourth rank had five dishes, a box of fruit, and two pitchers of wine, while the fifth-rank officials got only three dishes and one pitcher. Pictures and calligraphy by the famous artists Wu Daozi and Dong Yuan were hung for the feast. Just as the number of courses symbolized the emperor's political power, the antiques and artworks at the banquet represented the emperor as the carrier of Chinese tradition, his appreciation and mastery of the essence of the culture. The fabulous quantities of the finest food, the best to be had in the world, revealed the emperor's inexhaustible resources and his power to command pleasure for the senses rather than for the pleasure itself (Zhou Mi 1957, 491–504).

Mirroring the imperial power, high officials also threw endless amounts of money and resources into food. Cai Jing, the prime minister of the late Song, whom Ximen Qing had adopted as his "godfather" in the novel *The Golden Lotus,* was said to have had hundreds of cooks in his enormous kitchen. The gifts Ximen sent him for birthday or tribute consisted of gold, silver, and silk as well as large quantities of local food products. However, for officials, intellectuals, merchants, and commoners, especially if they lived in cities, eating could still be enjoyed for pleasure as much as for its ritual and social function. Food rituals at restaurant and family dinners, however, were designed more to enhance food than to affirm social and political power. As is described in Meng Yuanlao's *Dongjing meng hua lu,* Song restaurants were noisy places where customers shouted out their orders, and the diners were fickle and demanding (1957). To be a qualified waiter required much training, even for a waiter in a noodle shop. When customers sat down around the table, he would ask each for their order. Some wanted hot noodles, some cold, some with broth, some with broth on the side. The waiter memorized the orders, which were often complicated and numerous, for a noodle shop could have a wide variety of noodles. Soon, he came out with three bowls in his left hand, and another twenty bowls of noodles lined from his right hand up to his shoulder. He had to hand each order to the customer without a single mistake. Otherwise, the client had the right to complain to the head man. The waiter would be scolded, fined, even fired (Meng Yuanlao 1957, 4:27). The customers' fickleness reflected their extravagance and indulgence, on the one hand, and their expectation of restaurants to serve as places for social service and gathering, on the other. When friends (sometimes acquaintances and strangers) encountered each other on the street, they often ended up in a wine shop, eating and drinking while establishing a friendship or conducting business. Such scenes were common in Ming and Qing literature.

The Song painter Zhang Zeduan's *Spring Festival on the River (Qing ming shang he tu)* gives us a vivid picture of the life of the Northern Song capital city Kaifeng, its people, and particularly the food that people ate. As the scroll enters the city along the country road and the river with great squat boats bulging with grain for the capital, we see streets crowded with restaurants elaborately decorated with scaffolding, flowers, and fluttering official flags, and simple food stalls and vendors hawking every delicacy known in the empire. Culinary richness and variety are suggested everywhere. *Meng liang lu* lists 216 dishes that were available in the city of Lin'an in the Song, some of which were:

One hundred spice soup
Ten-color head soup
Five-soft soup
Chicken turtle soup
Turtle chicken soup
Scallop soup
Chicken and goose bamboo five-spice chicken
Lamb steamed in wine
Lamb head and fish
Lamb hoof with bamboo
Five-spice young chicken
Conch in wine sauce
Wine oyster
Deep-fried fish
Fermented fish
Sautéed eel
Shrimp ball
Mustard shrimp
Spicy crab
Wine crab honey partridge Lotus cake
Crab dumpling

Marco Polo marvels at the abundance of Hangzhou markets in his book *The Description of the World*:

There were ten principal open spaces, besides infinite others—a Chinese description says 414—for the districts which are square, that is half a mile for a side. And on each of the said squares three days a week there is concourse of from forty to fifty thousand persons who come to market and bring everything you can desire for food, because there is always a great supply of victuals; that is to say of roebuck, francolins, quails, fowls, capons, and so many ducks and geese that more could not be told; for they rear so many of them at [West] Lake (which borders the city), that for one Venetian silver groat may be had a pair of geese and two pair of ducks. (1938, 328)

Eating was so intimately connected with the pleasure of drinking as well as sex that many Song restaurants in Kaifeng, and many wine shops and tea houses in Hangzhou employed singing girls or prostitutes, or were adjacent to the pleasure quarters in the same lane. *Meng liang lu* vividly describes the scenes:

> In all of [Kaifeng's] wine shops, they tie bright festoons in the doorway, but in the best establishments, after entering the gate, one went straight through the main corridor for about one hundred paces. To both sides of the courtyard were two passageways, both of which had little side doors, and towards evening lamps and candles twinkled and glittered, upper and lower reflecting each other, and the elaborately adorned sing-song girls— several hundred of them—would crowd along the corridor and, holding out wine, would call to the guests, so that gazing at them was like seeing fairies. (Quoted in Freeman 1977, 159)

In such a world of luxury and pleasure, where "wind and rain, cold and heat do not occur, and day mingles with night" (Meng Yuanlao 1957, 16), visitors often gave themselves up to sensual indulgence, leaving behind the call of duty and ritual for a few hours, sometimes a few days. Hangzhou, the capital city of the Southern Song, was known for its beautiful women and great food. When Marco Polo traveled here and saw all the restaurants, public baths, women in luxurious clothes and jewelry, banquets, servants, music, and people, including the emperor himself, living as if intoxicated and dreaming day and night, he believed that Hangzhou was "the greatest city which may be found in the world, where so many pleasures may be found that one fancies himself in Paradise" (1938, 326). Even today, the Chinese still say that "there is a paradise in heaven, and there are Su Hang [Suzhou and Hangzhou] on earth."

Marco Polo describes the Song emperor's extravagance in food and sex, his palace in Hangzhou—the "City of Heaven"—in a straight, matter-of-fact tone, yet his wonder at China's richness and craftsmanship is mixed with his contempt for the emperor's indulgence in sensual pleasures:

> The other two parts of the enclosure were distributed in groves and lakes, and charming gardens planted with fruit trees, and preserves for all sorts of animals, such as roe, red deer, fallow deer, hares and rabbits. Here the King used to take his pleasure in company with those damsels of his; some in

carriages, some on horseback, whilst no man was permitted to enter. Sometimes the King would set the girls a-coursing after the game with dogs, and when were tired they would hide to the groves that overhung the lakes, and leaving their clothes and swim about hither and thither, whilst it was the King's delight to watch them; and then all would return home. Sometimes the King would have his dinner carried to those groves, which were dense with lofty trees, and there would be waited on by those young ladies. And thus he passed his life in this constant dalliance with women, without so much as knowing what arms meant! And the result of all this cowardice and effeminacy was that he lost his dominion to the Great Khan in that base and shameful way that you have heard. (Quoted in Forman and Burland 1970, 129)

In *The Golden Lotus,* women, especially women with money and social rank, entice men with wine and food. Both Li Ping'r and Madame Lin prepare a feast for Ximen Qing when he first visits their houses. Almost every sexual scene between Li Ping'r and Ximen Qing is accompanied by drinking and eating. Often, she sets up a special low table in bed. Inside the bed curtain, their drinking, eating, and gambling gradually lead to sex, to food again, and then back to sex. Sometimes their eating and copulating go on for hours and days, particularly if it occurs in a brothel. Throughout the book, Ximen rides his horse, half-drunk, hopping from one mistress's dinner table to another's bed. Food and sex are intertwined and depicted in such sensitive and painstaking details that it is fair to say the whole plot of *The Golden Lotus* and the full development of the characters are realized through these two types of experiences. Other sensual props—clothing, jewels, furniture, houses, gardens, flowers, music—are used as background to bring these two major modes into a sharper and higher focus.

The infamous love scene between Pan Jinlian and Ximen Qing in his garden (chapter 27) is traditionally considered by scholars as the most obscene in Chinese literature. However, as a scene of total sensual involvement, it provides a great example of how the author brings food and sex together as counterparts and how the two major characters come to a tragic end by inflicting uninhibited sensuality on themselves and others.

On an intensely hot summer day, Ximen wanders in his garden with his hair loose, watching his servants water flowers and having them plucked for his wife and concubines. Two of his favorite concubines, Pan Jinlian and Li Ping'r, enter the garden hand in hand, their summer clothing and beautiful faces described in the most sensual details:

Golden Lotus [Jinlian] and the Lady of the Vase [Ping'r] were both dressed in the lightest of silver silk, with skirts of dark red and a fringe of gold thread. The Lady of the Vase was wearing a short crimson cape and Golden Lotus had one of silver and red. Golden Lotus wore nothing on her head but a blue Hangchou head-dress, through which four braids of hair peeped out. On her brow were three flowers made of kingfisher feathers, which enhanced the beauty of her white face and glossy hair, her red lips and pearly teeth. (*Golden Lotus* 1:377)

The colors and texture of their clothing—white, red, and light—are used to accentuate the women's fair skin and red lips, which eventually lead to Ximen's favorite parts of the two women's bodies: Li Ping'r's white bottom and Pan Jinlian's red flower heart (vagina). All the details of the garden, the flowers, the weather (heat and shower), the music, jewelry, clothing, especially food, are used to set up the scene for sexual pleasure. Even his lovemaking with Ping'r can be seen as part of the foreplay for his final sexual game with Jinlian.

When the three meet in the garden, they decide to have something to drink and eat as well as to play music and sing. Jinlian offers to fetch other ladies, but returns to eavesdrop on Ximen and Ping'r, who immediately engage in sex. Jinlian learns that Ping'r is pregnant. This stirs up her jealousy. When other women arrive with musical instruments, Jinlian refuses to sing or play and constantly flings mocking remarks at Ping'r. It is only after all the ladies finally leave, and only Jinlian and Ximen remain in the garden, that she agrees to sing for Ximen. By then, the garden becomes more luscious, more colorful and sensual after a summer shower (which can also be seen as an emotional as well as sexual shower). Ximen orders the maids to bring wine and food to the vine arbor. The description and contents of the food add a wider range of colors, textures, and flavors to the display of luxury and leisure. More important, food is not only used to initiate the sexual foreplay but also becomes the prop of the game:

One maid enters carrying a pot of wine, followed by another with a covered sweetmeat box atop which there is a bowl of chilled fruits. Ximen Qing turns to this box and opens its lid. Within there are eight divisions containing eight foods: ducks' webs cured in rice-wine dregs; shreds of cured pork cut in a special way; flakes of icefish; sliced pullet wings in jellied sauce; green lotus seeds; fresh walnut meats; fresh pond horned-nuts; peeled raw water chestnuts. . . . The center division of the box contains a small but elegant silver wine ewer, two pairs of ivory chopsticks. (Quoted in Mote 1977, 251)[2]

The two connoisseurs of food and love sit on porcelain stools, continuing their numerous games while they eat. Soon Jinlian feels sleepy from the wine and lies down on a mattress stark naked, her white skin in contrast with her crimson lotus shoes—the same color tones as those worn by Ping'r (her crimson underwear and white bottom). Ximen ties Jinlian's feet to the posts of the grape arbor. The act suggests that Jinlian has become part of the fruit, ripe and available to be plucked and eaten. Then he plays with her red "flower heart" with his toes while drinking the wine and eating the fruit. His foreplay is interrupted by the arrival of the maid Chunmei (spring plum). He drops Jinlian, who is immobile on the mattress with her feet still tied to the posts, and runs after the maid. When he comes back with her and seats her on his lap, he continues the amorous dalliance with Jinlian, throwing chilled plums at Jinlian's enflamed vagina. He drinks and eats and dallies with Jinlian, who begs him to stop tormenting her sexually. Ximen ignores her plea and decides to take a nap, keeping Jinlian strapped to the posts with her feet up in the air. Only after he feels he has punished her enough for her jealous attack on Ping'r does he take out his love tools and engage in sex with her.

Food and drink play an indispensable role in creating the full range of sensations of smell, taste, color, texture, temperature, feelings, and actions, and more important, the display of luxury and power. Climax is reached in a calculated, leisurely manner, so that readers can experience all these sensations through linguistic maneuvers along with the protagonists. The variety and quantity of the food presented in this fictional scene are much less compared to the daily menu and food at real-life royal banquets, yet they are carefully chosen and symbolically arranged to create the notion in the reader's mind that the food/fruit is one with the female body and her sexual organs. The dishes that the maid brings to the garden—ducks' feet, fish, lotus seeds, water chestnuts, and pond horned-nuts *(ling jiao)*—are all euphemisms for bound feet.

Soon after part of the food is eaten and the wine drunk, Ximen ties Jinlian's tiny feet to the grape vine and starts throwing plums (highly suggestive of the female genitals) at her flower heart, occasionally inserting some of the fruit into her mouth and vagina. Thus, the differences between the two orifices are erased. Both function now as digestive and sexual organs at once. The connection and flow between the two are made possible by the word *plum,* its dual symbolism for sexual pleasure and poison already embedded in the language. *Mei* (plum) not only suggests the female genitals, femininity, and sex, but also poison, disease, death. In fact, the characters for syphilis in Chinese are *mei du*—literally, "plum poison."

It is not a coincidence that Jinlian's maid is called Chunmei (spring plum). She is not only her mistress's sole confidante and ally, but also an active participant herself in the erotic games. While Jinlian is alive, she is her mistress's sexual playmate for Ximen Qing. After Jinlian's death, she establishes her own haven of orgies in her new home. As the first lady of a high-ranking official, she has the full power and control to satisfy her desire. She brings in Jinlian's ex-lover Chen Jingji as one of her sexual partners, claiming that he is her long-lost brother. She pushes her mistress's licentiousness to a further extreme. While Jinlian only tries to seduce her brother-in-law and sleeps with her son-in-law, Chunmei turns her lover into her "brother." Of the three most important women in the novel (their names form the title of the book—*The Golden Lotus* stands for Jinlian, Ping'r, and Chunmei), only Chunmei has the power and means (social, financial, as well as linguistic) to fulfill her dream: to sex herself to death. She dies of *se lao,* oversex, whereas her mistress Jinlian is brutally killed by Wu Song, and Ping'r bleeds to death.

The highly refined atmosphere, created from the cooked food together with the expensively kept garden and luxuriously groomed women, is set in contrast with the raw fruit, the naked body, the stripped bound feet, the fully exposed genitals, and especially the dirty words that spurt out of Jinlian's mouth during lovemaking. These contrasts are mingled and melt into the ocean of words—words of daily life, of dialect, of blasphemy and obscenity that bring the erotic game to its climax, just as all the opposites are melted in the furnace of footbinding.

Why do food and sex go hand in hand? Why is the urge to link sex and food an indispensable part of the expenditure? And why does a beauty have to become edible before she can be consumed sexually and economically? What makes this connection between food (oral) and sex (foot) possible and keeps the flow going? To answer these questions, it is necessary to examine the ritual and cultural importance of food, and how it is affiliated with sex/foot by language.

Behind the facade of grand banquets and display, eating for the Chinese is a serious business. What they eat and how they prepare the food mark the degree of civilization they have attained. In Confucius's *Liji (The Liki)* we find that people who do not eat grains or food cooked with fire are classified as "barbarians":

> The people of those five regions—the Middle states, and the Jung, Yi (and other wild tribes round them)—had all their several natures, which they could not be made to alter. The tribes on the east were called Yi. They had

their hair unbound, and tattooed their bodies. Some of them ate their food without its being cooked with fire. Those on the south were called Man. They tattooed their foreheads, and had their feet turned in toward each other. *Some of them ate their food without its being cooked with fire.* Those on the west were call Jung. They had their hair unbound, and wore skins. *Some of them did not eat grain food.* Those on the north were called di. They wore skins of animals and birds, and dwelt in caves. *Some of them did not eat grain food.* (Legge 1967, 229; emphasis mine)

What make these people different from Chinese people are their fashions and their foods. Some have unbound hair, tattooed bodies; some wear animal skins and have their feet turned in toward each other; and most important, none of them eats food (meat) cooked with fire or grains. These are all the signs that mark them as barbaric, non-Chinese, uncivilized. Like sex that goes beyond the mere function of reproduction, food is more than just the vital part of the chemical process of life. The process of cooking with fire marks the transition and transformation from the raw to the cooked, inedible to edible, contaminated/contaminating to pure/purifying, wild to tamed, savage to civilized, nature to culture. In other words, cooked food establishes order, difference, and hierarchy. Its importance and position are established as early as Chinese history, appearing as an indispensable part of sacrificial rituals, fortune telling, medicine, and so forth. In fact, Confucius (551–479 B.C.) regarded it as a matter so essential that even the art of the military, which was crucial to a country's survival during a period of war, could not compete with it. When the Duke Ling of Wei asked him about military tactics, he replied with utter contempt: "I have indeed heard about matters pertaining to *tsu* (meat stand) and *tou* (meat platter), but I have not learned military matters" (*Lun yu*, "Wei Ling Kung," in Legge 1983).

Since it is eating raw and nongrain food that makes people barbaric, alien, contaminating, and dangerous to Chinese civilization, one of the ways to tame them is to introduce them to cooking through delicious Chinese gourmet methods. In the Han dynasty, Jia Yi (who died in 169 B.C.) proposed a menu for the Han restaurants along the border, in which roasted meat was prized as a main dish to attract the Xiongnu (Tartars) to China's side. He predicted optimistically that "when the Xiongnu have developed a craving for our cooked rice, keng stew, roasted meats, and wine, this will have become their fatal weakness" (Jia Yi 1937, 4:41). We do not know whether his strategy to fend off the Xiongnu's aggressive attacks worked or not. But his proposal suggests that while cooking establishes the differences between civilization and barbarity, order and chaos, control and impulse, it can also become a fatal weakness for a culture. Refinement and civilization indeed lead to a transcendence of savagery and barbarity, but also a loss of masculinity and virility. This dual nature has always been embedded in the Chinese concept of food. If one keeps a balanced diet, then food works as a good medicine that ensures one's health and longevity. But an unbalanced diet, overindulgence, or paying no heed to what one puts in one's stomach can turn food into poison.

The lotus foot, the symbol of Eros, once entering the realm of plant/food, is associated with all the signs, functions, and rituals of this food culture. Like cooking that transforms the raw and savage into something edible and refined, footbinding cooks the wild and primitive force of nature—the female body and its sexuality represented by the feet—into a piece of art, an object of desire. In his *Classification of the Qualities of Fragrant Lotuses,* Fang Xun states that the human lotus is superior to the loveliest flower because it understands human speech, perseveres in overcoming pain, and resists seasonal change. As mentioned earlier, footbinding was encouraged and spread as a way to establish the differences between men and women, high and low, barbarity and refinement, yet the result was a conglomeration of fused oppositions.

Both food and sex were used by Taoists as crucial ingredients for immortality pills. In Taoist sexual alchemy, human bodies become symbolic furnaces where elixir could be extracted through sexual union between yin and yang. This practice was later turned into *cai yin shu,* a sheer harvesting of yin from female bodies through intercourse. A man gathered or stole yin from as many women as possible to repair his broken yang until he gained health, longevity, and even immortality. Because food can be either medicine or poison, foot/sex carries the same ambivalent force. Moderate sex and controlled erotic pleasure are the best tonic for health and longevity, whereas overindulgence in sex brings only disease and death. This theme appears in every Chinese erotic novel and story, whether ironically or in earnest. In the early seventeenth century, Ming scholar Qu Sijiu made a proposal to the court to save China from the Juchen invasions. He prescribed women who could snatch souls with their tiny feet:

> The reason these barbarians are able to leave their own territory easily and swiftly and come to invade us from a great distance is that there are no beautiful women in their northern regions. If we want to control these northern barbarians, we should bring it about so that they have many beauties and cause their men to be ensnared and deluded by feminine charm. We should teach them footbinding and persuade them to imitate us in dress. They will prize women with a willow waist and a lotus gait [the way women with bound feet walk] and a weak and alluring attitude. Barbarians

who have been deluded by such women will then lose their cruel and harsh natures. (Quoted in Levy 1992, 32)

This immediately reminds us of Jia Yi's proposal sixteen hundred years ago. The ingredients may differ, but the concept is the same: to use the ambivalent forces of food or foot as a weapon, to take away the power of barbarian enemies by refining their tastes in food and sex. Yet this weapon is doubled-edged: it cures and infects; while it can be used to destroy the enemy, it often turns around to destroy its own user.

The ambivalent, double-edged force of food and the lotus foot calls up the language that Jacques Derrida uses when he describes what writing represents. In Plato's *Phaedrus,* Socrates treats writing as a *pharmakon,* a dangerous drug that is both remedy and poison. When used properly, it can cure the weakness of memory, but an overdose causes death. The *pharmakon* itself, however, has no proper or determinate character; rather, it is a neutral, common element, a medium that can go in any direction. As Derrida argues,

> The *pharmakon* is "ambivalent" because it constitutes the element in which opposites are opposed, the movement and play by which each relates back to the other, reverses itself and passes into the other: (soul/body, good/evil, inside/outside, memory/forgetfulness, speech/writing, etc.). It is on the basis of this play or this movement that Plato establishes the oppositions or distinctions. The *pharmakon* is the movement, the locus, and the play (the production) of difference. (Quoted in Culler 1982, 127)

This ambivalent, double-edged nature of Western writing is characteristic of Chinese speech, which I have discussed in my earlier chapter on the different languages of Jinlian and Wu Song. All of the common elements and possibilities of food and lotus foot are actually the ambivalent, dualistic workings of language—particularly, euphemism. Euphemism connects food and foot (sex) linguistically in the spectacle of expenditure and display, keeping the flow between the two. And most important, it works as a furnace to transform the raw, the wild, the untamed into the cooked and civilized. Women (beauty, femininity, sexuality) are like wild beasts: they look beautiful but are dangerous and contaminating. Such is not true beauty, because it cannot be used or consumed. Beauty is good only after it has gone through the "furnace" of language/euphemism, where feet are transformed into lotus, red beans, water chestnuts, dumplings, and so on, all cooked and edible. *Xiu se ke can*—beauty is edible—is thus not a casual Chinese saying. It carries all the significance and meaning of how language works and functions in aesthetics, sexuality, and daily life of the Chinese.

Let's look at what *euphemism* means. According to *The American*

Heritage Dictionary, the root of the word is from the Greek *euphemismos* and *euphemiszein,* to use auspicious words (*eu,* good, well, true; *pheme,* speech). Euphemism is then the act or an example of substituting a mild, indirect, or vague term for one considered harsh, blunt, or offensive. For example, one uses "slumber room" as a euphemism for funeral home. Two things are important for euphemism. One is the concept of substituting; the other is the content of this substitution. The so-called harsh, blunt, and offensive are actually the violent, bad, infected/infecting elements of reality, such as death, disease, violence; and these elements must be substituted (or covered up and transformed through "cooking") with the so-called good, auspicious words—words that are mild, indirect, or ambiguous. This is exactly the function of fire in cooking that transforms the raw to the cooked, and the function of footbinding that transcends women's "raw" body into a piece of art, into a beauty that can be feasted on visually and orally. Euphemism works as a metaphor, a metaphor specialized in substituting violent with mild, straightforward with vague, bad with auspicious, original with simulacrum.

Both cooking and footbinding mark the first stage of transformation: fire cooks the raw into edible food while binding turns the female body into beauty. This stage involves unspeakable violence. For cooking, it involves slaughtering, skinning, and dissecting animals, then all the boiling, broiling, grilling, sautéing; for footbinding, it means crying, bleeding, rotting, putrefying, and deforming of the feet. Confucius thus advised that a gentleman should keep a safe distance from the kitchen. And men often traveled or kept away from the inner chambers to avoid hearing their daughters' painful cries or seeing their tears from footbinding. Further, violence lurks behind the mild, tasteful presentation of food on the table, behind the layers of wrapping and the beautifully embroidered shoes, threatening to break through all these civilized "cover-ups." Such food and beauty are still not consumable until they are further "cooked" through words—prayers or euphemisms. Language here works as a final barrier that keeps the unspeakable violence at a safe distance, an outmost skin to cover (or seal) the killing, blood, pus, disease, and death. Through euphemism, the harsh, violent, and unspeakable reality becomes acceptable and speakable and is therefore ready for consumption.

Language, through euphemism, is thus the agent and medium that link and blend the borders between food and sex, mouth and foot, dead and living, divine and human. It transforms the unspeakable violence and uncontrollable savageness into something good, useful, speakable, and edible. The pleasure of the gods and the dead in Chinese culture is orally oriented in a similar way. Like humans, they love to eat: human bodies as sacrificial food, slaughtered animals, and cooked food. They cannot consume this gift, however, until it is delivered with another kind of food: words of prayer, chanting, songs, and other rituals that involve language. Here prayer and rituals work like euphemisms for footbinding. They cover and veneer the violent and unspeakable, tricking gods and ghosts into accepting the sacrificial food from humans, as is shown in Qu Yuan's *Chu ci* poems "Zhao hun" (Summon the soul) and "Da zhao" (Great Summons):

> O soul, come back! Why should you go far away?
> All your household have come to do you honor; all kinds of good food
>   are ready:
> Rice, broom-corn, early wheat, mixed all with yellow millet;
> Bitter, salt, sour, hot and sweet: there are dishes of all flavors.
> Ribs of the fatted ox cooked tender and succulent;
> Sour and bitter blended in the soup of Wu;
> Stewed turtle and roast kid, served up with yam sauce;
> Geese cooked in sour sauce, casserole duck, fried flesh of the great crane;
> Braised chicken, seethed tortoise, high-seasoned, but not spoil the taste;
> Fried honey-cakes of rice flour and malt-sugar sweet meats;
> Jadelike wine, honey-flavoured, fills the winged cups;
> Ice-cooled liquor, strained of impurities, clear wine, cool and refreshing;
> Here are laid out the patterned ladles, and here is sparkling wine.
>
>   (In Hawkes 1959, 107)

> The five grains are heaped up six ells high, and corn of zizania set out;
> The cauldrons seethe to their brims; their blended savours yield fragrance;
> Plump orioles, pigeons, and geese, flavored with broth of jackal's meat;
> O soul, come back! Indulge your appetite!
> Fresh turtle, succulent chicken, dressed with a sauce of Ch'u;
> Pickled pork, dog cooked in bitter herbs, and zingiber-flavored mince;
> And sour Wu salad of artemesia, not too wet or tasteless.
> O soul, come back! Indulge in your own choice!
> Roast crane is served up, and steamed duck and boiled quails,
> Fried bream, stewed magpies, and green goose, broiled.
> O soul, come back! Choice things are spread before you.
> The four kinds of wine are all matured, not rasping to the throat:
> Clear, fragrant, ice-cooled liquor, not for base men to drink;
> And white yeast is mixed with must of Wu to make the clear Ch'u wine.
> O soul, come back and do not be afraid!
>
>   (In Hawkes 1959, 111)

Behind the mouth-watering food and enticing menu lies bloody violence. No wonder the deceased and the gods are afraid and have to be persuaded with beautiful words to come and enjoy the sacrificial banquets.

In the Chinese language, food and sex overlap and blend into words of sensuality and violence. Apart from the bound feet that become edible through euphemisms, words also turn the rest of a female body into food. Her eyes are "almonds," her mouth is a "cherry," and her nose is "white and shiny as soap made from the whitest goose-fat" (Cao Xueqin 1973, 1:359). Her face is as shapely as a sunflower seed or goose egg. Her cheeks are as sweet and tender as a ripe peach or a "melon ready for cutting" (Shen Fu 1960, 54). Her neck is as white as a tender lotus root. Her breasts are "chicken's heads." Her fingers are slender and pointed like freshly peeled spring onions. The list is endless, and all the metaphors can be generalized into one saying: *xiu se ke can*—beauty is edible. This obsession with edible beauty, however, hides a violent instinct deep in our bodies. We humans, like gods and ghosts, love to eat our own species.

There are also many proverbs, slang expressions, and idioms that blend food, sex, and love. *Tou tao bao li*—give a plum in return for a peach—comes from a love poem from *Book of Songs,* its sexual and love symbol quite obvious. *Ju an qi mei*—raise the tray to the brows—indicates that the husband and wife live in such harmony and mutual respect that when the wife brings food to her husband, she lifts the food tray up to her eyebrows to show her respect. *Zao kang bu yan*—do not discard husks and chaff—praises those husbands who do not abandon their old wives. *Zao kang,* which translates as husks or foodstuffs that the poor eat, is a metaphor for a wife who has shared hardships with her husband. *Lan hama xiang chi tian e rou*—a toad wants to eat swan meat—mocks those who are ugly, poor, or low in society trying to run after high-priced women.

The interlocking and interaction among food, sex, and language seep into every aspect of Chinese culture, influencing how people think, look at things, and express their emotions. Food and drink become the most convenient and effective lures to sex. Preparing a meal for a lover, children, or guests is regarded as the best, subtlest, and most direct language to show tenderness, love, and respect. Ximen Qing rarely shows his emotion for any woman he lives with or sleeps with except in giving them money or gifts, either because he is simply heartless or lacks the words for such expression. Even when he mourns Li Ping'r who has died of grief over her son's death, the only channel he can find to express his sorrow is food. Once, after a song, when a friend asks him why he is sad, he replies: "If she [Ping'r] had been alive, she would have prepared my dishes herself. After her death, they leave servants alone to manage this. You see what this looks like. Not a single piece is really tasty" (*The Golden Lotus* 4:179). What Ximen Qing misses is not only the food Li Ping'r prepares for him, but also the charming words that accompany her food. Unlike Jinlian, who seduces and kills with her "oily mouth," Li Ping'r pleases Ximen Qing with her soothing and flattering words.

Food accompanied with insulting words can bring about such turbulent emotions that they cause a country to fall, just as beauty can bring down a nation. *Jie lai zhi shi*—food that is handed out in contempt (with contemptuous words)—is from a story of the Spring and Autumn Period. During a serious famine, a man named Qian Ao prepared food by the side of the road for hungry people. A man walked by, stumbling from starvation. Qian lifted the food and shouted to him, "Hey, you, come and eat!" The hungry man stared at Qian and said, "I fell into such a state because I refuse to eat food that is handed out with such contemptuous words!" He walked away and soon died. Another example of this is found in *Zuo zhuan: xuan gong si nian,* which records this story: the Country of Chu sent Duke Zheng a turtle as a gift. Prince Song Zigong heard of it and wanted to taste the delicacy. Duke Ling learned about his wish and decided to insult him. He summoned his officials and invited them to taste the turtle soup. He also invited Song Zigong yet did not offer him the soup. Zigong watched everyone eating, talking, and laughing, while he alone was ignored. Suddenly he ran over, dipped his finger into the cauldron, put it in his mouth, then left the palace without a word. Insulted by his act and silence, Duke Ling decided to kill Zigong. But Zigong was faster and killed the duke instead. Thus a country was destroyed by a pot of turtle soup.

"You are what you eat." On the one hand, the link between foot and food represents the desire to obtain the primal force of nature through the magic of imitation. Hence, little girls eat dumplings made from cooked grains and red beans when they are initiated into footbinding, hoping that their feet might become as soft and small as the food they consume. In the process of their first binding, girls would bite the tip of a writing brush or grasp a water chestnut so that their feet would become as thin and pointed as these objects. On the other hand, this magical imitation implies a deeper desire to return to the primal state of being—death—through the pleasure of food and sex. As Freud points out in *Beyond the Pleasure Principle,* the death instinct is the most powerful life force, the fundamental drive of every living thing to return to an inorganic state. The organism "wishes only to die in its own fashion" (Freud 1989, 39). Thus "the pleasure principle seems actually to serve the death instincts" (63). For the Chinese, the death principle has been fulfilled through spectacular spending on food and sex. They have been living up to Confucius's saying *wei zhi sheng, yan zhi si*—without knowing life first, how can one understand death? To eat oneself to death and sex oneself to death: this is not only the principal theme of the erotic novel *The Golden Lotus* but also the undercurrent that runs through Chinese history. The pleasure in food and sex, the connection and flow between the two, are made possible through language. Thus, it is not enough for little girls just to eat dumplings and grasp water chestnuts in their initiation to footbinding. The magical imitation works only when it is accompanied with prayers and linguistic rituals. Food and foot cannot be enjoyed unless they are blessed by words. Language is the sorcerer behind all the spectacles of food and sex, order and chaos, logic and impulse, life and death. In that sense, "you are what you eat" can be phrased as "you are what you speak." It is no surprise that Socrates, the master philosopher who possesses the most potent medicine, *pharmakon* (writing, knowledge), is arrested in Athens as a sorcerer, as a magician who seduces youth through the enchantment of words. And he is sentenced to death by drinking his own medicine—*pharmakon*.

Alas, who could say it is a coincidence that nearly sixteen hundred years later, a Chinese scholar Wang Shizhen (1526–67), who was believed to be the author of *The Golden Lotus* under the pen name Xiao Xiao Sheng, used writing to poison his enemy?[3] Only he was more crafty and knew the secret that poison, in order for it to work better, must be blended with sweets: food and sex. When he wrote the book, he did not realize that it would become the most popular erotic novel among the Chinese, a classic of the genre in the history of Chinese literature. He did not intend it to. His only motive was to kill his enemy, a descendant of the evil minister Yan Song (1480–1567), who murdered his father Wang Yu (1507–1560). The method was odd but made perfect sense. He wrote the book with poisoned ink (some said that the pages were soaked in poison) and delivered it to his enemy as a present (Is it another coincidence that the etymology of *gift* in English goes back to the word *poison*?). He was confident that the mouthwatering food and soul-snatching sex scenes in the novel would compel his enemy to read on and on, licking his finger so as to turn the pages faster. By the time he finished the book, the poison he licked off his fingertips would be enough to kill him. Here, Xiao Xiao Sheng/Wang Shizhen materializes Plato's metaphoric connection between *pharmakon* and writing. Words seduce and kill. And they do so by way of the mouth.

Silken Slippers:
Footbinding in Chinese Erotica

In books, you will find a golden house.
In books, you will find women as beautiful as jade.
                    —Chinese saying

Words do address bodies directly; they do tell a story of sex and violence.
Language being spoken by a speaker but also becoming a speaker itself
and speaking the author.
                    —Jean-Jacques Lecercle, *The Violence of Language*

DENG XIAOPING DIED without any title in the Chinese government or the Party. In fact, the former Party president, suffering from Alzheimer's disease, had withdrawn from the political scene entirely in his final days. Yet when he died, all Chinese flags were lowered to mourn him, and newspapers all over the world reported his death and his funeral. Jiang Zemin, the president of China, was pictured in the *New York Times* crying like a son at Deng's funeral.

It didn't matter that Deng had resigned his positions in the government, party, and the military force, or that he had Alzheimer's. Deng Xiaoping had been the Father of the State, the column of the nation, or to use a Western term in a slightly playful mode, the Phallus, ever since he took power from the hand of Hua Guofeng, Mao's appointed successor after his death, just as Mao had been the Red Sun, and before him, Sun Yat-sen had been revered as *guofu*—Father of the State—and all the past emperors had been called *tianzi,* sons of heaven. Such is the mold of the Chinese feudal system (even the socialist regime cannot escape its shadow):

the state is seen as a family; the emperor/president is Father, Heaven, and all his sons/subjects bow and kowtow to him. The same patriarchal structure is mirrored in individual families: the father is foremost, and women follow their father before marriage, their husband when they get married, then their sons. *Junjun, chen chen, fufu, zizi*—King (must act like a) king; minister (like a) minister; father (like a) father; son (like a) son—is the Confucian hierarchy and relationship set up for the government and family. It has been the foundation of Chinese feudal society and is deeply imprinted in the consciousness and subconsciousness of each individual.

The fact that Deng continued to function as China's linchpin even in reclusion is evidence that it is not an actual Father who is ultimately the most important to the order of the government and families but, rather, the Name-of-the-Father, a symbolic father whose power is invisible but everywhere. This symbolism is close to Jacques Lacan's notion of the Phallus as the mythic, veiled signifier associated with maleness and power, as well as language and desire: "The phallus is the privileged signifier of that mark in which the role of the logos is joined with the advent of desire" (1977, 318). The initiation into language is also the entry into desire: "The fact that the phallus is signifier means that it is in the place of the Other that the subject has access to it. But since this signifier is only veiled . . . it is this desire of the Other as such that the subject must recognize" (1977, 288). However, because the phallus is symbolic, no one, including the male who is endowed with a penis, actually possesses it. According to Lacan, all human subjects are caught between having and being a Phallus that one can never possess. Thus, a sense of permanent "lack" arises.

Can the obsession of bound feet be partially explained psychoanalytically as the Chinese man's desire for the phallus? In other words, can one borrow Freudian's speculation on the fetish as a penis substitution arising from castration anxiety, or Lacan's notion of the phallus, or even the Marxist theory of commodity fetishism as false consciousness to examine a Chinese practice and obsession that is a thousand years old? On the one hand, such an application will certainly cause problems because it immediately raises the question of whether Western theories can and should be used for the analysis of non-Western materials, and whether they (Freudian, Lacanian, or Marxist) can be applied as a "master key" to the global cultures of different eras. On the other hand, if we put aside the theoretical controversy temporarily, and just look at and compare the cultural phenomena, a certain logic and link begin to appear. Chinese men's craving for the pointed, upward, penis-shaped feet does seem to resonate with Freudian fetishism, just as Bataille's meditation on eroticism and expenditure highlights the fact that bound feet intensified Chinese men's desire so much that they squandered their resources to acquire and possess tiny-footed women as well as their shoes. And when one looks at the Chinese obsession with the size of male genitals in literature as well as in reality,[1] and looks at it together with their obsession with the size of bound feet and language (the written characters particularly), it inevitably reminds one of Lacan's Phallus as the privileged signifier.

My justification for bringing Western theory, particularly that of psychoanalysis, into the study of footbinding and its related literature, is that I do not intend to use it to explain the Chinese cultural phenomenon or prove the universality of Western theory. Rather, I hope that the speculations on the Western psyche and culture will work to open my discussion, or to borrow a Chinese term, *qiao men zhuan*—a brick to knock on the door that opens to the vast historical and literary materials on footbinding. Meanwhile, I understand and keep in mind that each of the Western theories can only work as a mirror or metaphor for the one-thousand-year-old mystery of this Chinese male erotic fixation. And the reflections from the mirror are as fragmentary and partial as the fetishistic gaze itself. Footbinding, so widespread (in terms of regions and classes) and so long enduring in Chinese history, should be viewed not as an individual "fetish" but as a culturally produced aspect of male desire deeply rooted in Chinese culture—its political, social, and economic systems and dynamics, especially in language.

In what follows, I concentrate on the ways that the cultural fetish of bound feet acquired erotic, sexual content, in other words, how a more complex fetish form achieved male erotic dominance in a variety of literary forms: essays, short stories, and erotic novels from late imperial China to the contemporary period. I suggest that a fetishistic fixation on female body parts goes hand in hand with the fractal, synecdochic element in much of Chinese male writing when it comes to desire and erotic fantasies. Often, their fetishistic gaze is translated in poetry, essays, and novels as a manic collection—classifying, inventorying, categorizing—a linguistic taxonomy of female body parts.

The male authors I examine in this chapter showed the tendency to textualize, fetishize, and categorize the female body in their writings, with the tiny feet as the paramount focus of their gaze. The eighteenth-century scholar Fang Xun's *The Classification of the Qualities of Fragrant Lotuses* is an inventory of the various human lotuses and the best scenes and environments for their erotic pleasure. The writing in the Ming erotic novel *The Golden Lotus* is so saturated with the synecdochic details of food and sex that they hold more meaning than the plot. Lost in the luxurious sensuality of the metonymic descriptions, one finally gives up reading to identify with its characters and instead wallows with the author in the careful depiction of the props. In Li Yu's (1611–1679) book of essays on drama, music, food, and gardening, bound feet, like the rest of female body parts, were classified, appreciated, and analyzed like painting and poetry (Li Yu 1996). The taxonomization, classification, and textualization of the tiny feet were even further dramatized in the contemporary writer Feng Jicai's novel *The Three-Inch Golden Lotus,* which instantly became a popular book when it was published in the early 1980s.

The writing of these and other authors turned the female body into fractal and metonymic parts, then treated these parts as if each were whole. With the same fervor to collect art and money for social status, the authors (or their male characters) collected tiny-footed women and foot-related objects such as shoes, socks, wrappings, as well as linguistic and historical knowledge of footbinding. The foot competition for women always turned into a fierce battle among men; in other words, the naming of women's feet became a means of beating other men in the possession of cultural capital, and the whole category of fetishization became a domain of discourse and knowledge in its own right.

The fetishization of writing/knowledge through the female body reflects Chinese men's desire to be part of the phallic power manifested in written Chinese language. Words are associated with maleness, desire, power, money, and social rank; meanwhile, they also castrate and destroy. Such ambivalent forces of language are vividly represented in the Qing writer Pu Songling's short story, "The Bookworm." Similarly, the story of the female poet Shuangqing, presented in fragments through Shi Zhenlin's (1693–1779) memoir *Xiqing sanji* (Random Notes of West-Green) makes an interesting case in which a woman's voice (her poetic talent) and her body (beautiful, virtuous, but terribly abused) are fetishized into the image of *jiaren* (beautiful woman) in order to serve as a mirror for the ill-fortuned *caizi* (talented man), and as a vehicle for male imagination and writing. It is a case that demonstrates how the discourse of the female body becomes that of the male body. Shuangqing's poetry, however, escaped Shi Zhenlin's textualization over the years, and she became one of the most distinguished woman song lyric writers of the Qing dynasty, whereas Shi and his writings were known only to a small circle of intellectuals. The relationship between the creator (Shi as Shuangqing's discoverer) and the created, the fetish agent and fetish object, is reversed.

As the female body is categorized, the fetishized body part (the lotus foot) achieves a life of its own as art, poetry, history. The fetishized object begins to haunt and hunt its users. Men, the agents and creators of the fetish, end up being fetishized and castrated by their own creation. The authors lose control of their narratives; instead of speaking language and characters, it is now language and (female) characters speaking them and speaking through them. Since the ambivalence of language is revealed and works through the ambivalence of the female body (bound feet, female virtue, writing), the discourse of the female body as well as that of the male body constantly undergo the violence of language. And the most dramatic form of writing/inscription on the body is perhaps manifested through China's most cruel punishment—the thousand cuts. The prolonged process of cutting the flesh into a thousand pieces as symbolic writing on the male body is quite similar to the way the female body is fetishized into edible beauty to be consumed visually, orally, and linguistically.

An Inventory of the Human Lotus

As discussed in chapter 2, the first poem praising bound feet was written by the Song poet Su Shi, but the fixation on feet did not flourish in literature until the late imperial era. With the spread of footbinding, poets, especially lyric song poets, and fiction writers could no longer talk about the beauty and sexual charm of the female body without mentioning lotus feet. The metaphors and idioms about bound feet, however, never escaped the frame set by earlier writers: feet as pointed as the new moon, as delicate as willow branches in the eastern wind, as fragrant as fruit, as delicious as dumplings, or lotus steps as light as if the woman were floating on the surface of water, her feet so tiny that she could dance gracefully in a man's palm. Such clichés are scattered throughout poems, songs, short stories, and fiction as well as essays.

By the eighteenth century, an aristocrat who called himself "Doctor of the Fragrant Lotus" under the pen name Fang Xun wrote several essays that were among the earliest works dedicated entirely to women's feet. As mentioned earlier, the first, *The Classification of the Qualities of Fragrant Lotuses*, names, classifies, and inventories various bound feet, giving critical commentary on the aesthetic of tiny feet. The second, *A Golden Garden Miscellany (Jin yuan za chuan)*, collects sayings and proverbs related to lotus feet. The third, *Guan yue zha*, and the fourth, *Lotus Picking Boat (Cai lian chuan)*, analyze drinking games in which shoes play a principal role.

Classification botanizes bound feet by imitating the thematic arrangement of Zhang Gongfu's famous botanical work *Qualities of Plum Blossoms*.

Fang lists fifty-eight varieties of bound feet, arranging them according to five principal styles—lotus petal, new moon, harmonious bow, bamboo shoot, and water chestnut. Under the style of lotus, he names and defines eighteen kinds of feet:

"Lotus petal on all sides"—perfectly narrow and arched, three to four inches long.

"Lotus with silk linen sides"—correctly bound, an inch longer, preventing the wearing of sharply pointed shoes.

"Long hairpin lotus"—shaped like a bamboo shoot, but too long and thin to satisfy critical aesthetic standards.

"Single leaf lotus"—soles narrow and flat.

"Buddha's head lotus"—instep very full, hunched like a knot on the head of Sakyamuni.

"Piercing heart lotus"—hidden high-heeled shoes.

"Double flowers"—toes pointing outward.

"Intertwined hearts"—callused heels. (*Xiang yan cong shu* 1914, 4:8; quoted in Levy 1992, 109)

At the end of the list is "Tibetan lotus," a large-petaled flower from Tibet, indicating that the foot is larger than the normal standard because the girl starts the binding in her adulthood. This is an inferior form but still preferable to the lotus of "Jade well," referring to a natural foot disguised by wearing a pointed sandal.

In Fang Xun's botanical garden of human lotuses, the artificial "plants" surpass natural ones because the lotus feet, having overcome pain in their creation, become immortal. A woman's face may wrinkle, but her feet never fade, age, or become subjected to the cycle of seasons as long as the body lives. Feet are separated from the body and serve as a fixed object of male eroticism. Peeking at lotus feet, stealing lotus shoes, washing, massaging, smelling the feet as well as inserting the pointed toe into the nostril—all are parts of sexual fantasy and foreplay. A lotus foot is praised and worshipped as if it encompassed the beauty of the entire body: glistening and white like skin; arched like eyebrows; pointed like jade fingers; round like breasts; small like a mouth; red like lips; and mysterious like private parts (*Cai fei lu* 2:336–37). The part, having completely substituted for the whole, has indeed become whole in the eyes of fetishists. And the metonymic nature of the fetish classification is associated with the process of contour sharpening with the very essence of erotic fixation.

Fang also arranges the feet according to nine official ranks. These nine qualities are:

Divine quality (A1): neither plump nor slender but as perfect in size as the ancient *beauty Xi Shi,* who looks superlative in every posture.

Wondrous quality (A2): weak and slender, like a willow branch leaning for support and bending in the breeze.

Immortal quality (A3): straight-boned, independent, and not of the common herd. She is as spiritual as the *Taoists who live in the mountains and eat only pine seeds,* though thin and cold like the *poems of Jia Dao and Meng Jiao* [both Tang poets].

Precious article (B1): conspicuous and brilliant as a peacock, but the back of her foot is too wide and disproportionate.

Pure article (B2): long and thin, like the neck of a goose with outstretched throat crying aloud or a duck with its neck elongated in flight.

Seductive article (C1): fleshy and short, relatively wide and round, like the royal concubine *Yang Yuhuan's dance and song.* Frailty is the mark of femininity, but a woman with this foot shape can easily withstand a blowing wind.

Excessive article (C1): narrow but not smooth, slender but insufficiently pointed, reminding the beholder of *Mi Fei's* [1051–1107] *landscape painting with one strong rock but crumbling clouds and precipices.*

Ordinary article (C2): plump and almost common, like a red water chestnut in the autumn water and the distant green on the spring mountain. If placed among chickens, it can still stand out like a crane.

False article (C3): it has such a large heel that she gives the impression of a climbing monkey, as Yang Xinshu described, "A madam whose origin is from a low family tries to act like a lady, but can't pass." (*Xiang yan cong shu* 1914, 4:8; emphasis mine)

Fang compares bound feet to pines, bamboo, and plum blossoms, which have become the tropes and symbols of integrity, uprightness, and perseverance in Chinese painting and poetry. The taxonomy of the bound foot is only the first step. The human lotus needs to be initiated and transformed further into art, poetry, writing, and power (official rank). To rank bound feet with official titles is analogous to scholars' identification with the courtesan in the late Ming, which, as pointed out by Dorothy Ko, "was integral to the operation of the civil-service examination, the process that reproduced the empire's political and cultural elites" (1997b, 82). Bound feet, like the late Ming courtesan, once included in and elevated to the world of *wen* (writing, power, politics), become part of a Chinese man's "rites of passage to elite manhood and his eventual prize to claim" (82).

Fang emphasizes three precious qualities that make a pair of excellent lotuses: plumpness, softness, and fineness. *Plumpness* implies voluptuous beauty, *softness* gives an enticing skin texture, and *fineness* provides a mystic elegance. While the first two qualities can be achieved physically and appreciated visually, fineness can be grasped only through the spiritual understanding and exchange between a footbinder and her feet, between a lotus lover and lotus feet. Such understanding and exchange are realized only with the help of language, through the historical knowledge of footbinding, the mystic transmission (oral and written), the aesthetic taste acquired from education in poetry and painting. In the final stage of this linguistic transformation, however, language no longer suffices. According to the lotus lovers, no words can ever describe the mystic beauty, elegance, or spirit of superb lotus feet. The process of making a pair of such bound feet is similar to painting and writing poems about pines, bamboo, and plum blossoms. Just as one cannot produce a good piece of work without first spiritually (linguistically) entering and becoming one with these plants, a woman cannot make superb bound feet without understanding and grasping the immortality and divinity of the human lotus, nor can a lotus lover truly appreciate the lotus foot without knowing its linguistic and historical origin.

Translating the female body into art, poetry, and political power is by no means Fang Xun's invention. Li Yu (1611–79), the acclaimed dramatist, essayist, and fiction writer, had already emphasized in his *Occasional Writing on Casual Emotions (Xian qing ou ji)* that physical appearance alone did not suffice to make a beauty. A woman of ideal femininity must also be skilled in poetry and painting, musical instruments, singing or dancing, just as he insists that a pair of ideal lotus feet must be thin, small, and agile: "Both sayings like 'every step produces a lotus blossom' and 'standing slim and graceful like jade' indicate that only [women with] tiny feet who could walk around freely and come in and out of a painting at ease should be regarded as treasure." In other words, Li Yu's ideal beauty is a living painting that can first of all satisfy men's visual pleasure. "The more a man gazes at a pair of tiny, thin feet, the more pitiful [lustful] he feels. That's the function of small feet for the day time" (*Xian qing ou ji* 1996, 124). By the same token, he believes that teaching women how to read adds tremendous charm to their beauty: "Women learning how to read and write are already a great visual pleasure for men even from the beginning, let alone the benefits after they have mastered the skill: when she opens a book, holding a brush at the green window, it is already a painting" (156). Teaching women to play chess has the same visual effect. A man can easily lose his soul by watching her holding a chess piece between her slender fingers, hesitating where to go. Seeing such a lovely picture, Li Yu comments, no man on earth has the heart not to let her win the game (158).

Li Yu's intention to teach women how to paint, write, and play chess is not to make them men's equals, but to make them better objects of men's gaze and erotic satisfaction. To Li Yu, the fetishistic process involves not only physical violence like footbinding but also linguistic enforcement. A beauty cannot be consumed unless she is first "cooked" by language and nurtured by culture. Once her body is inscribed with such cultural artifice, she becomes a medium that leads men to a visual orgy, a linguistic intoxication and erotic gratification, while she herself remains mute and neutral, a living painting that will not threaten to usurp the master's position.

Li Yu's ideal woman was revived again in the 1980s. In his popular novel *The Three-Inch Golden Lotus,* Feng Jicai created a living painting and a poem out of Fragrant Lotus's feet, according to Li Yu's and Fang Xun's modes. Fragrant Lotus was born with the best raw materials for the making of beauty: she had a pair of the softest, smallest, and shapeliest feet. After she went through several violent processes of footbinding, first by her grandma, then by the old maid who was an expert binder, her master (also her father-in-law) gave her Li Yu's *Occasional Writing on Casual Emotions* and Fang Xun's *Classification* to read. He assured her that these books would help her understand the spirit and secret language of lotus feet. Only when she had fully comprehended the books would she be able to turn her feet into something divine, spiritual, something beyond language. And she would become a foot champion. Fragrant Lotus followed his advice, studying the books while attending to her feet daily. When she appeared at a foot contest, no one could recognize her. She was no longer the girl with too much emotion and desire, or with too much flesh and blood. Now she was all spirit, her body rid of the dross, carnality, and other earthly qualities. Her subtle yet highly erotic costume and makeup, her averted face and downcast eyes that gave a mixed impression of being shy, demure, yet highly confident, grasped every man's eyes at the contest and affected them like "a little bug that tickled and tickled and tickled but eluded capture" (Feng Jicai 1986, 115). This modest, shy, and passive figure soon turned into an athlete who played breathtaking tricks at her shuttlecock game with her barely visible tiny feet, tickling the audience's desire to the point of explosion. Finally,

she extended the other foot to have the shoe tip catch the shuttlecock, and
it lighted softly. This move was designed to reveal her foot, to give the audience an eyeful. Her foot was fine, thin, narrow, pretty, and tiny, just like a
slice of melon. But one must not show too much of a good thing, so
Fragrant Lotus gave the shuttlecock a kick, and it rose in the air and returned to her hand. Her tiny feet were once again hidden beneath her skirt.

Fragrant Lotus again stood gracefully, her gaze cast not toward the audience but shyly downward. The period of exertion left her bosom rising
and falling lightly with breath, which made her even more tender and
adorable. (117)

The effect is stunning, sending the male spectators into crazed intoxication. They either shouted like lunatics, totally losing control of themselves,
or became speechless. When they finally calmed down, Mr. Qiao, a poet
who often acted as the spokesman of his friends, heaved a sigh and said,
"This is just like poetry, painting, song, dreams, mist, and wine; if it leaves
us enchanted, intoxicated, mindless, even dead, it is worth it" (116–17).

Fragrant Lotus is an incarnation of Li Yu's ideal of feminine charm. To
use Li's own words, she is a tiny-footed beauty "who can walk about freely
and come in and out of a picture at ease" (124). As the emblem of femininity,
she becomes equivalent to poetry, art, or spirit, something too ephemeral to
be described or comprehended. As the foot gains a soul and a life through
language, the fetish has now taken over the rest of the body, substituting
for the whole and usurping the subjectivity of the master and creator.

The Female Body as Fetishized Language

Lotus feet enhance men's visual pleasure during the day and gratify their
erotic desire at night. But they have an even more important task to do,
that is, to teach men moral lessons. The ambivalence of footbinding helps
reveal the violence and corruption of language and brings men back to the
right track. It is with this goal in mind that Li Yu wrote *Occasional Writing
on Casual Emotions*. For the first third of the book, he goes into great detail
about the theory of playwriting, music, and performance. Then he turns to
women in the third chapter, "Voice and Appearance" (speech and image),
giving detailed advice on how to pick and train beauties, and he ends the
book with his comments on houses, gardens, furniture, food, plants,
health, and enjoyment. Such an arrangement may seem strange to readers at
first glance, yet it makes sense if we look into Li Yu's anxiety over language,
and his ambition in channeling its ambivalent force to the advantage of so-

ciety and humanity. In the introduction, he emphasizes the effect and affect of language that permeate every sphere of humanity and society. He warns that language corrupts and destroys, leading people and society astray. The corrupting force of language is manifested in plagiarism and clichés, the two leading elements that poison human hearts and morals. The only way to prevent and correct the corruption is to constantly revitalize language by transfusing fresh meanings into words that have become clichéd, inventing new writing styles, and producing new thoughts. Language corrupts, but if it is well channeled, it also brings peace and joy for the body and mind: "In order to correct the corrupting custom, one must first reform people's hearts" (*Xian qing ou ji* 1996, 6). But since men only love to read casual books and hate listening to the moral lessons of the teacher Zhuangzi, the only way to sneak some teaching into their ears is through women, art, music, interior design, and other topics of refinement, taste, and pleasure: "From refinement to Zhuangzi, from shallow to deep, no reader will be scared away" (6).

If *Occasional Writing on Casual Emotions* is meant as a medicine to cure society's disease caused by language, Li Yu in this case uses the fetishized female body as a *yao yin,* an inactive ingredient added to enhance the efficacy of a dose of medicine.[2] Of all the ingredients (theater, music, food, ornaments), the female body is perhaps the most alluring, most tasteful, and most dangerous. So potent and sweet is the *yao yin* that the added supplement replaces the main ingredients. Readers enjoy his advice and comments on women so much that the rest of the book is soon forgotten. The result is ironical but also inevitable. When a woman is endowed with the power of image and language, her fragmented and fetishized body also obtains (or is infected with) the ambivalence of words. When the body becomes a medicine to fight the infection of language, or a bait to lure men into learning the values of modesty, simplicity, and integrity, it is just a matter of time that the medicine turns into poison, and the bait reveals its deadly hook.

The obsession with language derives, it may be speculated, from the cultural adherence to Confucius and his lifelong devotion to *zheng ming,* the rectification of names. No moral precision was conceivable, Confucius believed, without absolute concentration on language, as he put the idea to one of his brightest but most impetuous students, Zilu:

If the names are not correct, language is without an object. When language is without an object, no affair can be effected. When no affair can be effected, rites and music wither. When rites and music wither, punishments and penalties miss their target. When punishments and penalties miss their target, the people do not know where they stand. Therefore, whatever a gentleman conceives of, he must be able to say; and whatever he says, he must be able to do. In the matter of language, a gentleman leaves nothing to chance. (Quoted in Legge 1983, 263–64)

The tight rein Confucius put on language indicates the dangerous wolf that lurks behind and inside words. Names are the incarnation of social law and authority, and the act of naming is theoretically constitutionalized, embedded with power, authority, and social status. A word like *father* implies a series of rules that determine the behavior of the individual bearing this name as well as the power and privilege it carries. But language also depends on its object, which is often sexualized and fetishized in order to exercise its power. And the female body, in a patriarchy, becomes the most convenient and efficient object for such fetishization.

In *The Golden Lotus,* Ximen Qing facilitates his sexual relations and enjoys his power with women as a *gan die*—adopted father, especially of women with lower or equal social status, like all his concubines, maids, servants' wives, and prostitutes. At the same time, he acquires political power by offering himself as a *gan er*—adopted son—to the Imperial Censor Cai Jing. His sexual partners' verbal acknowledgment of his identity as their "father" or "husband" during sexual intercourse gives him the greatest satisfaction and enhances his sexual pleasure. Sometimes he even goes so far as to dictate words for the woman to repeat, as is the case with Ru Yi, the wet nurse of Ximen's short-lived son. The setting and progress of the scene are marked by a gradual revelation of power that reaches its climax in Ru Yi's verbal recognition of Ximen Qing as her father/husband. As Ximen plunges more deeply into a sexual frenzy, his health soon deteriorates. That day, he goes to Ru Yi to get her milk as a medicine for his backache, a sign that in Chinese medicine is identified as a weak kidney as well as weakened virility due to excessive sex and loss of semen. After taking the pills, he settles down in bed for drinking and eating, summons Ru Yi to lick his penis, promising her silk and money if she serves him well. Still unsatisfied, he tells her that he has a particular urge to burn incense on her body. Ru Yi obeys, offering him any part of her body he desires. He places one stick of incense between her breasts, one on her abdomen, and one on her mount of Venus, then engages in sexual intercourse with her. When she can no longer bear the burning and begs him to spare her, he shouts,

> "Zhang Si'er [Ru Yi's maiden name], you whore, whose wife are you?" The woman replied, "I'm yours, Father." Ximen corrected her: "You should say

that you were once Xiong Wang's wife, but today belong to your darling daddy." The woman repeated, "I was once Xiong Wang's wife, but today belong to my darling daddy." (5:78; my translation)

Upon hearing his own words echoed back from Ru Yi's mouth, Ximen Qing is overwhelmed with passion and desire, and his semen gushes out like a spring. Here, the fetishization of language becomes so literal and intense that words equal sexuality/virility, which equals semen, which equals power. All this can take place, however, only through and on the fetishized body of Ximen Qing's mistress. First, her milk was used as a *yao yin* for his medicine, then her body as an incense burner to enhance his sexual pleasure, and finally, her mouth as a tool to echo his words so that he can reach an orgasm. Without such a physically and linguistically fetishized body, Ximen Qing's language would just fall into a void, and so would his power.

The fetishization of language was so culturally central that in the case of footbinding, the fetishized feet were no longer real or sexual: they had become the fecundity of language itself. In other words, naming lotus feet, collecting tiny-footed women and shoes, and accumulating the knowledge of footbinding became a domain of discourse and knowledge in its own right. As *The Three-Inch Golden Lotus* shows us, the intense foot competition is actually a fierce battle among men for power, sex, and social status. While women compete ferociously during foot contests and in their daily life for survival as well as rank within the family, men get together to compete about their knowledge of bound feet and their ability to name, invent games, and write poems on the topic. One of the games is to name sayings related to lotus feet. The list Mr. Qiao gives resembles Fang Xun's book:

"All right. Use your ears and listen, and use your mouth and count—this is called the twenty-four criteria of the golden lotus," said Mr. Qiao. "These twenty-four are divided into four categories: shape, essence, air, and spirit. Each category contains six terms. Six times four is exactly twenty-four. Shape is fine, pointed, short, thin, curved, and poised; essence is light, tender, fragrant, swift, firm, and bewitching; spirit is leisurely, refined, transcendent, secluded, charming, and light. (Feng Jicai 1986, 110)

The losers not only have to drink wine as a penalty, but they lose face, and worse, they lose their authority and authenticity to speak and be listened to. This is the case with Lu Xianqing, the self-named "lotus-loving recluse" from Da Tong, a city in Shanxi known for its women with perfectly bound feet. Lu comes to Tong Ren'an's foot contest to challenge the authority of Tianjin's number-one lotus expert and collector, who has bought four women with the most beautiful feet for his four sons. After he loses his first battle to Tong over the origin of footbinding, he loses his power and right to speak. All he can do is sit "utterly defeated, his mouth gaping, eyes staring blankly" and "totally at the mercy of the others" (Feng Jicai 1986, 54, 56). When he returns for the second foot contest, he barely speaks again. When he tries to talk, he is received in silence, with contemptuous looks. His loss in this linguistic battle reduces him to a "no man." In other words, he is castrated when words are taken from his mouth. In contrast, Tong Ren'an wins the title as one of the "four marvels in Tianjin" after beating Lu Xianqing in the foot contest. His linguistic triumph is sure proof of his manhood.

Understanding the power of speaking, naming, and writing, every man took great pains to say the most remarkable, the most knowledgeable things about bound feet. Even Niu Fengzhang, the dumbest and most vulgar figure in the book, manages to squeeze out a poem in the contest:

> Lovely is the golden lotus.
> The feet of Eldest Young Mistress
> Kicked the shuttlecock eight yards high;
> Whoever says her feet aren't good
> Should be forced to drink cat's piss!
>
> (113)

As the fetishization of the female body takes place and finds completion in the repetitive accumulation of words, anecdotes, and knowledge about women—a fetishization of texts—the male fetishists in *The Three-Inch Golden Lotus* are often swept away and lose control of their bodies or, more accurately, their voices. When they see Fragrant Lotus's bound feet, the wonder they have created collectively under the leadership of Tong Ren'an, their reactions are "stunned," "speechless," "eyes popping out," and "shrieking in a strange falsetto" (111). A foot contest becomes a site where men of different backgrounds and ranks gather, worshiping and competing for words and knowledge in the name of the phallic feet. Through the female body men are either marked as masculine and veneered with the phallic power, or they are feminized, silenced, and finally castrated.

Words, once fetishized through the female body, pave the path that can lead men to power, desire, and masculinity. The more words one collects and owns (in the case of footbinding, the more knowledge about and names for bound feet), the more powerful and more virile a man becomes. Ximen Qing practically cannot have an orgasm without hearing women's oral recognition of his authority as father/husband/man. Likewise, Tong

Ren'an, the main character from *The Three-Inch Golden Lotus,* could not have won the title of "Tianjin's marvel" solely by his collection of women with the best bound feet; he has to beat all his rivals in the contest for the knowledge on footbinding. Fang Xun would not have dared call himself "Doctor of Fragrant Lotus" without his expertise on lotus feet. Li Yu, a man of letters known for his contribution to the theory of music and drama, also held the key to the secret of eroticism through his vast accumulation of knowledge on different subjects, his talent in playing with words and writing styles. Language and women are interlocked, both as fundamental materials of the cultural fetishism and as the focal point for erotic desire and political power.

The Ambivalence and Vengeance of the Fetishized

While fetishized language and women lead men to phallic power, they also carry the force to castrate and destroy. Chinese men's desire emerges in their essays as a fetishistic inventory of words, sayings, and naming of the female body. In their novels, particularly erotic novels, the fetishism of language and the body continues and reaches the point in which the synecdochic detail of an event, an object, or a body part suffocates the narrative and characters. Toward the end, there is often an inverted relationship between the authors and the writing, between agents and objects of the fetish. Instead of being the masters of their writing and the speakers of language, the authors are captured by what they have created (or fetishized). Words, plots, and actions no longer express the authors' or their characters' obsessions; on the contrary, they carry them away. When language strikes back, it inverts everything: the hunted become the hunters, and the fetishized objects usurp the positions of the fetish agents. This is what Jean-Jacques Lecercle warns us about: "Instead of using our words, we become their plaything. The master has been enslaved" (1990, 190).

The Golden Lotus can barely hold its plot against the massive details in the two major modes of the book—sex and food—along with the full depiction of clothing, jewelry, houses, furniture, gardens, flowers, music, and other objects of sensuous pleasure. This huge body of description gives the author an opportunity to display his inventiveness in depicting the humdrum events of daily life; yet when ways of saying something new and perceptive about sex and food and other props eventually run thin, the inevitably repetitive details gradually lose their power over the plot and the development of its characters, and turn the novel into, as Fredrick Mote points out, "an inexhaustible storehouse of Ming social history" (Mote

1977, 249). What makes the obsession with details interesting is that the principal character Ximen Qing is weakened, even buried by the piles of related and unrelated anecdotes, while some of the minor characters in *The Golden Lotus* become more vivid and memorable.

In the earlier chapters of *The Golden Lotus,* Ximen Qing has absolute control of the direction and result of his own actions. And accordingly, the descriptions of his sexual seduction and his financial maneuverings are revealed at a leisurely, multidimensional pace, and the narrative is inventive, fresh, and vivid. The love scene in the vine arbor, as analyzed in chapter 4, is a good example. It takes eight full chapters (2–6, 8–10) to narrate the scenes of Ximen's meeting with Jinlian, their mutual attraction, their passionate affair, their plot to murder Jinlian's husband, their bribery of the autopsy officer to cover up the murder, Ximen's narrow escape of Wu Song's deadly revenge, and finally Jinlian's marriage to Ximen as his fifth concubine and the family's celebration. The courting scene between Ximen and his sixth concubine Li Ping'r also takes up many chapters, though the story is scattered through chapters and diverted by other events, interrupted by Li Ping'r's marriage to a doctor before her final reunion with Ximen. As his triumphs over women pile up, the narrative picks up speed like a roller-coaster, and the details become repetitive until it is no longer Ximen Qing who desires and acts. He becomes the slave of his desires, going around to perform various sexual stunts like a robot. He can no longer guarantee his success with women or be in control of his own ejaculations, as happens during his fatal encounter with his colleague's beautiful wife Lan Shi:

> It would have been all right if Ximen had not met her. But the moment he set his eyes on her, his soul left his body. He ejaculated even without physical contact with her. Yueniang and the others greeted and introduced her to everyone in the rear hall. Then they invited Ximen to meet her. Ximen tidied his clothes and hair before he rushed in to salute the visitor. She appeared like the jade tree of the heavenly forest descending to the mortal world and the goddess of Mount Wu coming down in dreams. He made a bow, his heart shaken and eyes flustered, his self-control all lost. (*Jin ping mei ci hua* 5:38; my translation)

Lan Shi, with her aristocratic title and beauty, symbolizes the higher power and place that Ximen Qing desires. Since she is inaccessible, he falls into the vertigo of sexual frenzy. After a series of frantic sexual encounters with various women as substitutes for the unreachable Lan Shi, he returns to Jinlian. Exhausted and sick, he is unable to have an erection. In her despair, Jinlian takes advantage of his being half-conscious and overdoses him with sex pills and alcohol to pump up his penis. Throughout the book, Jinlian has been playing the role of sexual plaything. Now she plays the master, turning Ximen Qing into a sex object in her own bed. And Ximen Qing, the fetish expert, loses control of his body as well as his consciousness. Once his penis becomes erect with the help of the pills, it gains a life of its own, ejaculating semen and blood automatically and continuously until Ximen Qing falls into a coma. Even then, it refuses to subside until it rots, bursts, and kills the body.

In the earlier part of Li Yu's *The Carnal Prayer Mat* (1657), the protagonist Weiyang Sheng's sexual adventures are inventive, playfully didactic, affectionately satirical, and leisurely paced. The story meets Li Yu's own high standards for writing, especially when it comes to inventiveness of language, style, and content. He wrote *The Carnal Prayer Mat* partly to warn society against unrestrained sexual desire and indulgence in libertine adventure, through the lesson of Weiyang Sheng, a typical scholar of the age, and his downfall. And partly, Li Yu wanted to show the public how erotic literature could be written with novelty and imagination. It didn't have to be like the stale, often imitative pornographic books that flourished in the Ming publishing market, or like popular romantic literature written to a fixed formula: a handsome scholar falls in love with a beautiful maiden and finally, through overcoming various obstacles, marries his beloved. Indeed, his scenes of the animal implant for penis enlargement and the orgy outdo all the other erotic fictions of Li Yu's age. Still, he cannot escape the pattern of the genre: the relentless quantification of sex, the obsessive accumulation of conquered women, of their names, and the analysis of their bodies. As the quantification adds up in a repetitive pattern and the narrative picks up speed, an inversion takes place. Weiyang Sheng gradually becomes the prisoner of his unrestrained desires as well as of the women he has been hunting.

The book begins with Weiyang Sheng setting off as a hunter after women, but toward the middle of the book, the hunter is already turned into a plaything in the hands of three young women. They decide whom he should sleep with each night; he does not have a say in the matter. Finally, he is carried stark naked in a trunk used for storing antique books and paintings into the house of Aunt Flora, a woman in her thirties with an expertise in sexual experience. Weiyang Sheng, the fetishizer, or the phallic desirer, becomes the hidden, fetishized, and feminized object. Now it is his turn to be enjoyed, used, and manipulated in the hands of women as art, literature, antique/treasure, and commodity:

> Opening the lid and glancing inside, she [Flora] discovered the smooth,
> snow-white body of a man across whose thighs lay a flesh-and-blood laun-
> dry beater that was woefully limp but still big enough to shock. She could
> only imagine what it might look like when stiff.
>
> Confronted with such rare merchandise, Flora felt a natural impulse to
> monopolize it. (Li Yu 1990, 248)

Determined to keep this rare commodity as long as possible for herself,
Flora has a long, hard-nosed round of bargaining with her three nieces.
While they discuss how his body, now fractured into a piece of merchandise, art, and the big "penis," should be divided among the four women
and how long Aunt Flora could keep the captured "stolen goods," Weiyang
Sheng is shut in the trunk, never allowed to come out from hiding. In the
end, he is carried away to Flora's place as her "old paintings," her "rare
commodity." There, he is possessed first by Aunt Flora alone, then shared
by the four women together. He is released only when he is depleted of his
sexual power and becomes useless goods.

Since language is fetishized through the female body, it strikes back also
through women's hands. (In the case of footbinding, it is the bound feet.)
In Feng Jicai's *Three-Inch Golden Lotus,* Tong Ren'an creates the phallic
woman, Fragrant Lotus, through her feet. Once she is made the foot champion, she is the automatically acknowledged head of the inner chambers.
But before long, she takes over the entire household and Tong Ren'an's
business, including his body.

The book begins with Tong Ren'an as the master of a big, rich household, a collector of women with the best bound feet in Tianjin, and the
owner of the city's best art shop, which has a vast collection of priceless old
paintings. He seems to be on top of everything and everybody. No one surpasses him when it comes to the expertise in art and bound feet. In many
ways, his excellent taste, his keen eyes, and superb training in female beauty
strongly resonate with the author of *Xian qing ou ji*—a "real gentlemen"
who has mastered the balance between hedonism and asceticism through
a true understanding of Confucianism, Taoism, and Buddhism and the
genuine appreciation of worldly pleasures. In fact, Tong is not only a reader of Li Yu's; he also passes his essays to his first daughter-in-law, Fragrant
Lotus, as a family treasure, guaranteeing her success in the next foot contest if she reads and comprehends the book thoroughly. This master of self-
composure, however, drops to his knees when he sees Fragrant Lotus's feet
and says in a quivering voice, "It's you who can help me" (91). He believes
that her feet can help him transcend the flesh and allow him to enter the

realm of the spirit and divinity, the realm beyond language. To use Western fetish theory here, although its limitations are now obvious, in Fragrant Lotus's feet he sees the potential for creating and possessing a Phallus. Indeed, after Fragrant Lotus wins the foot contest, she becomes statue-like: always keeping a calm, distant expression and manner, barely speaking unless to give orders. All her energy goes toward maintaining her status as a Phallus—the foot champion as well as the head of the inner quarter. She is feared by every woman in the Tong family, including her most cruel and fierce rival, Golden Treasure, her sister-in-law and a former foot champion.

Yet once Tong Ren'an has the "phallus," in the form of her transcendent feet, he begins to lose his control of it. The first sign starts in his antique shop, his financial resource, another form of the phallus. As the biggest art collector and dealer as well as the best antique appraiser of Tianjin, Tong has a full store of priceless, genuine paintings. Yet he never sells his collection. His antique and art store is just a cover for his counterfeit business. He hires a painter to imitate the paintings and sells them as genuine. The imitations appear to be so real that his customers never suspect anything and treat the reproductions as original, the imitations as genuine. At the same time, the real paintings are hidden in the back of Tong's store. Only two people are trusted to watch and care for the treasure, his second son, Tong Shaohua, and a half-witted dwarf, Living Sufferer, who can barely see or speak because of his birth defects: "When Tong Ren'an saw his [Living Sufferer] eyeless, mouthless, breathless, spiritless form, he immediately hired him as a storeroom watchman, treating the dead as if alive, and the living as if dead" (25). Living Sufferer resembles *hundun* (Chaos), the primeval force and the earliest state of the universe according to Chinese mythology, when earth and sky were still together, and the universe was just a huge ball without eyes, nose, ears, or mouth. *Hundun* also means innocent child, which puts Living Sufferer in the same category as women. Since he cannot talk or think, he is the perfect person to guard the art, and his body becomes the best safe to store all the secrets. Tong becomes his eyes and speaks for and through him. In this sense, Living Sufferer also represents the language and knowledge that Tong Ren'an can fetishize and possess. Thus, together with the paintings, antiques, and bound feet, Living Sufferer completes Tong Ren'an's fetish collection.

The dead, however, comes alive and haunts the living. This Living Sufferer robs his master's collection of ancient art secretly and slowly, by peeling half of the painting off the real work, substituting it with the imitation, then selling the half-real, half-fake piece as the original. Using his muteness and blindness as a mask, the half-witted servant fools his master and destroys Tong's masquerade with a trickier scheme, a more deceiving masquerade. The trick is not exposed until the half-real, half-imitation paintings become mass-produced and enter the black market. When Tong Ren'an discovers the truth by accident, the whole shop has been looted— not a single painting remains whole or genuine. Everything is half-real, half-fake. All the authentic and original art is now "contaminated" by the fakes and imitations. And Tong Ren'an, the owner and master imitator, is also contaminated. The real disaster is, however, that without the real as a backup, and with all his secrets leaked out by his runaway servant, he can no longer continue his counterfeit business. Without that facade, this master connoisseur of art, women, and knowledge is worthless. So horrified is Tong that he collapses from a stroke, which turns him into a speechless, immobile living corpse. The "contamination" of inauthenticity that stems from the fetish now runs amok, be it fool or female foot. Fragrant Lotus, the phallus that Tong has created, becomes the master of the family and rules the all-female household with an iron hand. The only male, Tong Ren'an, although still functioning as a phantom leader of the family (quite similar to the status of Deng Xiaoping in his last remaining years), is at the mercy of Fragrant Lotus. He has become a real living sufferer, who can neither move nor speak. The inversion between master and slave, fetishizer and fetishized, is now complete.

The vengeance of language is violent and merciless. As writers, poets, as well as scholars of Chinese classic texts, the authors of *The Golden Lotus, The Carnal Prayer Mat,* and *The Three-Inch Golden Lotus* are all aware of the dual, ambivalent power of writing as a potential remedy or curse, of its gripping and corrupting power over its creators. And they all consciously or unconsciously try to keep the middle road, to maintain their control of their writing while gearing it to the designed destination, whether as a cure for social problems (Li Yu's writing) or as a poison for his enemy (Wang Shizhen/Xiao Xiao Sheng's *Jin ping mei*). But language always triumphs in the end. The real master, as it turns out in each of the cases discussed above, is not the speaker but the words. As Martin Heidegger states poetically, "Language is the house of Being. In its home man dwells" (1978, 193). And this house is also an institution full of violent vengeance. In all these writings, language seems to be used in the beginning as the medium of a didactic or erotic tale, with its sardonic comments and facile moral lessons. But soon the tables are turned. The speakers lose their grip on their plots, characters, and words. The language they use as a tool to tell their stories becomes the subject of the tale. Instead of having the author speak the language, it is now the language that is speaking through the author, speaking the author. And it tells its own tale, a tale of sex (bound feet) and food mingled with violence, the violence of murder and mutilation, seduction and incest, intervention and interaction, that is written or inscribed on the body—not just the body as individual or biological, but also the body as political, social, economical, and sexual. It is out of this violent collision and subversion between words and body, however, that meaning becomes possible: "So there is a natural, serial link between reading, writing, action, and destruction. . . . And the destruction in question is both a source of pain and a cure—a painful remedy, like language itself" (Lecercle 1990, 230).

The Expanded Penis and Reduced Feet: A Vicious Circle

The overall collecting, quantification, inventory, and classification in the texts of decorated, fetishized female bodies, which extend to styles, plots, and actions in essays, fictions, and erotic literature by male authors from late imperial China to the contemporary period, can be seen in part as a linguistic affirmation for what men try to possess or become a part of—to borrow the Western term, a phallus.[3] The fetishism of language through the female body, however, is superseded by the inability to substitute for the substitute, and soon the power of the fetish itself becomes overwhelming and destructive, leaving Chinese men with a permanent feeling of inadequacy and lack as sons, forever kowtowing in fear and awe to the silent, invisible, yet omnipresent Father, the Son of the Heavens.

This feeling of inadequacy and lack comes out as an obsession with the size of the penis and the length of erection. "[Penis] size is an expression of phallic power" (Stratton 1996, 129). Both of the principal male characters in *The Golden Lotus* and *The Carnal Prayer Mat* have somehow enlarged their sexual organs. Weiyang Sheng chooses an animal implant. Although Ximen Qing does not take such a drastic method, he does receive a hundred magic love pills that look

> like earth or dung.
> But, when its merits are known, its worth is more than jewels.
> No gold will buy it.
> And jade is valueless compared with it. . . .
> Take but a speck of this, set it upon you, then
> Rush like a whirlwind to the bridal chamber.
> There you will find Spring always young. . . .
> The first engagement will leave you full of vigor.
> The second, even stronger than before. . . .

In a hundred days, hair and beard will be black once more.
In a thousand days, your body will know its power.
Your teeth will be strong, your eyes more bright,
Your manhood stiffened.

(*The Golden Lotus* 2:310)

The Indian monk who gives out the pills warns him that the medicine has double-edged effects. On the one hand, it goes beyond mere sexual pleasure and ecstasy. When taken properly at the right dosage, it is an elixir that will bring Ximen Qing manhood and immortality. On the other hand, if he is not careful and takes too much of it, it can bring harm and death to the body. To Taoist and sexual alchemists, sex is not its own end but a tool that leads men to health, masculinity, longevity, and finally, to the phallic image of immortals and gods. This concept partly comes from the Taoist and Buddhist practice of sexual alchemy, in which women's bodies are used both as raw materials for extracting their yin element to repair men's broken bodies and as stoves to make the elixir for immortality. The key to this art is *coitus reservatus,* which requires lifelong discipline, restraint, and cultivation in morals, aesthetics, and religion. Yet Ximen Qing will have nothing to do with these. He wants a shortcut to the phallic power through the gratification of his unrestrained desire, even if it means the ruin of his body.

Such male obsession goes hand in hand with the fetishization of the female body, which in footbinding manifests itself as the reduction of women's feet. This has a dual affect on men's relation with women. The desirability and sexuality of the fetishized female body (the feet) are drastically heightened and brought into the spotlight as the passive, phallusized woman; at the same time this highlighted body, which now carries the dual power for healing and castrating, brings out more fear and anxiety and pushes men into a frantic effort to expand their body size, accumulate more wealth, acquire more political power, and achieve better linguistic manipulation—to outdo what they have created. It is a vicious cycle. The more men fetishize the female body and text as the phallic power, the more they need to expand their own bodies (physical, political, economic, and linguistic) to keep the power struggle in balance, and the faster they are brought down by their own creation. Their fall, as presented in the texts by these male authors, often ends in sterilization or self-mutilation.

Again, take the example of Ximen Qing from *The Golden Lotus.* Although he has a wife and five concubines plus numerous lovers in and outside of his household, he does not have a male heir. To be more accurate, he cannot bring up any of the sons his wife or concubines have given birth to. They expire one way or another: the son by his sixth concubine, Li Ping'r, dies at an early age; his wife Yue Niang has two boys, one lost in a fifth-month miscarriage, the other doomed to become a monk (another form of sterility and self-castration). His fifth concubine, Pan Jinlian (Golden Lotus), seems infertile, for she has never gotten pregnant during her two marriages. Yet after Ximen's death, she is immediately impregnated by his son-in-law and gives birth to a son, drowned the moment he is born. The only child Ximen is able to bring up into adulthood is his daughter, who in the Chinese patriarchal system is considered an outsider. Even this outsider, Ximen's only descendent by blood, is sterilized; therefore she is unable to produce a child who will inherit Ximen's name, a last resort in the Chinese custom to prevent the extinction of a family. So when Ximen dies (and he dies from a kind of castration, since it is his penis that rots and erupts), he leaves behind him a huge household occupied only by women under the care of his wife, Yue Niang, whom Ximen has constantly praised as obedient, generous, and good-natured. But the first thing this model wife does after Ximen's death is to expel her son-in-law, the only man left in the house. Then she sells Ximen Qing's favorite maid and concubine, Chunmei (Spring Plum), who is Jinlian's right hand. Soon after that, she easily sells her rival Pan Jinlian, whose golden feet once symbolized Ximen Qing's highest achievement in his fetishism of women, language, and power. Her rigid, merciless rule gradually drives away Ximen's other concubines: one returns to her old vocation, prostitution; one runs away with a servant; one manages to remarry. In the end, the entire estate falls into Yue Niang's hands alone. Nothing is left under the name of Ximen Qing, nothing of his once-powerful kingdom of masculinity filled with tiny-footed beauties, money, art, music.

With Weiyang Sheng, the protagonist from *The Carnal Prayer Mat,* his decision to have an animal implant—the self-mutilation of the genitals— comes from his anxiety and humiliation over his penis size, and from his desire to expand his body in order to gain unlimited access to women, whose bodies will help him gain direct access to language and its phallic power. The beginning of the book already hints at the paradox that the "castrating" of the female body (feet) allows for the male expansion of language, sex, and power, and such an expansion eventually falls into the male fear of castration. The novel opens with Weiyang Sheng's visit to an enlightened monk on a deserted mountain. The two immediately get into a heated discussion on what is the quickest way to reach enlightenment. The monk believes in cleansing the body of all earthly desires, including the final purification of language—silence. Weiyang Sheng insists that one has to first read all the books and possess the most beautiful women on earth. These two—a talented man and beauty *(caizi jiaren)*—are interlocked and indispensable to each other. Without the beauty, a talented man loses his object; a beauty without a talented man is likewise incomplete. What underlies Weiyang's argument is that the possession of knowledge (fetishism of language) is achieved only through the fetishized female body, and fetishized language guarantees a man his manhood, sex, money, and power, just as the Chinese saying goes: there is a golden house and beautiful women in books.

When Weiyang Sheng realizes, to his horror and humiliation, that his body size (penis) is too small to allow him to reach his goal, he is willing to go through anything to repair that lack, even if it means having an animal implant, a genital mutilation that may leave him sterilized. But this physical expansion is not his ultimate goal. The enlarged penis is only a prop to help him get women. It is through women that he reaches the highest level of expansion—the expansion of language. Claiming the title of the most talented man on earth has meaning only when he has many women's bodies as his foundation. The paradox is, however, that while he possesses and fetishizes women, he himself is being possessed and fetishized. And once he loses these women, his wife, concubines, and lovers, all the talents and knowledge he has accumulated are reduced to nothing. No longer eloquent or arrogant, he has no choice but to return to the monk, begging to be admitted as a Buddhist monk. He is joined by his thief friend Sai Kunlun and his rival Honest Quan, both symbols of masculinity and virility. Together in the temple, under the guidance of their master monk, Lone Peak, they learn how to renounce all worldly and physical desires through silence—a linguistic castration. Even that is not enough for the author, Li Yu, who has his character cut off his own sex organ at the end of the book as a final measure to denounce the body.

Tong Ren'an plays both a castrating and castrated role in *The Three-Inch Golden Lotus*. As the father of four sons, he is the only man who has access to the women (his four daughters-in-law and servants) in the household, the only man healthy, normal, and capable of running the antique shop. His first son, mentally retarded, dies of hunger and fear after his wife stands up for herself for the first time, a potential castrating threat. His second son works for Tong Ren'an in the shop, but no matter how hard he tries, he is constantly insulted and put down by his father and is cast out of his own bedroom when his wife wins the foot contest. His father orders him to move his bed to the shop's storeroom. His wife curses him away whenever he sneaks back home because she has to make herself available to her father-in-law's frequent visits. He finally collaborates in robbing his own father's shop with the servant Living Sufferer, runs away with all the cash and remaining treasure in the shop when their scheme is discovered, and is murdered a few years later. The third son is exiled to a faraway place to run his own business, and when he plans to return home, he wounds his foot and becomes immobile while his wife leaves him behind to join her father-in-law's household. The fourth son dies of a heart defect he has had from birth, leaving behind him a young wife and a daughter for his father's enjoyment. None of Tong's four sons leaves a male heir. Tong Ren'an is the only phallic figure in a house full of women with perfect bound feet, like an emperor with a whole troop of beautiful women hidden deep in his palace. Also like Ximen Qing, who becomes a plaything in his favorite concubine's bed when he is sick, Tong is at the mercy of his fetishized woman, the foot champion Fragrant Lotus, once he is paralyzed by a stroke. When he dies, his entire property, his prized women, come under the strict rule of Fragrant Lotus.

What's in a Book? Words and Woman's Body in Pu Songling's "The Bookworm"

"There is a golden house as well as beautiful women in books." This old saying summarizes how the system of Chinese civil service examinations works and how it has affected every Chinese man who aspires to gain access to wealth, rank, fame, and women through the system. Theoretically, every man who has mastered the Chinese classics and writing the eight-legged essay *(bagu wen),* an extremely rigid and formalized prose, has the potential to pass different levels of examinations—county, provincial, and metropolitan—and to be appointed a position in the government. Today's peasant boy could be tomorrow's prime minister. This highly hierarchical society was also highly flexible, at least in theory. In reality, however, only a very small percentage of the candidates ever passed the exams. The extremely competitive examinations, and the mountainous amount of words and texts a student had to memorize, required vigorous study that dominated men's lives from childhood. According to Miyazaki Ichisada's estimation in *China's Examination Hell,* boys had to memorize passages totaling more than 400,000 characters in classical Chinese texts, which amounted to two hundred characters a day for six years, just to prepare for the first level of competition (cited in Ropp n.d.). Words, like the fetishized female body, led men to the world of power and fame. They also led to the destruction of their spontaneity, creativity, even the sanity of many Chinese men. Lin Yutang sarcastically lists *bagu wen* (the eight-legged essay) and bound feet as two of the three national treasures of the Qing dynasty. Yet at the same time, he can't help admiring the euphemism for bound feet—*fragrant lotus*—praising it as a fine transcendence from *golden lotus*: "The use of 'fragrance' is very meaningful; it indicates that rich Chinese families, especially their studies, are filled with the sweet smell of female flesh, that many masterpieces were written in such erotic studies" (Lin Yutang 1995, 156). The woman's body and male writing are integral and inseparable.

Castration and erection, terror and excitement, fear and desire are intertwined in much of men's writing throughout late imperial China. Qing writer Pu Songling's (1640–1715) story "The Bookworm" reveals an intense male anxiety over castration, and the fierce power struggle between the fetishizer and the fetishized. As a failed candidate himself, Pu created hundreds of the most erotic female ghosts and foxes in his masterpiece *Liaozhai's Records of the Strange (Liao zhai zhi yi)*.[4] "The Bookworm" satirizes a scholar, with much affection, who knows nothing about the world except for reading, believing that everything, including food, money, and a beautiful wife, would come out of books. The male protagonist, Lang Yuzhu, has nothing in his house except for thousands of books collected and passed down by his ancestors. The only thing he knows how to do is to read those books aloud, believing that everything he needs and desires will come out of the words.

One day, he finds a female figure cut out of woven cloth between the pages of the famous *Han History*. On the back is written "the weaving girl," a mythological fairy who weaves clouds for the goddess.[5] To his surprise, it stands up and turns into a beautiful woman. She calls herself Yan Ruyu—beautiful as jade—a name from the saying "there are women as beautiful as jade in books" *(shu zhong zi you yan ru yu)*. They live together like husband and wife. The first things she tries to teach him are how to give up reading and how to gamble and play chess and musical instruments. She succeeds in pulling him away from books only by disappearing into the words several times. One day, Lang asks his wife why she hasn't produced a child like all other women. Laughing, she tells him that it's because he knows nothing about sex. So she starts to show him the art of the bedchamber.

Soon a boy is born. By then, Lang no longer reads books but drinks, gambles, sings, dances, and socializes with other scholars all day long. His wife tells him he is now ready to take the exams for officialdom, but she warns him that his books will bring him a terrible disaster unless he burns them or lets her go back where she came from. Lang refuses to do so, telling her that those books are his life as well as her parents. How could she have the heart to destroy both? Soon, the official in Lang's county hears about the beauty of Lang's wife and demands to see her. She disappears into the books. The official puts the husband in jail and interrogates him with the cruelest torments to make him tell where she is. Finally, Lang's maid reveals that Yan Ruyu has come from the books and is probably hiding among them. Facing the huge collection of Lang's books, the official realizes that he will never be able to read through each page to find the woman. He orders all the books to be burned.

In this short, fable-like story, words and texts, fetishized whole-heartedly by Lang and his ancestors, have obvious castrating power. They render him totally ignorant and powerless as a social and sexual being, a virgin in every sense. The woman, who is literally created by words and from worshiping words (Lang reads aloud the books passed down from his ancestors without necessarily comprehending their meaning), has the ambiguity of phallic power. On the one hand, she transforms Lang from an ignorant bookworm into a sophisticated social being, teaching him how to prepare for the examinations and the art of sexual performance. In other words, she initiates him into manhood and the realm of the Phallus with her body. On the other hand, the process of becoming masculine also makes him feminized. As soon as she stands up from the book, that is, from the phallusized to the phallic, she not only lures the man away from his reading into the feminine realm of art (music, dance, chess, and sex) but also wants him to burn the books that are his life—a complete castration. Since she was born out of the books, burning them means cutting her off from her linguistic origin, and her fetishistic creator. Once this is done, she will have no possible retreat, no past to go back to, but must remain outside books as a "phallic woman" forever. Once again, the relationship is reversed. The creator is controlled by his own creation, Yan Ruyu, the woman who comes out of words, is literally made of words, who now threatens to destroy her master.

Even though Yan Ruyu is the direct cause of the book burning, the actual castration is done by the real phallic symbol—the county's official. His action resonates with the deeds of the first feudal emperor in Chinese history, Qin Shi Huang (259–210 B.C.), who is remembered for the Great Wall he built as well as *fen shu keng ru,* burning books and burying scholars alive. Since then, the fear of being castrated (to have one's books burned and, worse, to be buried alive) and the anxiety and desire to face the phallus (the emperor), to become part of his phallic power, have seeped deeply into the Chinese male's conscious and unconscious. As an example, at the end of Pu Songling's story, Lang Yuzhu is released from prison, passes the official exam, and becomes the boss of his enemy who has persecuted him. Lang has his final revenge: he fires the official from his position and takes the man's favorite concubine for his own pleasure. Once again, woman's body is used as a trope for the ultimate power struggle and transaction between men, between a winner and a loser as well as the sacrifice for men's success (Yan Ruyu's disappearance is her symbolic death). Thus Lang Yuzhu, having gone through a series of painful initiations and punishments, finally enters the world of phallic power and becomes part of the castrating machinery.

Inscribing on the Agonized Body: Shi Zhenlin and Shuangqing, the Story of Caizi jiaren

In Pu Songling's story, Lang Yuzhu created Yan Ruyu (the Weaving Maiden) through reading books of history and classics, and she then reeducated him into a man with her charm, wisdom, and sexuality. Her body, and the disappearance (a symbolic consumption) of her body, paved the path for Lang's entrance into manhood—sexually, socially, and politically. If Pu created the story as a fantasy, then Shi Zhenlin's story of Shuangqing hangs between dream and reality, fantasy and history, ambiguities and graphic details. Shi Zhenlin (1693 to about 1779) recorded the life and works of Shuangqing in his personal travelogue and diary, *Random Notes of West-Green (Xiqing sanji),* during his visits in their native Jiangsu from 1733–35. Shi Zhenlin's presentations of this beautiful, talented peasant woman poet, as noted by Paul Ropp (n.d.), is full of ambiguity and contradictions that made some modern and contemporary scholars believe that Shuangqing might have been Shi Zhenlin's sheer creation.[6] But it is exactly because of Shuangqing's unique voice and style that Grace Fong and other contemporary scholars argue that there was a real rural woman with poetic talent behind Shi Zhenlin's writing. (Shuangqing's lyric songs will be discussed in the next chapter.) It is probable that Shi Zhenlin "edited" her work and her life story in order to aestheticize and subjugate her image to his vision of ideal femininity and to the tone of his male voice (Fong 1997, 466). Regardless of the controversies, what makes the case most interesting here is the way a woman's body is fragmented, eroticized, and aestheticized through pain and writing (be it real or imagined), and the way this fetishized body is consumed visually and linguistically by Shi Zhenlin and his elite friends during the two years when he was preparing for his provincial and metropolitan examinations. The consumption of Shuangqing's agonized body and writing shares striking similarities with the consumption of footbound women.

Shuangqing embodies all the qualities of an ideal of femininity—*jiaren* (beautiful woman): beauty, virtue, and talent. What makes her so outstanding, however, is the intense pain that she bears with utter grace and patience. It is true that ill fortune and suffering of various degrees are essential components of *jiaren* represented in literature and history. Yet no one can compete with Shuangqing in terms of the intensity, frequency, and cruelty of the pain she has to endure. Shi Zhenlin records his friend Ningxi's reaction after reading Shuangqing's song lyrics throughout the night:

> He [Ningxi] pulled open my bed curtain and yelled: "For this kind of young woman to exist in the world is truly a miracle of Heaven and earth! In talent and in beauty Shuangqing is incomparable, and in poverty and sickness she is also incomparable. On top of that she has an evil husband and a cruel mother-in-law who fiercely yell at her and compel her to work and suffer all day long. . . . Now all the other ill-fated beauties in the world cannot match Shuangqing in talent, beauty, poverty and sickness." (Quoted and translated in Ropp n.d., 11:1)

Not only is she afflicted with chronic malaria; she must also live with constant abuse from her husband and mother-in-law. The worst pain, however, is her ill fate. She is endowed with the most remarkable beauty and talent in poetry but is doomed to be born in a poor family, and worse, to be married to an illiterate brute. Unlike a *jiaren* of an elite family, who has leisure, security, and support to cultivate her talent, Shuangqing has to toil in the house and fields from morning until night despite her illness, is too poor to buy ink or paper for her writing (thus has to write her poems on leaves with pollen), and is totally unappreciated and alienated in her environment. However, she rises above all of these ill fortunes, a true lotus blossom rising out of the mud. The pains she suffers and bears glorify her virtue, beauty, and talent, to such a degree that she is worshiped as a "banished immortal," leaving her admirers "filled with admiration, pity and awe" (Ropp n.d., 4:22).

Random Notes is written in fragments and anecdotes, a collection of Shi's observations, records, and meditations over what he witnesses and hears in his wandering. Shuangqing's story and poetry, embedded in unrelated anecdotes, seem even more fragmented, enigmatic, and problematic. For example, though she has been praised for remaining absolutely loyal to her abusive husband, her virtue is often challenged by Shi Zhenlin's orthodox Confucian moralists, who accuse Shuangqing of being unvirtuous for exchanging poems with Shi and his friends. Shi has to employ his friends' voices for her defense or have Shuangqing defend herself (see Ropp n.d., chap. 10). Even her lyric songs, presented in the context of Shi's writing, appear quite flirtatious from time to time. But one thing is consistent throughout his recording of Shuangqing: his graphic description of her pain, especially the physical abuses from her husband and mother-in-law, her backbreaking labor and hardship, and the malaria that burns away her already frail, battered body. The following anecdote is a good example:

> One day Shuangqing was pounding rice with the mortar and pestle. Out of breath, she stood still for a moment, holding onto the pestle. Her husband saw her standing there and suspected she was just loafing. He gave her a hard shove and as she fell down beside the mortar, the pestle fell on top of her midsection with a loud crack. She bore this pain in silence and just got up and resumed pounding the grain. Her husband glared at her, and she smiled apologetically and said, "I'll soon be finished with this pounding."
>
> She was then heating their gruel for lunch when she suffered a malarial attack. The fire flared and the gruel started to boil over. Shuangqing panicked and hurried to pour cold water into the boiling gruel. Her mother-in-law grabbed her by an earring and tore it off, yelling, "Get out!" Her earlobe was torn and blood ran down on her shoulder. She tried to cover her ear and started to cry. Her mother-in-law waved the ladle at her and yelled, "How dare you cry!" She just wiped the blood up in silence, but because she had let the gruel boil over, her husband forbid her from joining in the noon meal. Shuangqing just smiled and kept on grinding grain with the mortar. The neighbor lady asked if she was hungry. When Shuangqing answered, "No," the woman sneeringly laughed and said, "So, the toad has some fire in her belly after all! Perhaps that has filled you up!" (In Ropp n.d., 6:1)[7]

This episode is followed by Shuangqing's request to be buried with Shi Zhenlin's *Random Notes* when she dies, and her exchanging a series of nine poems, written with rouge on a head kerchief, with one of her admirers (also her landlord), who stained the poems with his tears. Many of Shuangqing's works are introduced in such a dramatic, painful setting, apparently intended to arouse readers' (within and outside the text) intense feelings and reactions, be it pity, empathy, admiration, awe, or Eros. Shi seems to have achieved his goal. In even more graphic details, he describes how his elite friends become crazed when they hear Shuangqing's tragic stories, read her poems, or see her portrait. Some cry and shout like lunatics (like the lotus lovers in *The Three-Inch Golden Lotus* who lose self-control when they see Fragrant Lotus's feet). Some lose appetite and sleep, burned by the desire to see her or exchange poems with her. And others loiter around the places where Shuangqing lives and works just to have a glimpse of her (Ropp n.d., chap. 11). The obsession of these admirers with Shuangqing is comparable probably only to that of the lotus lovers for bound feet. Although Shi Zhenlin never mentioned whether Shuangqing had bound feet or not, her tortured body as well as her writing apparently served as a much more refined substitute for their erotic gaze and consumption.

Why did Shi Zhenlin take such pains to portrait Shuangqing's suffering and introduce her poetry in such an agonized and agonizing context? True, her poetic talent is the "driving force behind the literati's obsessive interest in her" (Fong 1997, 275). True, as Grace Fong suggests, "as her poetry becomes a symbolic extension of her own body and own person, desire is displaced onto it, making it the object of male longing" (Fong 1997, 275). What makes the connection between the body and writing, however, is the pain she suffers, and her heroic endurance of that pain. In other words, pain cleanses, procures, "cooks" her earthly body into something utterly beautiful, spiritual, and immortal, transforming the flesh into writing—poetry. Such a procured or "cooked" body (physical as well as linguistic) eliminates all the boundaries of class, sex, and gender, as Shi claims repeatedly through his friends' as well as Shuangqing's mouths. Without her suffering or her stoic endurance, her beauty or talent would not be worth a thing. Such a belief has already been made clear before Shi and his friends meet Shuangqing. The following discussion in *Random Notes* on the virtue of *jiaren* among Shi Zhenlin, Zhao Fengqi, and Duan Yuhan is recorded right before Shi encounters Shuangqing:

> Heaven has endowed the ideal woman *[jiaren]* with a spiritual heart and beautiful form. She should cherish and protect herself well. If she, because of a moment's pleasure, forever becomes stained, what endless remorse would there be! It would be better to endure and endure in order to keep oneself pure and whole. . . . Qingmou [Tang Xianzu] would cry bitterly for not having met an ideal woman, I [Zhao Fengqi] on the other hand would cry bitterly for an ideal woman who has lost her purity. (In Fong 1997, 273; her translation)

Duan Yuhan, who later turns out to be one of the crazed admirers of Shuangqing, has an even harsher opinion on this issue: "A fallen *jiaren* should first cry for her lost virtue; if she doesn't cry for herself, why [should we] waste our tears on her?" (my translation).

Like the pain of footbinding that "cooks" a woman's body from a raw, savage thing into cultural artifice, Shuangqing's "incomparable" pain exalts her to a *jiaren* as a cultural icon. While the deformed bound feet become the source and inspiration for writing, Shuangqing's battered body and her heart-wrenching poetry (as an extended body) stir up men's passion and imagination. According to Shi's description, whoever encounters her poetry and story immediately falls into the impulse to write song lyrics or prose to match Shuangqing's work. Her pain becomes their fountain of creativity. It explains partly why Shi and his friends flock around Shuangqing as sympathetic admirers, obsessed voyeurists, and crazed worshipers, but none makes an effort to help her. The only person who suggests any financial help for Shuangqing is Bi Keshan, who wants to raise funds to build her scenic memorials such as the "Delivering Lunch Pavilion" and to buy some land so that she can plant melons and dig a pond for washing clothes (*Random Notes* 4:40). These activities and sites have appeared in Shuangqing's famous song lyrics and Shi Zhenlin's poetic descriptions. They are also the spots haunted by her crazed admirers for inspiration. So Bi's proposed memorial really has nothing to do with relieving Shuangqing of her poverty and pain; it has to do with celebrating her writing and suffering as a permanent source for the male imagination.

For Shi Zhenlin, her pain is "necessary" for a more important reason: it ensures his own path to the realm of truth, imagination, even immortality. In describing (inscribing) Shuangqing's suffering, her poetry, and the circle of her admirers, Shi "was also collecting advertisements for himself and his memoir. . . . Many are so profoundly moved by Shuangqing's story and her poetry that they nearly lose their bearings. Lovers of literary talent above all else, they admire Shi Zhenlin as much as or more than Shuangqing" (Ropp n.d., 11:24). Bi Keshan traveled a thousand *li* to obtain a copy of Shi's *Random Notes* and carried it with him wherever he went. He claimed that Shi's story of the talented scholar and beautiful maidens was so well written that it was even more valuable than the Buddhist sutras (*Random Notes* 4:42). Equally high compliments for the power of Shi's writing are carefully recorded throughout *Random Notes*.

Although Shi Zhenlin appears to have no interest in seeking rank and fame through the examination system and is "more attuned to the romanticism, idealism, and religious ferment associated with the late Ming period rather than the Confucian orthodoxy" of the eighteenth century (Ropp n.d., 4:19), he does show great ambitions in writing, the kind of writing that leads him to a world of dreams, emotions, imaginations, and creation other than the "real world" of politics and money. For a marginalized intellectual like Shi Zhenlin, who seems to have no powerful political connection or wealth but his own refined taste for aesthetics, his ability in writing, and his sensitivity, the world he created in *Random Notes* is his alternative to escaping the anxiety of a highly competitive, success-craving age. Shuangqing, her tormented body and writing, is his best vehicle to enter that world: "In one's life, bitter tears should be shed for two things only: one for his writing unable to be appreciated, the other for the fallen [*caizi*—genius] unable to meet a *jiaren*" (*Random Notes* 2:28; my translation).

This statement, as Kang Zhengguo notes, can be used as a guideline for reading the *Random Notes* (1994, 90). The ill fortune of *jiaren* mirrors the fate of *wenren* (literati) or *caizi* (genius), especially those whose talents are unrecognized all their lives, who fail to pass the civil service examinations although they have accumulated a vast amount of knowledge in classics and can write exquisite poetry and prose. Thus, when Shi Zhenlin and his literati friends cry bitterly for Shuangqing's pain, they are actually crying for their own suffering. The more tragic Shuangqing's story becomes, the better it will convey the feeling and sentiment of a *caizi*. In that sense, Shuangqing's talent is their talent, her beauty their beauty, her virtue their virtue, and her pain their pain. Here, the discourse of the female body is used to mirror that of the male body. This mirroring is implied when Shi Zhenlin describes how Shuangqing, when mocked by her neighbor for her suffering, sighs and makes a vow to herself: "Heavens! I hope that this life of Shuangqing's can atone for all the world's most beautiful young maidens, and that after I absorb all the endless sufferings and tribulations of this world in their stead, young beauties will never again have to bear what I Shuangqing have had to bear" (in Ropp, n.d., 6:1).

How Shi Zhenlin had access to this soliloquy made by a peasant woman in her kitchen is an interesting matter itself. But Shuangqing's vow immediately reminds one of Du Fu's famous "Song of My Thatched Hut Damaged by Autumn Wind." After describing a series of disasters that he and his family experienced—exile, a damaged house, leaking roof, cold and torn blanket, hunger, civil war—the Tang poet made a vow that had been imitated by poets ever since: "May there be ten thousands of solid, spacious houses to shelter all the poor intellectuals on earth! When I see the happiness on their faces, I'd be content even if I alone died of coldness in my broken hut." While Du Fu was willing to suffer for the happiness of all the poor intellectuals, Shuangqing was willing to suffer for the happiness of all the young beauties. The parallel is subtle but clear: by comparing the pain and lofty ideal of a peasant woman poet to that of the greatest male poet in Chinese history, Shi Zhenlin turned the discourse of *jiaren* into that of *caizi*.

For Shi Zhenlin, Shuangqing's poetic talent also becomes the vehicle for his own ambition in making a literary name for himself: "By his self-proclaimed discovery of the brilliant and beautiful peasant woman poet, he demonstrated his profound understanding of literary talent, his deep sensitivity to the suffering of the down-trodden, his superior ability to recognize great beauty in surprising surroundings, and his keen aesthetic sensibilities" (Ropp n.d., 4:21). Shi Zhenlin had been seeking such a vehicle by communicating with female immortals through *fuji* (planchette writing). But once he discovered Shuangqing in the middle of the second chapter of *Random Notes,* she became the major focus of his writing nearly until the end.[8] When he visited the place where she lived, he recorded her daily life, her hardship and illness, the abuse from her husband and mother-in-law, her poems as well as song lyrics, and the behavior of her enamored admirers. When he was away, he showed her portraits and writing (that is conveyed through his own writing) to his elite friends. The female immortals that Shi Zhenlin communicated with were fine tools to help him connect with the world of dream and imagination, but Shuangqing, the banished immortal whose flesh and blood made her available to men, apparently served as a much more successful vehicle. Female immortals may be beautiful and talented, but they don't suffer, nor do they need to be pitied or rescued. Shuangqing, though embodying all the qualities of a female immortal, is poor, sick, and extremely vulnerable. Such an ill-fortuned beauty *(jiaren)* can and must be pitied and treasured (*lian* and *xi*) by her male equivalent—genius *(caizi)*. Shi Zhenlin gained a reputation not only for discovering Shuangqing and spreading her name, but also for his own writing. After all, it is through his pen that Shuangqing is discovered, cultivated, and preserved. Without his fine taste and eloquent writing, Shuangqing would have perished without a trace. In that sense, Shi Zhenlin created Shuangqing with his words, through his fragmented textualization. As his creation, Shuangqing's own text (her stories and poetry) always remains as a symbolic body, forever tormented, beautiful, and virtuous, forever available to be textualized and eroticized. Such a relationship is made clear in the long letter Shi Zhenlin had Shuangqing write to her passion-crazed admirer Yuhan on a *Jixiang* leaf (a kind of thin-leafed grass) with powder. After defending her unconventional behavior of exchanging poems with men and repairing Yuhan's winter clothes, she told Yuhan, "I must preserve my body like a fine jade; you must treasure your writing like rare gold" (*Random Notes,* quoted and translated in Ropp n.d., 10:17). Shuangqing is doing more than just drawing a parallel *(shou shen ru yu, xi mo ru jin)* between the female body and male writing: she is actually equating the two—the body *is* the writing.

Through Shuangqing's body, Shi Zhenlin entered a world of dreams and imagination. Ironically, it also seemed to have opened his path to the world of success, the world Shi Zhenlin feigned to have no interest in. In 1735, after his last record of Shuangqing's story, he took the provincial exam and became a *juren* (a successful candidate in the imperial exams at the provincial level during the Ming and Qing dynasties). In 1737, he went to the capital to participate in the metropolitan exam and became a *jinshi* (a successful candidate in the highest imperial level). During Shi's two years of wandering in and out of his native Jintan, Jiangsu between 1733 and 1735, and his preparation for the coming civil service examinations, Shi Zhenlin wrote for and through Shuangqing's body. After his great successes, however, she is never mentioned again in *Random Notes.*[9]

The fetishized, however, is not forgotten so easily. In the case of Shi Zhenlin and Shuangqing, the relationship between the fetishizer and fetishized is once again reversed, as is true for each case I analyzed earlier. Over the years, Shuangqing's poetry has been anthologized with or without mentioning her origin (the person who discovered and recorded her). As she gradually got away from the textualization of Shi's narrative, she even acquired a surname, *he,* which she never had in the *Random Notes,* a new birthplace, and she became a "gentrified" peasant woman poet, the woman *ci* poet of the Qing period. Shi Zhenlin recorded Shuangqing's story and poetry in order to preserve and spread her name. In the end, it is mostly through Shuangqing's song lyrics that Shi's name is mentioned and remembered.

From the Golden Lotus to a Thousand Cuts

The female body, fetishized through physical and linguistic violence either as the golden lotus or poetry, became a theatrical stage for political power struggles and ideological, ethical discourses.[10] The spread of footbinding and the flourishing publication of women's poetry were echoed by the dramatic rise of exemplary women, the incidence and commemoration of widow chastity and suicide in the Ming and Qing periods. These seemingly controversial phenomena were the products of the same discourse on the body. As beauty was achieved through the violent deformity of feet, and as a *jiaren* was established through her poetic talent as well as her suffering, virtue in the Confucian tales of exemplary women was enacted through physical ordeals and gruesome self-mutilations. As Katherine Carlitz points out, "women's bodies were always available for use—ideological, physical—by men" (1994, 124). The body does not belong to oneself but to the family, the clan, and ultimately the monarchy. In her insightful discussion on Ming Confucian tales of exemplary women that flooded the publishing market, Carlitz suggests that the dedicated female body becomes in fact an arena to display loyalty at any cost:

> The characteristics of the female body gave it unique possibilities as a theater for the drama of virtue. Women's breasts, providing essential nourishment, could be offered in filial service. Penetrable, woman's body was the site where the drama of resistance to invasion could be acted out. Weaker, it could shame men unwilling to rise to the same heights of virtue. Procreative, it was a resource to be sold or controlled. Attractive, it offered opportunities to men to prove their moral worth by exercising self-restraint. (110)

As neo-Confucianism rose in response to national crises (the foreign invasions and the nationwide indulgence in expenditure and sex), the female body, fetishized through footbinding and acts of chastity (often resulting in facial and bodily self-mutilations), was pushed to the front to combat social and cultural decadence, to appease male anguish over their identity crises in race, gender, and hierarchy, and to meet their need to fetishize language for phallic power. Not only were women's bodies both objects and subjects for commercial, moral, political, and sexual consumption, but they were also consumed in many male authors' writing as a linguistic fetish—or, more bluntly, as a linguistic extension of the male sex organ.

The discourse of the female body, as shown in the above cases, often comes out in male writing as an equally extensive discourse of the male body on scrutiny and self-scrutiny, self-mutilation, even self-castration. The violence that is inflicted and written on the female body, be it physical or linguistic, is also inscribed on the male. As women entered history and literature through physical ordeals (their chastity as the symbol of moral uprightness and political integrity, their tiny-footed beauty as the muse for art and poetry, and their poetic talent as a vehicle for the male voice), Chinese men hoped to become part of the phallic power through the female body. However, as the fetishized female body took on the dual nature of fetish and the ambivalence of language—to heal and poison, to empower and destroy—the fetish agents were soon overwhelmed by the power of the fetish and its vengeance. They were often forced to turn to themselves, like the protagonists in *The Golden Lotus* and *The Carnal Prayer Mat,* inflicting mutilation, even castration, on their own bodies.

The Ming dynasty is a good example of the female body discourse as a manifestation of the male body discourse. No other period in Chinese history focuses more on the body than this one. While footbinding and the cult of exemplary women spread rapidly, and while women's poetry was widely anthologized, and the published writings on exemplary women, women of chastity, erotic prints, and sex manuals flourished, the dynasty was also marked by the most restrictive laws and the most cruel punishments inflicted on its subjects—commoners as well as officials. The Ming is known for the rapid growth of the number of castrated and self-castrated males and the eunuch system. Although many were castrated as prisoners of war and political criminals, most of the castrati were the result of poverty and personal trauma.[11] And some were prompted by their ambition for power, money, and fame by taking this "short cut." Despite all the punishments and the chance of failure, it was still easier to get a job from the emperor as a castrati than by devoting one's whole life to studying Confucian classics and writing eight-legged essays to compete in the civil service examinations.[12] At the risk of being executed or exiled, parents castrated their sons or young men performed the self-castration with the hope that they might one day serve in the palace and even become part of the royal power network.[13]

At the beginning of the Ming, there were only about a hundred castrated men. But this number rose to ten thousand in the 1520s, and near the end of the dynasty, it reached one hundred thousand (Tsai 1996, 26). As the excessive mob of castrati swarmed the capital looking for and even demanding opportunities to serve in the palace, they became a serious social and financial problem. Many of them were never hired as eunuchs and had to live miserable and poverty-stricken lives. For those who were fortunate enough to be chosen for the royal service, they were only treated as slaves and servants. Only very few rose to power. The most famous were perhaps Grand Eunuch Admiral Zheng He (about 1371–1435) and Grand Eunuch Nguyen An. A genius navigator and explorer, Zheng He led seven maritime expeditions in the world's largest fleet between 1405 and 1433 and visited some thirty states in Southeast Asia and along the Indian Ocean coast, reaching as far as Africa (Tsai 1996, 153–63). Nguyen An was brought to China as a tribute from Annam (Vietnam) near the end of the fourteenth century. A talented artist, ingenious architect, and expert civil engineer, he designed and constructed the magnificent Forbidden City in Beijing for Emperor Yongle (reign, 1403–24) around 1420 (1996, 202–3). The most infamous eunuchs in Ming history were Wang Zhen, Wang Zhi, Liu Jin, and Wei Zhongxian. They controlled important military, political, and financial positions in the court, their influence on the emperors often stronger than that of ministers. They also accumulated material, gold, and property at an astonishing speed. Since the rule of Zhu Yuanzhang (Ming Taizu, 1328–98), only eunuchs were appointed to be in charge of the secret police agency such as *Dongchang* and

Xichang (Eastern and Western Depot). These eunuchs reported directly to the emperor on the actions and words of government officials and ministers. They became symbols of the imperial power. Once they gained power in the court, they inflicted the most violent physical torture and terror on the bodies of officials, intellectuals, and the masses.

The power concentrated in the Ming eunuchs' mutilated/castrated bodies "reflects the Ming regime's dualistic characteristics—a system evidently distinguishing the eunuchs from the civil and military bureaucracies and yet at the same time allowing the two different elements to check on and balance one another" (Tsai 1996, 58). It is also the dialectical opposite of the fascination with bound feet or mutilated faces of exemplary women. The violence these eunuchs exacted on themselves and later their victims and the violence inflicted or self-inflicted on the female body suggest that the two phenomena derive from the same discourse: the discourse of the body that undergoes the violence of fetishism/mutilation, the violence that eventually haunts its fetish agent with vengeance. Ironically as well as symbolically (but by no means coincidentally), one of the favorite torture machines invented by the eunuch Wei Zhongxian (1568–1627) was called the "red embroidered shoes." These iron shoes were heated until they turned red. The torturer then forced them onto the victim's feet. Whoever wore the shoes would be severely crippled for the rest of their lives, just as women who bound their feet became crippled (Wang Yongkuan 1991, 58).

For Chinese men since the Tang, the path to power and government positions was through the civil service examinations; that is, through the accumulation of words and knowledge of the classics and history. Often, by the time he passed the highest exam and became a *jinshi* (if he was lucky enough), he was in his forties, and his best years were already consumed by the preparation. The reward of a successful fetishism of language and knowledge was the access to women, money, and power. Paradoxically, the linguistic fetish was often achieved through the fetishism of the female body. Some took this paradox at face value and believed that women were the obstacles that prevented them from passing the official exams or writing books. In reality and in many Ming and Qing stories, men usually moved away from women into isolated study to prepare for the exams. And of course, they often ended up being seduced by neighbor girls, prostitutes, passers-by, fox spirits, or ghosts in the masquerade of irresistible young women.

Some intellectuals actually inflicted castration on themselves to show their determination to do away with women so that they could concentrate on their studies and writing. During the Jiajing reign period (1522–66), Ke

Weixiong castrated himself so that he would not be distracted by his sexual desire while writing his *New Edition of Song History*. He claimed he was just following the example of the Han historian Sima Qian (about 135–? B.C.), who wrote *Tai shi gong shu* (also called *Shiji*), the first book of Chinese history presented in a series of biographies. Sima Qian completed the book after he was castrated by the emperor's order for defending a captured general. During the Wanli reign (1573–1620), there was a story of a teenage student who castrated himself because he could not repress his sexual interest in women, which, he believed, had seriously damaged his concentration on his studies. Like the bookworm Lang Yuzhu from Pu Songling's story, they all took the phallic power of words and their fear/ desire for women to the extreme. Unable to use the female body as a fetishistic substitute to act out or release their fear, anxiety, frustration, and desire, they felt they had no choice but to turn to their own bodies. Their self-castration was an effort to inscribe/write on the male body—to take a "short cut," like the eunuchs, to power. Instead of entering writing and history through the fetishized female body, they tried to do so through their own mutilated bodies.

The most dramatic example of writing/inscribing on the male body, however, is perhaps manifested through China's most cruel and highest punishment from the monarchy—*ling chi,* the thousand cuts. The term *ling chi* literally means a hill that slopes gradually, a metaphor for a slow, gradual death. It was first recorded in the Five Dynasties (907–60) period. According to Ming law, the only persons subjected to such a punishment were those who committed the highest crimes, *mou fan da ni*: conspiring against the state or plotting to destroy the state ancestral temple, mausoleum, or palace. Again, the Ming dynasty had the most instances of recorded *ling chi* executions. The two famous cases were Liu Jin, a eunuch who used his power to have endless numbers of innocent people and political rivals murdered, and Zheng Man, a renowned scholar unfortunately involved in political intrigues. Both were accused of *mou fan*—conspiracy (Wang Yongkuan 1991, 1–12).

In the fall of 1510, the emperor ordered that Liu Jin be executed by *ling chi* in a period of three days, during which he would be kept alive until all of his flesh was cut out. The whole scene was recorded by the execution supervisor Zhang Wenlin:

> According to the rule, the total cuts are 3,357. On every tenth cut, the executioner calls the number out loud. On the first day of the execution, Liu received 357 cuts, each the size of a thumb nail, starting from the chest. [He]

bled a little at the first few cuts, then no more blood came. It was said that when the executed person was in such an extreme state of shock, all his blood reversed into his abdomen and calves, and would spurt out only when the chest was chopped open at the very end. . . . That night, [we] brought him back to the prison in Wanping County, untied him, then fed him with two bowls of porridge. . . . The next day, he was taken back to the execution ground at the east of the city. As he had exposed a lot of palace secrets during the previous execution, [we] stuffed his mouth with walnuts. After ten more cuts, he stopped breathing. When the sun rose, we reported to the emperor and were ordered to have Liu Jin, after getting the [3,357] cuts, dismembered, but his head could be spared. Many people grabbed his flesh to offer it as sacrifice for their relatives who had been killed [by Liu]. (*"Ming Zhang Ruiyan,"* quoted in Wang Yongkuan 1991, 6–7; my translation)

Spectacular and theatrical public executions and bodily torture were set in contrast to the writing that concentrated on the accuracy of minute details, including the exact cuts on the body and the meals fed to the executed, to the point of total detachment and lack of emotion. Such style brought out more mystification, shock, and the spectacle of the punishment and vertigo of language. But the physical mutilation and display were only the first step. The fetish of the male body was completed and finalized only through words and by words, just as the female body was fetishized first through the physical binding of feet, then through the linguistic manipulation of metaphors and euphemisms, through the inventory and category of tiny feet in much of the male writing of this period. The difference is that in *ling chi* the fetish site moved from the female body to the male, from private inner chambers to a public execution ground, from silence to loudness, from surface to interior.

If the eunuch Liu Jin deserved a thousand cuts for his evil deeds, the scholar Zheng Man's punishment seemed a mere political scandal and display of the capriciousness of royal power. Zheng was a *jinshi* of 1622, known for his literary talent. He was accused by his political rivals of flogging his mother and sleeping with his sister—the two worst offenses apart from conspiracy against the state. Like the writing on Liu Jin's execution, the record of Zheng Man's death was written with exactness and detachment:

At dawn on the twenty-sixth day of the eighth lunar month in the twelfth year of the Chongzhen reign (1639), the emperor sentenced Zheng Man to the *ling chi* penalty, to be executed the same day. Early in the morning, workers built a stage at the Eastern Pailou for the execution supervisors. Before the stage, a thick cross was hoisted up. Soon the executioners arrived with hooks and knives in their baskets and started to sharpen their weapons. Around nine o'clock, Zheng Man was brought to the ground in a big basket, stripped of his hat and shoes. While waiting for the execution, he talked nonstop to his pageboy, instructing him on things that needed to be taken care of in his household after his death. By then, thousands of spectators had gathered around the execution ground, blocking all the streets and squares, covering all the roofs nearby. . . . The execution official announced the emperor's decree, his words drowned out by the noise of the crowd, except his last sentence: "According to the law, [Zheng Man] must receive 3,600 cuts." All the executioners responded to this with a roar, which thundered above the frightened crowd, sending shivers and chills through their spines. After three cannon shots, the execution began. The crowd stirred violently as everyone pushed and strained his neck to see the cutting. . . . After a long time, a rope was suspended from the post, then a bloody bundle was hoisted all the way to the top. It was lungs and liver. It indicated that all the flesh had been cut from the condemned. Soon, the internal organs were put down, and a head was lifted. Finally, the executioners lifted Zheng Man's torso, displaying his back with countless pieces of shredded flesh that hung loosely like porcupine's needles. Two officials waved red flags, galloping on horses toward the palace to announce the result of the execution to the waiting emperor. When it was over, the executioners sold Zheng Man's flesh to the crowd as medicine that cured malignant boils. (*Yu qiao hua Zheng Man ben mo,* in Wang Yongkuan 1991, 7–9; my translation)

Several details stand out from both records. One is the authors' obsession with the number of cuts, including the exact figures given by the emperors, the loud recitation of the royal decree from the executioners, and the cuts that had to be fulfilled even after the condemned had stopped breathing. In contrast to this very public precision of description is the absence of the recording of pain suffered by the condemned, which is all the more more noticeable considering that both cases were recorded by eyewitnesses.[14] The authors chose to ignore the extreme horror of this prolonged agony and death by *ling chi,* the same way as the lifelong violence and pain of footbinding were covered by the beautiful surface of the embroidered shoes and the flowery language of poetry and prose written about lotus feet. Perhaps as they witnessed the spectacles of bodily mutilation— whether it was footbinding or the thousand cuts—these writers all, to different degrees, experienced the vertigo of fetishism and writing (the thousand cuts as the most symbolic form of writing/inscribing on the body). The violence was so horrifying that it became unspeakable, therefore, unwriteable. Perhaps this was the same reason behind the lack of details on how the horror and pain affected the crowds. One can only guess from the silence between the words of the Ming executioners.

Ironically, the only visual evidence of this form of Chinese torture is found in photos taken by a French photographer, Carpeaux, who witnessed a *ling chi* scene in Beijing in 1905 (perhaps the last one, since the punishment was banned by law in 1905). Interestingly, Georges Bataille received these photos from the French psychoanalyst Dr. Broel twenty years later. The condemned man's expression in the photos—seemingly smiling seen from the profile and ecstatic from the front view—greatly puzzled as well as excited Bataille. He believed that the pain and terror of the punishment were so shocking to the body that the condemned man had reached "the point of ecstasy." Bataille himself experienced such "ecstasy" through his obsessive meditation over the photographs of this Chinese man being cut into pieces on a post. This moment of revelation so stunned his body that it enabled him to make a giant leap from the unspeakable to the elevated, that is, to make the fundamental connection between apparent opposites—extreme horror and divine ecstasy (1989, 206, 207).[15]

In the pictures that so fascinated Bataille, the victim's face did appear calm and celestial, his eyes rolled up as if receiving a message from the heavens. The intolerable agony and horror that were supposed to fall upon the condemned body seemed to have transferred to the crowd of onlookers. They were obviously terrified, their faces pinched and stunned, their mouths speechless. Yet the naked, dismembered body hoisted on the cross kept pulling them closer to the scene (figure 11). They stared, perhaps in a similar way to how spectators stared at a pair of three-inch bound feet. Perhaps their pity and anguish over the terrible violence on the body would lead them to the ecstasy that was experienced by Bataille. One can only speculate. But we are certain of this: the thousand cuts displayed the sovereign's power at its highest and grandest level. When the emperor's words roared out of the executioners' mouths in repeated unison, his power reached each individual of the huge crowd. And the body, in the prolonged process of horror, transcended from low to high, small to grand, hidden to public, base to sacred, and finally, from the most condemned to the most celebrated. This is the same passage of transcendence that Chinese women had been walking with their terribly deformed bound feet, the passage through which Chinese men hoped to gain access to the highest power.

Just as the female body was compressed into a pair of three-inch lotus shoes, mutilated into the model of female virtue and chastity, through all kinds of emotional and physical pain to be molded into the image of *jiaren, ling chi* turned the public execution ground into a gigantic stage where the male body was stripped, displayed, then cut into pieces under the intense gaze of thousands of spectators, until the entire body was carved into a living skeleton. This is the moment when the body of a man, through the most violent, most painful festishization, became connected with sovereignty. The body was gazed at with pity, terror, and awe, just like the gaze on the fetishized female body, only on a much grander scale.

Once again, like footbinding, the fetish was completed through language. The thousand cuts started with the executioners who shouted out the emperor's order in unison. After every ten cuts, the executioners would call out the numbers to the crowd. In the end, the horsemen would bring the death announcement to the emperor at the palace. Words traveled between the execution ground and the palace, connecting the condemned and the common spectators to the sovereign. The punishment thus turned the victim into a work of writing in every symbolic way. His body was dissected into thirty-six hundred pieces (in Zheng Man's case), a figure that coincides with the approximate number of characters a Chinese person needs to know in order to read and write. His fragmented flesh acquired the dual, ambivalent power of writing—to cure and to curse. After the torture, the victim's flesh was sold as the most effective medicine for incurable

Figure 11. A *ling chi* scene on April 10, 1905, in Beijing.

diseases or the most powerful sacrificial food. "Words not only name parts of the body, they mingle with them," says Jean-Jacques Lecercle (1990, 94). In the case of footbinding, female virtue and talent, and *ling chi,* words also hunted the body and consumed it alive. As the mob ate the victim's flesh, blood, heart, liver, and brain for medicine and sacrificial food, and as the lotus lovers licked, nibbled, and chewed women's bound feet, a connection was made between food and sex, eroticism and violence, death and ecstasy.

PART II

Footbinding in Women's Literary Traditions

Binding, Weaving, Chatting:
Female Bonding and Writing

So much has been written on fans and paper,
Every word is soaked in blood.
  —"Song of Female Writing," *Nu shu*

Commoners produced the basic material goods necessary for human
life, and within this sphere weaving was the female counterpart of till-
ing the soil. The elite worked with culture, *wen,* and within this sphere
embroidery was a female counterpart of writing.
  —Francesca Bray, *Technology and Gender*

ALTHOUGH FOOTBINDING was an entirely female practice, the discourse
and literature that evolved around it over time were scarce and largely produced by men. They recorded and wrote most of the documentation of
footbinding, either through accounts of missionaries or in scholarly studies
or literary reflections. This general lack of data on footbinding, and particularly women's silence on the topic, is itself an interesting phenomenon. The
gap between social practice and textual expressions may indeed constitute
the enchantment of the Ming entertainment world and serve to highlight
the gender ambiguity on which the courtesan's aura rests (Ko, 1997b, 78,
97). But the silence, especially when it came from the majority of the female footbinders, also indicates that the practice, if it indeed can be interpreted as a female bodily writing, had been living as an oral culture exclu-
sive to women, who passed it on from body to body, mouth to mouth,
handiwork to handiwork for more than a thousand years.

Thus the other half of the story, that of women's reflections on their
experience, rituals, and feelings about footbinding, must be traced through

the oral history of women's culture, and what is embedded and suggested between the lines of their writing, though it rarely referred directly to foot-binding. Since the expression of the body is mediated by social and linguistic structures, any true understanding of footbinding and what it meant to Chinese women must be sought not only in and between the lines of their texts, but also within the context of their everyday living and work environment, of their social, economic, and linguistic backgrounds. I will demonstrate how women's writing, whether by upper-class gentry or rural women, is interwoven with their handiwork (especially weaving, embroidering, and shoemaking) and their oral communications. I will also explore how such writing/handiwork/speech allows them to express their individual creativity, feelings, and desires and build supporting networks and literary communities, and most important, helps them redefine and reconstruct their fetishized bodies as a whole.

In this chapter, I examine the writing of three groups of women, and how their labors at text and textile became the integral contents of their daily life, communications, and friendship. The first group is the female gentry poets of the Jiangnan region in the sixteenth and seventeenth centuries. With their leisure and education, these women were able to express themselves by exchanging poetry and needlework. Their verses allow us a glimpse into the female inner chambers where feet and shoes played an important role in their self-definition and their female liaisons. In the poems exchanged between Tu Yaose (1576–1601) and her sister-in-law, Shen Tiansun (about 1580–1600), and between Ye Xiaoluan (1616–1632) and her mother, Shen Yixiu (about 1590–1636), we see how educated women in the late imperial times borrowed the male language of poetic imagery, devices, and diction to identify their own desires and sexuality, to view their own bodies and work (both writing and embroidering) with fascination as well as pride. Their achievements defy simple dichotomies of men against women, or victims versus perpetrators, and they defy the male fetishization, physical or linguistic, of their bodies and lives.

The second body of writing I examine is the song lyrics by Shuang-qing, a poet of the early eighteenth century who was born a poor peasant in the Jiangnan region. She received an education through the charity of her relatives. Her poems went beyond mere lament over the miseries of women's lot: her unconventional poetic diction, style, and disturbing images managed to break through the stagnancy of traditional allusions and formats for poetry and started a dialogue with herself, a dialogue between mind and body. For the first time in the tradition of Chinese women's writing, her poetry openly challenged the identity and sexuality that were imposed on the female body through fetishism. For both these upper-class women and Shuangqing, writing was a tool not only for asserting individuality and expressing emotions, but also one used for dialogues, interactions, and networking. This usage gave their writing its vitality.

In the third group of writing, I examine the *nu shu* texts—female writing—that had secretly been transmitted from women to women for several hundred years in a small rural county of Hunan Province. These Jiangyong village women invented a secret language, written on fans, cloth, or paper, with the purpose of forming liaisons between two unmarried girls, a relationship quite similar to a marriage, and to form sisterhood relations among married women that often lasted as long as they lived. In the name of making lotus shoes, weaving, and embroidering, they gathered together to chat and sing about their misfortune or happiness in the secret language. *Nu shu* is indeed a written form, but its performance style, its oral transmission from one person to another, and its purpose for interaction and sharing all link it to handiwork and speech. In fact, writing, embroidering, and talking for the Jiangyong women are inseparable parts of their literature and lifestyle. *Nu shu* is a language that is interwoven with women's handiwork—embroidery, weaving, and footbinding, their stories and bodies—a language that lives from hand to hand, mouth to mouth, and generation to generation.

Female Gentry Poets

Both Tu Yaose and Shen Tiansun were elite women of the Jiangnan region in the late sixteenth century. And the lives of both were spent enclosed in their separate women's quarters. By exchanging writing and embroidering, however, these two sisters-in-law were able to break through this isolation to form a lifelong bond. As Ann Waltner and Pi-ching Hsu note, "Letters and poems are physical objects which break out of enclosure, connecting women with one another and forming imaginative connections with women in China's past" (1997, 29).[1] For Tu and Shen (as well as for many other writing women, as discussed later), products of embroidering and weaving serve a similar function as that of their poems.

In one of the poems Shen wrote to Tu, she depicted a vivid picture of two young women working on embroidered shoes:

Presented to Xiangling [Tu Yaose], no. 2

Your willow eyelids, downcast, shield inky pools;
Floral makeup dapples your eyebrows, their shape like distant mountains
With scissors and ruler you defeat me, working at your embroidery;
Every night in front of the lamp, I borrow your shoe patterns.

(In Waltner and Hsu 1997, 37)

The first two lines seem to borrow the conventional images and diction ("eyebrows like distant mountains" and "downcast eyelids") to describe a typical *jiaren* (beautiful woman). The third and fourth lines, however, go beyond the poetic convention. With a few words, Shen presents a lively scene of the elite women's daily life—working at embroidery day and night, their constant exchange of the needlework, and their friendly but intense competition. Since the product of their embroidery was for strictly personal use—the highly eroticized and private shoes for their bound feet (which Waltner and Hsu compared to underwear)—such frequent exchange "indicates an intimate as well as erotic bond between the two."

If read by itself, the poem seems to focus on the domesticity and femininity of the women's daily life. But if one reads it together with its companion poem, "Presented to Xiangling, no. 1," then it is layered with the author's aspirations that go beyond the enclosed women's court:

Presented to Xiangling, no. 1

Your two hibiscus cheeks reflect your silken dress.
With a smile you touch your hair ornament, and the pair of phoenixes fly.
I suspect that you are performing the strategy of the green cloth screen;
I know your can solve the young lord's dilemma.

(In Waltner and Hsu 1997, 36)

Again, the first two lines seem to follow the poetic tradition by focusing on the women's appearance and costume. But the word *suspect* subtly brings out these women's ambition that can't be confined by the codes for women set in a patriarchal society. The seemingly vain beauty actually has the intelligence, ability, and strategy to surpass even men. As pointed out by Waltner and Hsu, the "green cloth screen" alludes to a story of the calligrapher Wang Xizhi (about 321–79). In an argument with his guest, his sister-in-law helped him out from behind a screen. Thus the gesture of touching her hair, which could be seen as a gesture of feminine vanity, is actually her signal to help her brother-in-law out of an awkward situation. Her beauty—appearance and ornament—is only a disguise for her intellectual power, which, though confined to the boudoir, is vital and indispensable to her husband. And by helping her husband, even if with silent language, she breaks the confinement of the female quarter and enters the male world as an equal, even better partner.

The twin poems give us the portrait of a feminine ideal: she has beauty and virtue, talent and womanly skills, all integrated together, balancing and glorifying one another. What is interesting is that the author places needlework on an equal level with that of writing and intelligence. In both poems, beauty (appearance) is used as a prelude to bring out what are hidden—talent (writing, intelligence, knowledge) and womanly skills (embroidery, shoemaking). With skillful subtlety, the author suggests to us that the feminine tradition of womanly work is as important and worthy as the masculine capacity—talent. The importance of cultivating and keeping a balance between the two is also implied.

The exchange between Tu Yaose and Shen Tiansun shows how elite women in late imperial China bonded through their writing and handiwork, and how writing (text) was interwoven with embroidering (textile) and vice versa, and how such activities helped redefine their identity. As Francesca Bray points out, weaving is the female counterpart to men's toiling of the soil (1997, 266). In late imperial China, elite families no longer practiced the ancient mode of agrarian ideals—*nan geng nu zhi* (men till, women weave). Although women still embroidered, it was not always out of economic necessity[2] but was regarded as a hallmark of domesticity, refinement, gentle nurturing, and individual creativity, especially since some of their embroidery became so highly creative and imaginative that it was exalted to the level of art.[3] At about the age when their feet were bound, young girls of elite families were taught the art of poetry and painting along with the training in fine needlework as part of the essential womanly work: "When a little girl was taught to spin and weave, she was not only acquiring the skills to produce useful goods—through them she was learning diligence, orderliness, and respect for labor, the dignity of a wife and the responsibility of subject of the state" (Bray 1997, 242). Susan Mann also comments that spinning and weaving taught both the gender-neutral virtue of filial piety and the more specifically female virtues of thrift, frugality, and diligence. These were considered essential not only for poor households but also for the proper management of elite households (1994, 30). Writing and embroidery served as a means for moral cultivation as well as a way to define their body and mind, their position in and outside the household, and their bonding with other women.

Around the seventeenth century, the traditional concept of womanhood was reinterpreted according to a new formula: talent, virtue, and beauty (see Ko 1994). The scholar hero in *The Jade Tender Pear (Yu jiao li)* gives a summary of this ideal woman: "She who has talent but no beauty cannot count as a belle *[jiaren]*. Neither can she who has beauty but no talent. Even if she has both but lacks a resonance of *qing* [passion] with me, she cannot count as *my* belle" (*Yu jiao li xiaozhuan,* quoted in Ko 1994).[4] The traditional womanly work of sewing, embroidering, spinning, and weaving now takes on a new content. A woman cannot be considered skillful unless she reads and composes poetry. Writing is thus quietly added to "womanly speech," a traditional doctrine for female virtue. In the Jiangnan region, the number of women poets mushroomed, their poetry was shared and circulated within families and women's poetry clubs, through dialogues between mothers and daughters, through correspondence among friends, and through anthologies: "The verses they exchanged, although laden with poetic conventions, provide a glimpse into the central place occupied by feet and shoes in upper-class women's definitions of self and in their interactions with relatives and friends" (Ko 1994, 169).

Ye Xiaoluan, the beautiful, talented daughter of the poet/scholar Ye Shaoyuan and the upper-class poet Shen Yixiu in seventeenth-century Jiangnan, wrote the following poem about feet at age sixteen, just a few months before her wedding:

> They say lotus blossom as she moves her feet,
> But invisible underneath her skirt.
> Her jade toes tiny and slender,
> Imprinting her fragrant name where she stops.
> Her pure chiffon skirt swirls in a dance,
> Then steadfast like the new moon.
> Her silk garment sways and flows,
> As she kicks her jade hook halfway up.
> (Consort Yang) left her stocking behind at Mawei,
> Adding to the remorse of the Tang emperor;
> At the banks of River Luo the goddess treads with elegance,
> Bringing sadness to Cao Zhi.
>
> (In Ko 1994, 168)

As Dorothy Ko points out, the poem "is infused with an unspoken delight that a sixteen-year-old girl . . . found in her own small feet" (168). This delight, with a touch of pride, permeates her other eight poems on her body parts—hair, eyebrows, eyes, lips, arms, waist, and the full body, ending with a verse on the Double Seven Festival.[5] Such a fascination with the sensu-

ousness of her own body contradicts, however, her reaction to the praise
that was showered on her beauty by her relatives. According to her mother,
Shen Yixiu, Ye Xiaoluan didn't like people to praise her appearance. She was
displeased when her uncle wrote a poem on her beauty, saying that beauty
did not distinguish a woman, and after all, she was only thirteen (Ko 1994,
166). She once rebuked her father who had said teasingly that she had a
face that could ruin empires: "Why would a woman pride herself on having a face that can bring down a kingdom? Father, do not call your daughter such" (in Ko 1994, 167). This suspicion toward beauty resonated with
men's fear of the femme fatale as well as the traditional teachings on womanly deportment: women must not cultivate their looks at the expense of
their virtue. Feminine identity should be achieved, instead of being given
as a gift, through human work and will. A pair of well-bound feet not only
makes a woman beautiful but also good and virtuous. This explains why Ye
Xiaoluan viewed such praise with great suspicion. Yet her pride and fascination in her own feet overflow each line.

Drawing from nature as opposed to the artificial for imagery to symbolize the basic physical self—water, moon, wind, and living things—Ye
Xiaoluan revitalized the poetic format called "linked pearl" and created by
the male poet Liu Xiaochuo (481–539), which she used for her nine-poem
series. It gave a new twist to historical allusions and images like "jade toes" or
kicking "her jade hook halfway up" that had become clichés in men's poems
about the tiny foot. What is most interesting is that throughout the poem
the teenage girl is very much aware of her own steps and body movements,
which are designed for the pleasure of a beholder. As she mentions in her
other poem on the full body: "Beauty fills a beholder like a feast" (in Ko
1994, 168). Who is this beholder? As the Chinese saying goes, *Nu wei zhi ji
zhe rong*—a woman makes herself beautiful for the one who knows her. This
zhi ji, in a heterosexual relationship, could be her husband, fiancé, lover, or
simply a male admirer. On the surface, Ye Xiaoluan's *zhi ji* alludes to two
male models. One is Emperor Tang Xuan Zong (Li Longji 685–762), who
indulged in the sensuous charm of his favorite Consort Yang; the other is
the poet Cao Zhi (192–232), who wrote about the two legendary sisters who
were the wives of the Emperor Shun. They jumped into the River Luo after
the death of their husband and were believed to become the goddesses of the
river. By using these female models for their beauty and charm, and using
the male models as their *zhi ji*, Ye Xiaoluan seems to be putting herself in the
same category as a female charmer, who either brought down kingdoms or
became the muse for male poets. If we look into her family situation, the environment in which she composed these verses, it becomes clear that her *zhi*

ji are the female members of her family. Her poetry is a continuous dialogue with her mother and sisters, like the intimate chatting within their inner chambers. In fact, her mother, Shen Yixiu, wrote a poem in response to Ye Xiaoluan's foot verse. Such communications through poetry formed a tight, intimate bond among the female family members, even for the ones who were married. Ye Xiaoluan's eldest sister Ye Wanwan (1610–32) often returned to her maternal home to seek solace from her unhappy marriage. The three sisters often stayed up all night, dreaming of retiring together as hermits in a mountain to get away from all their misery and misfortune.

Ye Xiaoluan's longing to imprint "her fragrant name" with her "jade toe" is a cry from a well-educated and privileged teenage girl for self-definition, and a bold act of defiance against the conventional male poetics, which sexualize the female body as passive, erotic. With a teenage girl's audacity and ambition, she denounces this dominant tradition. Yes, she still volunteers her body for writing, but it no longer serves as a fragmented, sexualized text for the male gaze. Instead, the author clearly states that her "jade toe" is for writing her own name, her own text, in her own language and on her own terms.

Writing the texts with their bodies, however, means that there is little distance between their lives and their art. Beauty alone is often not enough for creating the best material for writing. A beautiful, talented girl or young woman who has gone through a lot of suffering provides the most exciting text for both men and women writers. In the poetry anthology of the women from the age of the *Book of Songs* to the contemporary *Anthology of Chinese Talented Women Poets* (*Zhongguo lidai cainu shige xinshang cidian* [Zheng Guangyi 1991]), nearly all of the poets had a tragic story to tell. They either lived as widows from their early twenties, suffered from the brutalities of their husbands or mothers-in-law, lost their homes in wars, or in many cases, died at an early age. Pain and death are often the price that women have to pay for attempting to write within the order of masculine logic and language.

Ye Xiaoluan's mother, Shen Yixiu, also a talented poet, is aware of what her daughter might have to go through for her ambition. In her response to Xiaoluan's foot poem, she subtly hints at how fragile and erasable the body/writing can be, since it is printed "on the green moss lightly." And such imprinting/writing could be done only when she is "alone" and "lost in thought," a warning against loneliness, waiting for the return of the man—the usual lot for a woman (Shen Yixiu 1935, 119). As a woman in her forties, Shen Yixiu knows how much a woman's life and writing depend on men in a patriarchal system, economically, morally, and linguistically, even though she and her daughters enjoy a privileged freedom. As upper-class poets, their writings have been collected and anthologized, and as the wives and daughters of liberal literati in seventeenth-century Jiangnan, they were encouraged to cultivate their female talent and beauty. Shen Yixiu herself is blessed with a so-called companionate marriage, in which conjugal love is expressed through a harmonious blending of the intellectual and emotional compatibility between husband and wife. She is the ideal woman, with beauty enhanced by her talent in poetry and art as well as her virtue. Her husband, Ye Shaoyuan, wrote soon after her death: "By propriety we were man and wife; in intimacy we were also friends" (Ye Shaoyuan 1935a, 147–48; in Ko 1994). He even believed that their marriage was destined by their previous lives: he as the reincarnation of the famous Song love lyric poet Qin Guan (1049–1100) and she as that of Qin's wife. Yet even such an ideal marriage couldn't avoid stormy conflicts between Yixiu and her mother-in-law, who demanded that her daughter-in-law serve the family with self-restraint and forbade her to write poetry; she also forbade her son to be close to his wife.

Shen Yixiu spent many years waiting for her husband's return from his official post thousands of miles away, going through the hardships of giving birth to sixteen children and bringing up twelve. Many of her poems collected in *Li chui ji* (1935) are about this waiting and longing. Feelings of loneliness, emptiness, and grieving permeate each line. If her separation from her husband was forced on them by social convention (men go away to seek government positions and women stay home to take care of the elders and children), then her eldest daughter's (Wanwan) unhappy marriage was caused by the best intentions of her parents. Shen Yixiu and her husband promised her to the son of their best friend, Yuan, when she was still a baby, assuming that it would be another companionate marriage like their own, but it ended in a disaster. Wanwan was completely ignored by her husband. The marriage turned into seven years of emptiness and grief.

With great gentleness and subtle images, Shen Yixiu was warning her daughter about the lot of women, especially women with beauty and talent. In the final line of her response to Xiaoluan's foot poem she compared women to fallen petals in spring:

> They say she leaves her footprint on the green moss lightly,
> Only as she stands alone, lost in thought.
> . . . .
>
> As spring befalls the emperor's garden,
> The fallen petals make a fitting companion.
>
> (1935, 119; my translation)

Ye Xiaoluan died a few months after she composed the foot poem, shortly before her own wedding, at the age of sixteen, as if her mother's warning had been an omen. Or perhaps she died because she did not want to suffer the same lot as her unhappily married sister. Her death is an ultimate defiance, a final writing (with the body) against the system. A few days later, her sister Wanwan died in grief, at the age of twenty-two, and their mother Shen Yixiu followed the path within three years. She was forty-six.

The body of writing these upper-class women left behind indeed entered the annals of history. But more important, their writing is by no means a mere imitation and continuation of male poetics. By bringing dialogue and interaction into poetry, by writing their feelings, desires, and pain into their handiwork, they not only refreshed the writing that was becoming more stagnant in men's hands but also turned it into an effective tool to assert their new womanhood and self-pride, their ambition and emotion.

He Shuangqing

By the early eighteenth century (around 1732), another young woman poet, He Shuangqing, illuminated the sky of women's poetry.[6] Her chronicler, Shi Zhenlin, describes her background and education:

> Shuangqing, a girl from Xiaoshan [Jiangsu Province], was born of peasant stock. Shuangqing was brilliant from birth; upon hearing anyone read she would break into a smile. By ten plus years of age she was adept at needle work. Her maternal uncle was a village tutor who used to teach next door to her house. When hearing her uncle teach, she would memorize everything. She would give her uncle needle work in exchange for *shi* and *ci,* which she would chant from memory. She studied the *xiaokai* style of calligraphy, and learned to make all the strokes extremely gracefully. She was able to write out the entire Heart Sutra *(Xinjing)* on a Cassia leaf. (*Random Notes* 2:34; translated and quoted in Ropp n.d.)

Her education, which was usually available only to girls from the gentry families or the upper classes, was a result of chance (her uncle happened to teach next to her house) and her self-reliance (she exchanged poems with her needlework). Yet her talent and beauty could not save her from ill fortune. Her parents married her off to a woodcutter. The husband and mother-in-law abused her physically and emotionally, making her toil both in the fields and house, even though she suffered from chronic malaria.[7]

The combination of her classic education and her life at the bottom of society gave her writing a fresh perspective, coloring her poetic diction with a living vocabulary connected to the soil, the sky, the countryside, people, plants, and other natural elements.

Although she never mentioned a word about footbinding except for one allusion in a lyric song to her girlfriend,[8] the self-awareness of her body, be it fragmented, wounded, sick, alert, or heart-broken, permeated each of her songs. For many women writers, and perhaps for Shuangqing also, bound feet provided an important definition and emblem for pride and self-identity as women, but feet were also part of the body, as natural and indispensable to the whole as the hands, nose, eyes, mouth, heart, and liver. In that sense, bound feet were everywhere, whether they were mentioned or not. Shuangqing's writing explored the poet's inner world through the representation of the body with disturbing images, syntax, and diction that came out of women's daily conversations and handiwork. Employing a tone of voice that is alternately conversational, monological, and challenging, she depicted the harsh environment, both physical and linguistic, that a woman writer of her time had to endure, and the fatal predicament for female writers who try to bring their bodies and minds together in harmony through a language that is not entirely their own.

Let's look closely at the words of her tune "Shilouyi":

> In this world only deep emotions are hard to reveal.
> Tears swallowed, now well up again.
> Twisting withered flowers,
> I lean against the screen, wordless.
>
> Shocked to see myself in the mirror:
> So thin, so frail.
> Not a face of spring.
> Not a face of autumn.
> Could it be Shuangqing?
>
> (*Random Notes* 2:35)[9]

The first stanza seems to be a typical song lyric written by a woman, judging from its feminine signs and symbols in the lines: tears, withered flowers, screen, mirror, and the gestures of a woman's sadness. All these give readers the impression of a lonely woman longing for her absent beloved. The first and last lines of the first stanza also seem to indicate the same theme: a woman being choked wordless by her longing and emotions. Therefore, she turns to the mirror, another seemingly typical feminine gesture. The mirror, a substitute for the male gaze, continues to mislead readers: it reflects an image of feminine beauty who has become too thin, too frail from either the fear of losing her beauty or from the endless waiting for impossible love. The last three lines, however, overturn the tone of the entire poem. By negating the two images that have been traditionally allotted to women—"face of spring" and "face of autumn"—as pointed out by Grace Fong, she discards the poetic tradition of how a woman is seen and how she sees herself and begins to question the identity and sexuality that have been engraved on women's physical and psychological being. It becomes clearer when we consider the context in which Shuangqing composed the poem. According to Shi Zhenlin, Shuangqing's previous poem "Wang Jiangnan" made fun of Huaifangzi (Duan Yuhan), her ardent admirer. When she heard he was offended, she wrote "Shilouyi," which made Huaifangzi so remorseful that he wrote more than a dozen lyric songs, hoping that Shuangqing would reply with matching rhymes (*Random Notes* 2:35). In "Shilouyi," the male gaze (of Shi Zhenlin as well as Huaifangzi) in the mirror is now replaced by an asserting of the self: "Could it be Shuangqing?" Although this self-identity is established through a question of self-doubt, the voice of a woman who finally sees herself through her own eyes is established.

By seeing herself, she denounces the fragmentation and textualization of female bodies that often appear in the male writing. Languorous desire and longing, as noted by Grace Fong, do not inhabit her words (1994, 125). Coquettish flirtation and begging, typical depictions of the female image, do not exist in her poems either. Like the gentry woman poet Ye Xiaoluan's foot poem, Shuangqing wishes for a double of the self and a female friend. This search for the self leads to another break with the Chinese poetic tradition, which emphatically avoided reference to the subject, especially the subject of the author. The absence of the subject, made possible by the unique syntax of the Chinese language, often gives a poem ambiguous and multiple layers. Shuangqing apparently goes out of her way to upset this tradition by saying her own name over and over again in nearly all her song lyrics. The calling was intense, as if she were beckoning the souls of all the women, including her own, whose names had been buried alive over thousands of years.

Shuangqing transforms the term *deep emotion* from the traditional topic of woman-longing-for-man into a search for the self or her double. The task renders her wordless, since both the language and power to do the job are denied to her. Yet she keeps trying, through negations and questions, with not only her brush but also her whole being. "In this world only deep emotions are hard to reveal." *Reveal* is translated from the Chinese character *tu,* which has multiple meanings: to spit (as in blood, silk, phlegm, and so on); to speak; and to reveal. The difficulty and urgency of revealing, spitting out all the deep emotions that have been locked inside the female body, couldn't have been emphasized as strongly if she had used the much more common word *su*—to speak, to tell, indicating a complaint.

The need to expose and discard the forced and false identity is even more urgent in Shuangqing's song subtitled "Taking Meals to the Ploughing Field." Spring, a common metaphor for feminine beauty and youth, with the implication of its short duration and easy loss, is a favorite theme in women's, especially teenage girls', writing. Shuangqing's song begins with an idyllic scene as the author sets out to do her farm chores on a sunny spring day:

> Purple roads in spring weather.
> Slowly I tie a spring scarf around my head
> and eat alone for spring plough.
> The plum tree is thin in spring
> and fine grass blades glisten in spring light.
> Each step along the spring fields brings spring to life.
> ("Chun cong tian shang lai," *Random Notes* 4:47)

In the first stanza, the idyllic scene and almost languorous tone seem typical of a spring poem by a woman poet. Spring as a symbol for femininity and youth has a long tradition in Chinese poetics. Women have adopted this symbol but also transformed it into a personification of the other, to whom they reveal their feelings of secret longing, love, and disappointment:

> I remember that year in a fine spring
> I revealed my spring feelings
> to a spring swallow.
> And by now,
> I believe the spring letters and spring tears
> have all melted with the spring ice.

The author still seems to remain within the domain of conventional feminine poetics with the images of a swallow, letters, tears, and melting—doting on a failed or unfulfilled love. The swallow is a migrating bird that returns to its old nest every year. But this year, the bird hasn't returned. In this stanza, Shuangqing may be recalling her meeting with Shi Zhenlin and his literati friends in the early summer of 1733 and exchanging poems with them throughout the summer. Since they left that year, she hasn't seen them for two years. If the swallow serves as a symbol of the male literati who claimed to be her *zhiyin* (true friends), the failure of its return implies the unreliability of the emotions and the impossibility of communication. The ambiguous syntax of the last line further confirms this impossibility. The original *hua chun bing* can be translated either as "melted *with* the spring ice" or as "melted *into* the spring ice." The former implies that the author's letters and tears have been frozen in the past winter and have now melted in the fine spring weather; the second indicates a sudden return of cold weather in spring.

The next stanza becomes even more ambiguous and shocking with its images, metaphors, and peculiar word combinations:

> How many springs have I treasured and sympathized with spring?
> The spring oriole is locked
> in a veil of spring mist.
> Gifts for a springtime me,
> and I return with presents to a springtime you.
> Are you or I the spirit of spring?

The mist blurs everything: subject and object, self and other, feelings and values, and so forth. The verbs in the first line, *treasure* and *sympathize,* contain several layers in their original meanings in Chinese. *Lian* means to pity, to sympathize, with secondary meanings to love and to treasure. *Tong* is translated as pain, sadness, and hatred. Spring, in that sense, is treasured with pity, sadness, and hatred. The spring oriole, another symbol of femininity, contrasts with the free-willed, mobile spring swallow in the first stanza. The imprisonment of the oriole is stated with a subtle, yet striking image—locked in a veil of the spring mist. If the mist can be regarded as a symbol of the patriarchal system, then its influence penetrates things quietly. Just as the oriole is imprisoned in the mist without realizing it, women have internalized the male gaze to such a degree that they are unaware of whom they see or desire. If it is true, then the blurred, misplaced subjects and objects—you, me, and the third person, the spirit of spring—begin to make sense. "Springtime me" and "springtime you" are truly peculiar even if these two lines had subjects. The original has two possibilities. One is the above version, with spring as an adjective for the object. In the other version, if we switch the position of the word *spring* and interpret it as another object, the translation becomes "[You] give spring to me / And [I] present spring to you." The image of gift exchange as love tokens comes from the ancient *Book of Songs*: "[The girl] gives me a plum / [I] return it with a peach." Although the lines do not show the subjects, there is no mistaking that the poem is a love song between a young man and young woman, whose feelings for each other are mutual and reciprocated. And in Shuangqing's song lyric, the emotions are lost and misplaced (she reveals them to a bird that never returned). By dislocating the objects and omitting the subjects, Shuangqing echoes the theme of impossibility of emotional communication and exchange in the first stanza and subtly states the forced and dislocated identity/sexuality for women. By deliberately misplacing the objects, the poet creates a disturbing image of a woman who has gone mad inside an invisible prison. The repetition of the word and image *spring* becomes so frequent and intense that in the end it sounds almost like the continuous shriek of a mad woman.

As suspected by Shu Wu in her preface to Du Fangqin's *He Shuangqing ji*, something is about to explode under the smooth surface of Shuangqing's virtue (her stoic endurance of her suffering) represented and admired in the *Random Notes* (1988, 5). And when the veil of the spring mist is finally lifted, it reveals a demon:

> Even if I could count spring's beginnings and spring's ends,
> it's impossible to count how many spring dreams or spring awakenings.
> Which spring demon
> put me into the state of spring sickness?
> Spring has misled Shuangqing.

Awakened from slumber, Shuangqing calls out the shocking truth: "Spring has misled Shuangqing" in the last song lyric that appeared in Shi Zhenlin's *Random Notes*. Again, *misled* is only one of the meanings for the character *wu*. Its first connotation is mistake; its second is delay and ruin. Shi Zhenlin and his friends showered their affection, admiration, and pity on Shuangqing two years before, branding her a *jiaren* (beautiful woman)— the symbol of spring—and giving her the hope of spring. But this hope turned out to be not only short-lived and unreliable, but also false and destructive. To be lured into this endless dream is bad enough. But waking to see the truth is even more terrifying because the awakened is so alone, so powerless in a hostile environment. Unlike the Jiangnan upper-class women or the Jiangyong country women, Shuangqing struggled alone without a supporting network. The result is a masterpiece ("Fenghuang taishang yichuixiao") of disturbing visions and haunting images of loss and alienation, written for a female friend who returned to her husband's home after a short visit at her parents' village:

Inch by inch of sparse clouds,
ray upon ray of fading light,
flickering here and there, unable to vanish.
The soul that is being severed, now breaks,
but continues to shiver and reel.
Gaze after gaze at the mountains and streams,
the traveler is going farther and farther, indistinct.
From now on,
nothing but pain and plight
like tonight.

The blue sky is far away.
I ask the heaven, but it's silent.
Look at tiny little Shuangqing,
so frail and listless.
Who does she see and who sees her?
Who will pity the flower charm?
Who will look upon her joy and happiness,
stealing white powder to write and sketch?
Who still cares, age after age,
night after night, day after day?

(*Random Notes* 3:51)

The flickering images of the light, clouds, sky, and the figure that is going farther away among the mountains and rivers mirror the pain and plight Shuangqing bears. Although she is flocked and followed by a group of male literati who claim to be her *zhiyin,* the only person who really cares about her is her neighbor Han Xi, an illiterate village girl. She helps Shuangqing with her household chores, cries at her bedside when Shuangqing is ill. She asks Shuangqing to copy the *Heart Sutra* in her fine calligraphy and teaches her to recite it (*Random Notes* 3:51). But even this connection is severed by Han Xi's marriage. One day she returned to visit her parents and invited Shuangqing to dinner. Shuangqing was too ill to attend the party. Han Xi refused to eat without Shuangqing and brought the food to Shuangqing's house to share with her best friend. Seeing the farewell food, Shuangqing's soul runs after Han Xi along the mountain roads. Though her body is bedridden by a bout of malaria, her voice wails, loud and clear, at the sky and earth about the unjust fate of being a woman. The tradition of feminine poetics, especially for upper-class women poets, has always followed the principle of *ai er bu yuan*—bear the pains without complaint. In her song lyric, Shuangqing breaks the taboo not only of what women can write about but also of how they do it. The striking contrast between the agonized soul of an individual and the distant, indifferent surroundings presents a heart-wrenching picture of a lonely woman who refuses to give up or shut up. In this sense, her poetic voice contradicts the voice of virtue presented in Shi's *Random Notes,* who endures with patient smiles the constant physical and emotional abuse of her violent husband and mother-in-law. In other words, if the life of Shuangqing is fictionalized or aestheticized/fetishized according to Shi Zhenlin's vision, to "serve as some kind of signifier in both elite and popular culture" (Fong 1997, 280), her lyrics break the mode and frame Shi Zhenlin carefully set for future readers, speaking/wailing loudly and clearly to us between the lines. The late Qing critic Chen Tingzhou, puzzled as well as dazzled by her unique voice, raises the question: "So, is she an immortal fairy or a ghost? I can't name her realm *[ching]*" (quoted in Fong 1994, 130).

Guochao cizong xubian has this comment: "Shuangqing's song lyric is like a little girl engaged in small talk, chattering and murmuring. . . . The writer forgets that she is writing a poem, and the reader forgets that he is reading one" (Zheng Guangyi 1991, 1625). By introducing small talk into poetry, Shuangqing not only transfused fresh blood into a poetic genre that was becoming stagnant and rigid; she also pushed writing closer to speech, using it to question the established system and cultivate a new space for the female body and mind. This is a tendency already present among the seventeenth-century gentry women poets.

Forced to incorporate an alien language into her writing, Shuangqing, like many other women poets who died suddenly and in an untimely fashion, paid a heavy price in order to inscribe her claim as a woman and a writer within the prescribed male order. She paid with her loneliness and sense of alienation, with her body that was abused and afflicted with chronic malaria. Of course, this predicament is echoed by Western women writers as well. As Luce Irigaray sees the problem: "(How can we) disengage ourselves, *alive,* from their concepts" (1980, 75)? Annie Leclerc, in *La Parole de femme,* calls on women "to invent a language that is not oppressive, a language that does not leave them speechless but that loosens the tongue" (1982, 21).

Nu Shu

Such a language was indeed created by the country women of Jiangyong County in southwestern Hunan, a rural mountain area of China. Literally called female writing, *nu shu* is a syllabic representation of the local dialect, a secret script known, used, and passed down only by and among women for centuries until the mid–twentieth century. Though the authenticity of *nu shu*'s origin is debatable (it is believed to have started in the tenth century), the secret writing helped to shape a literary community among women writers, readers, and listeners. For *nu shu,* writing is inseparable from reading, singing, and sharing. Its form (the structure of the characters), content, and style are interlocked with these women's handiwork, living conditions, and lifestyle. Bound feet are not the focal gaze in their writing but appear everywhere as something taken for granted, something as natural and indispensable as limbs, eyes, noses, and other body parts. Footbinding serves as a basis for the self-awareness of body and desire, and as a code for seeking and recognizing female companions. Just as the verses by the seventeenth-century gentry women came out of their private inner chambers where they embroidered, read, and talked intimately with female family members and friends, and just as He Shuangqing's poems came out of her mixed and misplaced background and the conflicts between her inner world and hostile environment, Jiangyong women's *nu shu* came directly out of their embroidery rooms, where they gathered together regularly with their sworn sisters to chat, weave, and make lotus shoes.

Like footbinding, no one knows exactly who created this female writing or when. It, too, seems to have begun at the royal court. According to local legend (written in *nu shu*), a woman named Hu Yuxiu from the area in the Song (920–1279) was selected as a royal concubine for her intelligence and scholarship. Completely ignored by the emperor, she wrote home in a secret code she invented to complain about her loneliness and suffering. Hu's letter, whether it is authentic or not, set the tone for the female writings—to tell the pain and misery of being women, especially married women and widows, as expressed in the "Song of Female Writing":

> For all our lives we suffer and bend,
> No one has showed us any sympathy.
> Only through female writing
> Can our pain come out from the beginning.
> . . . .
> So much has been written on fans and paper,
> Every word is soaked in blood.
> If the tender-hearted read it,
> They'll all say "pitiful."
> If the ghosts and gods read it,

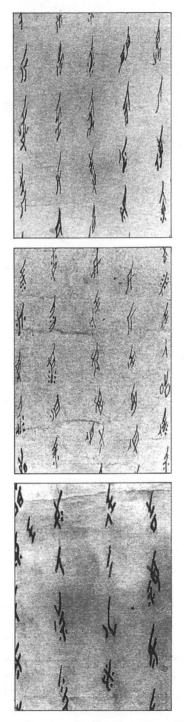

Figure 12. Patterns of embroidery. From *Nu shu*.

They'll shed tears for our stories.
If soldiers read them,
The world will be in chaos.

> (In Gao Yinxian and Yi Nianhua
> 1991, 10; my translation)[10]

This is also the theme for the gentry women's poetry, except that these country women write more straightforwardly and openly. And their purpose is also clear: by exchanging letters and singing out their stories with their lifelong female friends, writing serves not only as an important outlet for their emotion and consolation for their pain, but also as an indispensable tool to form a female literary community and support network. Since performing the texts with a group of women is such a crucial part of *nu shu,* Jiangyong women brought writing even closer to performance and oral interaction. Thus they escaped, to a certain degree, the fate of the Jiangnan gentry women poets and He Shuangqing, who paid for their writing with loneliness, alienation, sickness, even death.

In Jiangyong County, the division of labor was clear: men worked in the fields and women embroidered at home. Having had their feet bound when they were three or four, they spent most of their spare time in their embroidery rooms, alone or with their companions. This gave them an opportunity to get together with their female friends, discussing design patterns and colors for their embroidery and shoes, singing and writing their own or other women's stories in their secret language. For them, weaving, embroidering, making lotus shoes, chatting, and writing do not contradict one another. They are all interwoven, working together harmoniously and naturally, indispensable to each other as thread, needle, and cloth are indispensable to embroidery, or the loom and yarn to weaving. The embroidery room (often upstairs) provides these women a private space that excludes men, a space where women talk about things that are not for men's ears, writing in a language that men can't read, and producing their handiwork for practical and creative purposes. Like the Jiangnan gentry women poets who turned their inner chambers into female studies, Jiangyong women turned the workplace into a study.

Leisure (relatively speaking, compared to other peasant women) and space give them "a room of their own" for writing as well as handiwork. Gao Yinxian, one of the writers still alive when female writing was discovered, wrote in a letter to Gong Zhebin, "I have nothing else to do in the embroidery room, / So I spend all my time writing stories" (in Gao Yinxian and Yi Nianhua 1991, 314). The language they created and used (its thin,

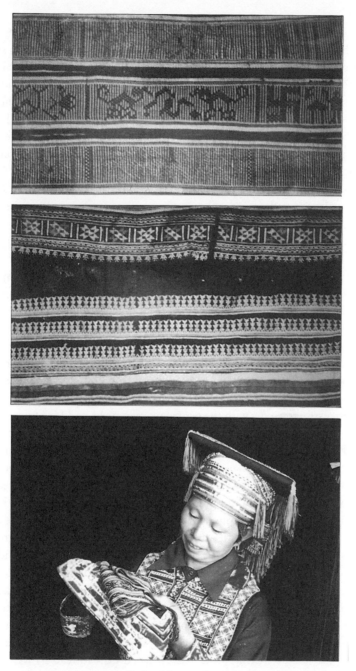

Figure 13. Patterns of weaving. Embroidery and weaving have been the major productions of the Jiangyong County women for many generations. The patterns of their handiwork have striking similarities to the strokes of *nu shu* words. From *Nu shu*.

rhomboid shape and its vertical lines that go from right to left) has a striking resemblance to their embroidery patterns (figures 12, 13, 14, 15). *Nu shu* was not restricted to paper but was also written on fans and embroidered onto fabrics. Sometimes one wrote a story and her sworn sister embroidered the writing on a handkerchief. Many writers made their own books with beautifully designed cloth covers. Women's handiwork and female writing have never been so naturally interwoven together as in *nu shu*. In that sense, *nu shu* restored the meaning of *wen*, which, according to *Cihai* (a Chinese encyclopedia), originally meant natural patterns such as those in the palm, then drawing and tattooing before it was used to represent words, language, and extended further for *wen ren*.[11]

Unlike the books written and published by male authors (including many of the anthologies of upper-class women's poetry), these books of female writing were not meant for the public (men's eyes) but were enjoyed as personal treasures and shared only among intimate female friends. Again unlike male authors, these women authors did not write in order to *liu fang bai shi*—leave a good name for a hundred generations. Before they died, they left wills to have their writing and books burned so that they could continue reading and singing these texts in another world (to the Chinese, the dead continue living as ghosts, with all the desires and needs of the living). It also prevented these texts from falling into men's hands. Such an act links *nu shu* with the gentry women poets and He Shuangqing, whose impulse to write, record, or anthologize their work often conflicted with their impulse to burn it. Such conflicting impulses, as pointed out by Kang-i Sun Chang, may have to do with the belief shared by many women poets, critics, and anthologists that women's virtue should be ranked higher than their talents (1997, 169). On the other hand, they reflect their belief in the inner connection among writing, handiwork, the body, and the oral, and their different attitudes toward eternality. It also reflects their intuitive distrust that once their work was printed and circulated in the hands of men, its authenticity and purity would be lost (a kind of male pollution).

Nu shu provides a literacy and literary community for women. Like the community of the Jiangnan poets, it starts within the family. The writing is passed down from mothers to daughters, or from grandmothers, aunts, or sisters-in-law, the same way footbinding is transmitted. Young girls who learned the female writing (or at least learned how to read it) were then able to reach out to girls of their own age, personality, class, often of the same foot size, for an intimate companionship called *lao tong* (its literal meaning—old same), something like sworn sisterhood. The procedure of forming such a relationship resembles that of marriage. First, the girl makes

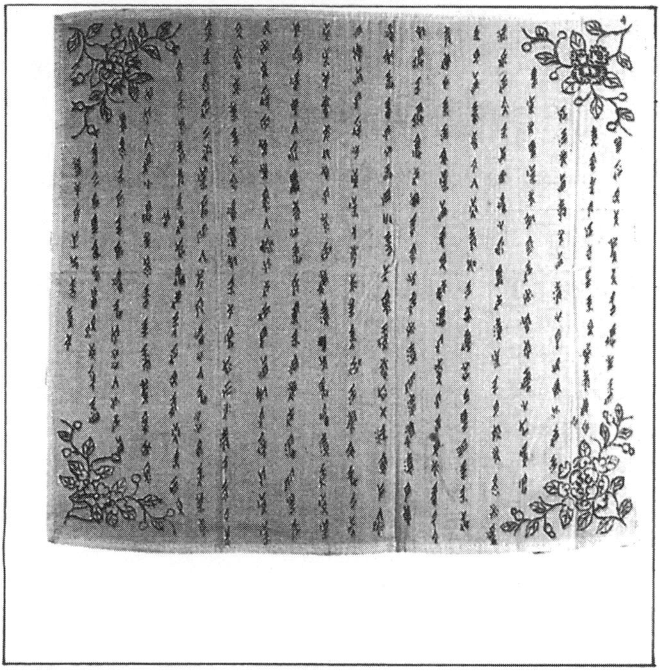

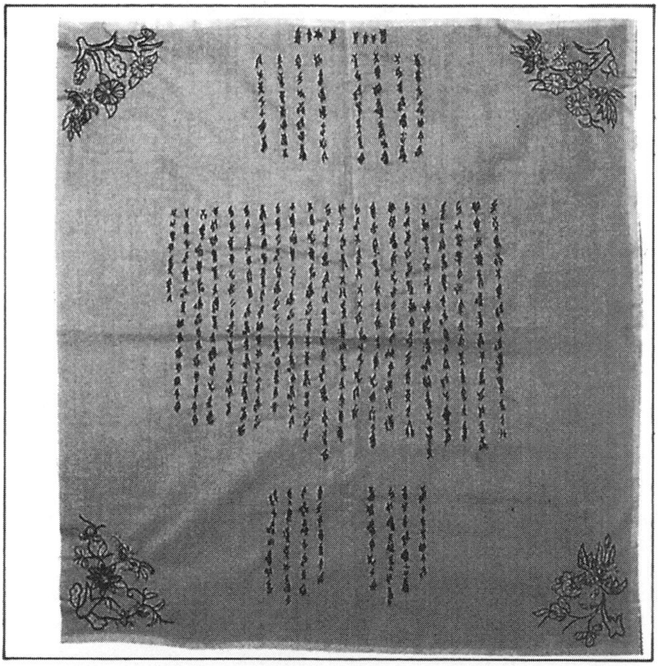

Figure 14. Two *nu shu* handkerchiefs. The text was written by Gao Yinxian, then embroidered by Tang Jinbao. From *Nu shu*.

a list of items to check about the girl she wants to befriend—her family background, personality, age, skills, and most interestingly, her foot size. If all match her own, she will then write a letter in the secret code asking for her hand. Female bodies and *nu shu* are thus knit together as intimately as their handiwork and writing. The body was the content and purpose as well as the subject and object of the writing. And since most women practiced footbinding, feet became a natural symbol for female identity and sexuality, the glue for female liaisons and bonding.

A *lao tong* letter often opens with metaphors in the Chinese tradition that are usually applied to heterosexual couples, often being sexually suggestive: lakes and ocean, the dragon out of its cave, the phoenix frolicking in water, mandarin ducks, among others:

> In the south of the lake as deep as the ocean,
> the dragon leaves its cave,
> treading the pearl endlessly
> in the crystal water.
>
> ("Letter of a *Lao tong* Expressing
> Her Feelings," in Gao Yinxian
> and Yi Nianhua 1991, 310)

These highly sexualized images are followed by the sender's praise for her ideal companion, often focusing on her body:

> A proper girl from a worthy family,
> You're intelligent.
> You talk in a gentle voice,
> Your eyebrows painted like distant mountains.
> Your hair as smooth and shiny as water,
> And you walk like Bodhisattva Guanyin.

Is such sensuality the same as the male gaze upon the female body? Even though the writer borrows some images from the male poetic tradition, such as the eyebrows that are like distant mountains (see Li Yu's *Xian qing ou ji*), the gaze does not possess or swallow the object. It actually serves as a self-evaluation in a subtle way, since the object of her praise is the same, and especially since the writer has to be modest about herself in the letter, saying things like, "You're ten times better than I." In her modesty, there is a genuine sense of pride and assertion of the self.

The metaphors she uses to describe the depth and eternity of their emotions and relationship are unique as well as domestic:

Snow peas and papaya,
Their vines long and deep.
The palm tree in the yard,
Standing tall for a thousand years.

Of course, as proper girls, their relationship needs to be approved by their parents: "Father and Mother agree," although only mother is really involved, since men are completely excluded from these women's activities. They are not even allowed to serve as deliverymen, because *nu shu* letters have to be delivered by women only. A *nu shu* letter touched, delivered, or read by a man is considered dirty, vulgar, and improper. Like the traditional couple, a *lao tong* relationship is also considered predestined. The two must be true to each other for the rest of their lives. They compare themselves to a pair of mandarin ducks, the old symbol for loyalty between husband and wife. Yet unlike the conventional heterosexual relationship in which a man can have as many wives as he can afford, and a woman must follow only one man, a *lao tong* relationship and sworn sisterhood do not restrict a women from forming relationships with other women. The co-author of *Nu shu,* Gao Yinxian had six sworn sisters after she married. When she met her last one, Gao Baojin, she was already in her sixties.

When two women decide to be each other's "same," they visit and stay in each other's houses for days, embroidering, talking, and sleeping together, just like husband and wife. Their letters initiating *lao tong* become their most precious keepsakes. If one of the *lao tong* gets married, she will receive *san zhao shu* (letter after three days) from her same three days after her wedding. In these letters, she is congratulated for her marriage, praised for her virtues, and reprimanded for breaking her vow that she will never abandon her same. Such letters are greatly treasured by the bride as part of her dowry.

Apart from the vows and metaphors that suggest a marriage, the letters between *lao tong* and sworn sisters are full of hints of homoerotic sexuality. The writer entices the other girl to become her same by promising that the two of them would embroider together upstairs, "thread our needles" and "speak in whispers, exchange sympathy" (*San zhao shu 2,* in Gao Yinxian and Yi Nianhua 1991). Such a promise appears repeatedly in every *nu shu* letter to a same or sworn sister. The obsession with talking, weaving, and embroidering forms part of women's culture. The oral—talking things over—is the most important element to *lao tong* and sworn sisters. It makes the female relationship focus heavily on the present. Even their writing does not aim for immortality like men's writing but serves as the text for singing and reading out loud at women's gatherings. It is more or less like the script of a play. After it serves its purpose, it is burned with the body of the deceased author or its owner. While men's writing, especially that which eroticizes women, tends to take her body apart and categorize the parts in order to immortalize her, the images that *nu shu* writers use are associated with living things and cycles of nature: flowing water, leaping dragons, frolicking phoenix, snow peas and papaya with long vines, palm trees of a thousand years. Like the cycles of nature, these women's stories are passed down through the mouths and hands of women. With the death of each author, the stories come back in a newer form through the mouths of the next generation. The burning of *nu shu* writing serves the same function. One folk song can have different versions in writing. In that sense, *nu shu* texts are like the cycles of nature. Things live and things die. Nothing remains the same forever; something always manages to return in a different form.

Whether the bonding between the women can be considered to be what Cathy Silber (1991) calls "female marriage" or "practice marriage," *nu shu* has certainly helped these women form a strong, widespread network of support and entertainment. Many of the *nu shu* correspondences are comforting letters to sworn sisters who have lost a loved one or who suffer from illness and the loneliness of old age. The family of a *lao tong*, especially the female members, often becomes the extended family for the other girl. The bonding among *lao tong* and sworn sisters lasts for life. It sometimes surpasses that of blood. Theoretically, the tie between mother and daughter and between sisters is transitory in China's patriarchal system. It ends with the marriage of the daughter/sister. Parents are no longer her parents, sisters no longer her sisters. She enters a new family, becomes a permanent member of it. To use a Chinese saying, she belongs to her husband's family forever, alive or dead. The bonding between *lao tong* and sworn sisters does not go through such a transition. Besides, sworn sisters usually live in the same village or nearby. Such relationships make it possible for them to visit each other often, if not every day, or at least comfort each other with their letters upon tragic occasions.[12]

Nu shu expanded the network for women on other social occasions such as fairs, temple gatherings, festivals. Jiangyong County was known for its monthly festivals. Some of them were exclusively for women. During the Lantern Festival (the fifteenth day of the first lunar month), women gathered together for a feast. For the Birds Festival (the first day of the second lunar month), women returned to their maternal homes; otherwise they would never be able to have children. During the Tasting Festival (the sixth day of the sixth lunar month), married women had to visit their maternal families with cakes, candy, and other gifts. On the Ghost Day (the fifteenth day of the seventh lunar month), women returned to their maternal homes to offer sacrifices to their ancestors. There were two especially important occasions for women. One was the Bull Festival, on the eighth day of the fourth lunar month, when women fed black rice cakes to bulls and got together to feast and read *nu shu* texts. It was an auspicious day to form *lao tong*. The other was the sacrifice to the Goddess Gupo (literally meaning aunt/grandma goddess) on the tenth day of the fifth lunar month. Days before the festival, women started preparing food, incense, and the other most important gift—*nu shu* texts written on fans and paper. When the day came, they gathered at temples, praying, reading their fans and paper to the goddess and to each other. And finally, there was the ritual of *da san zhao*. The sworn sisters and *lao tong* of the bride got together three days after the wedding, singing and dancing while reading out the *san zhao shu* they wrote for the bride.

Figure 15. *Nu shu* fans. Reading *nu shu* fans to each other or to a group is one of the most important activities for festivals, gatherings, and learning. From *Nu shu*.

Even in the texts of tragedies, humor and wit were everywhere. For example, the well-known story of Liang Shanbo and Zhu Yingtai has many versions. Each of them presents Zhu Yingtai as a beautiful, intelligent, but always well-behaved *da jia gui xiu*. Underneath her man's robe, she is a traditional lady. The *nu shu*'s version of this legend presents a witty and confident teenage girl who finds her way through the system's loopholes using her linguistic skills. She debates with her father about why she should go to Hangzhou to study, citing the examples of female heroes (for instance, goddess Guanyin and Empress Wu Zetian). Her argument is so convincing that she completely changes her angry father's mind and wins his total support. During the three years when she shares the study and bedroom with Liang Shanbo at school, she successfully keeps her transvestite masquerade with her language skill and quick wit (in Gao Yinxian and Yi Nianhua 1991, 120).[13]

Nu shu provided Jiangyong women a private and public space for intimate and social gatherings, lifelong bonding, and a widespread support network. More important, their secret language allowed them to write about things in a manner that the gentry women could not. Instead of hinting between the lines, they were able to complain bitterly and openly about their sufferings caused by men and the male dominant system. Since *nu shu* was created to be read or sung out loud to groups of women (either among friends or strangers) who were most probably illiterate, it allowed and required the writers to use a more lively style and vernacular so that the texts could be better appreciated.

All of these women's writings treated their bodies as whole, natural. We have seen that bound feet were regarded as the symbol of erotic and feminine beauty, but they were also the symbol for self-identity, the emblem of female pride and culture, and most important, the basis for female bonding and support networks. These women's writings were naturally interwoven with their handiwork and conversations. Through interactions, dialogues, and performances among writers and audience (listeners and readers), these women reconnected writing with speech in its vocabulary, content, and style and shortened the gap between writing and speech, just as they reconnected the fetishized lotus feet with their bodies through their handiwork, female bonding, and female literary communities. Their literature, together with their handiwork that often revolved around footbinding, revitalized language and enriched the oral tradition of women's culture. In these women's hands, writing and footbinding were no longer tools to reduce the body to fragments but, rather, parts of the living organism, whether it was language or nature. Instead of destroying their creators, they enhanced the harmonious unity between the body and mind. More important, they became a form of "womanly work" that did not serve men or the family but helped redefine womanhood, consolidate bonds between women, and cultivate women's culture. Writing, binding, chatting, and weaving/embroidering were interlocked with the ways these women lived, worked, and communicated. One cannot fully appreciate their writing without first understanding their living habits, including footbinding. And likewise, without looking into their literature through their living and working backgrounds, one cannot understand how these women transformed footbinding and its implications into their own language, their own heritage.

From Golden Lotus to Prime Minister:
A Woman's Tale Living from Mouth to Mouth

The storyteller takes what he tells from experience—his own or that reported by others. And he in turn makes it the experience of those who are listening to his tale.
> —Walter Benjamin, "The Storyteller"

Instead of a woman disguised as a man, I shall look like a man disguised as a woman. In truth, neither sex is really mine. . . . I belong to a third sex, a sex apart, which has as yet no name.
> —Theophile Gautier, *Mademoiselle de Maupin*

AROUND 1770, CHEN DUANSHENG (1751–1796) wrote *Destiny of the Next Life (Zai sheng yuan),* a verse narrative with seventy-seven acts in eight volumes.[1] Although Chen Duansheng came from a prestigious gentry family, well educated in composing poetry and lyric songs, she chose to write her play in *tan ci* form, a singing and telling performing art that was extremely popular among the common people, women especially, but that was dismissed by intellectuals and poets as low and unclean. It allowed Chen Duansheng to weave the dialects, idioms, and vocabularies of common people into her tale of female utopia, a tale that can be sung and performed as well as read. This proved to be a literary genre that reached the masses, especially women. Chen Duansheng brought writing closer to the oral tradition of women's culture than the seventeenth-century Jiangnan gentry women poets and Jiangyong country women.

Unlike most women writers, Chen Duansheng used bound feet as a major prop for her narrative and plots. The heroine of the narrative, Meng Lijun, has a pair of the most beautiful lotuses, which measure only 2.7

inches long. Such an emblem of feminine beauty, however, is hidden within men's boots, the mask of masculinity, throughout nearly the entire play, as Meng cross-dresses as a man to escape a bullying suitor. The double masquerade makes her a symbol of both femininity and masculinity. Once hidden in disguise (lotus shoes or men's boots), feet became women's most powerful language for self-assertion and self-identity and for forming female liaisons. The drama that centers on revealing what is behind the masquerade brings the tension between genders, classes, inside and outside, surface and depth, origin and simulation, writing and speech, body and mind, and all other opposites, to a boisterous climax.

Destiny of the Next Life celebrates a teenage girl, Meng Lijun. Her parents arrange to have her engaged to Huangfu Shaohua. But his rival, Liu Kuibi, plots to murder Shaohua so that he can marry Meng Lijun. When his scheme fails, Liu uses his father's political power to bring down the Huangfu family and force Lijun to marry him. Lijun escapes with her maid. Masquerading as a man, she places first in the official examinations, rescues her fugitive fiancé and his family, and rises to the highest position in court—*zai xiang* (prime minister). She marries her teacher's adopted daughter, Liang Suhua, who is actually Lijun's former maid and playmate, Su Yingxue. The transvestite Meng Lijun turns the patriarchal kingdom into an orderly, just, and harmonious utopia. But the story does not end here. The masquerade fits her so well that it becomes her second skin. She can no longer go back to her former identity as a woman. Thus the real drama begins to spin around the mystery of his/her sexual gender. She wears men's clothing, talks and walks like a man, and administers the country with the capability and wisdom that no man can match, yet her beauty constantly arouses men's desire and possessiveness (including the emperor's). Everybody wants her to return to her original identity in order to claim her. Her parents want her back as a daughter. Her fiancé wants her as a wife. Her fiancé's parents want her as their daughter-in-law who can bear them grandchildren. Her fiancé's sister wants her to marry her brother so that she will have no rival in the palace. Her companion, the woman she marries as her "wife," wants her to marry Huangfu Shaohua, her fiancé, so that the companion can become his second wife. And finally, the emperor wants her as his concubine. Besieged by men, women, and the whole system, Meng Lijun fights with her only weapon—her tongue. She speaks so well and convincingly that she fools everyone, including her own father and brother and the emperor. Language forms and protects her new identity and sexual gender until it is robbed by her female rival, who intoxicates her with drugged spirits and takes off her boots to reveal her lotus feet.

It is a story that defies and reverses everything in the prevailing patriarchal system: assumed identity and gender roles, the function of language and its games. Men still gaze at women, but only at their shadows (a picture or mask). Men no longer possess their bodies, physically or linguistically, even though women are still branded as wives and concubines, daughters and mothers. Through linguistic manipulation, women have emptied, substituted, and usurped the names that brand them as the oppressed and sacrificed, and they have managed to become masters to varying degrees. The best manipulator, of course, is Meng Lijun. By masquerading as a man and usurping male language/power, she achieves a new identity, an ideal model that is neither man nor woman, but one that combines the merits of both sexes. She has beauty—an enchanting face and a pair of 2.7-inch golden lotuses. She has talents that are often attributed to courtesans—painting and poetry. She has abilities and wisdom that traditionally belong to men's domain—medicine, government administration, and teaching. This ideal human model is in fact a transvestite, a great heroine in man's robe, a prime minister with lotus feet.

This chapter focuses on two aspects of the play. First are its oral characteristics, from its style and language to the way it is performed and shared by the audience, living from mouth to mouth. Second is the inversion that goes through every aspect of the play, the inversions between written and spoken, men and women, the oppressor and the oppressed, the narrator and narrative, and so on. Both themes provide crucial background for a comprehensive understanding and appreciation of Chen Duansheng's *Destiny in the Next Life* and its importance to further discussion of the relationship between footbinding and masquerade, transvestism and language.

The Oral Tradition of Tan Ci

The *tan ci* form is a telling and singing folk literature that is performed, mostly in southern dialects, accompanied by string instruments. It is divided into *tan ci* performance, which transmitted orally among performers, often without a text, and *tan ci* narrative or *wen ci*—literary *tan ci* (Zhao Jingshen 1960), which exists usually as text only.[2] The performance is, in most cases, a one-woman show. The actress plays, sings, and tells stories by herself. *Tan ci* focuses on storytelling. The genre often shares stories about people, women especially, their daily lives and struggles, their emotions and frustrations, their love and death. Even when the drama is about the royal, upper-class families, as *Destiny* is, the focus is still on women. The female characters in *tan ci* may be dressed in splendid silk robes and accompanied by maids, but their feelings and aspirations are closer to the experience and imagination of the audience, who are mostly commoners like peasants and city dwellers. Female masqueraders who achieve great things in a system that is usually closed to women become a favorite subject for such an audience as well as for women *tan ci* writers.

Tan ci attracts audiences through its narrative, plots, and characters. The story is detailed and complicated. Though its sources are often drawn from history and mythology, *tan ci,* especially literary *tan ci,* often "depict[s] and emphasize[s] the realm of domesticity, the one most closely related to women" (Hu Siao-Chen 1994, 312). It is written in rhymed seven-syllable lines that can be alternated with a three-seven syllable line or a three-three-seven syllable line for variation:

> Shi shi wo, she jian chun qiang qiang bu qiang. [three-seven]
> (Just try me, how powerful are my tongue of sword and lips of gun.)

> Xie miao juan, dai jia wen, yao ba ying cai xian di wang.
>   [three-three-seven]
> (Holding the elegant essays and examination papers, I'll present
>   the talents to the emperor.)
>
>   (Chen Duansheng 1982, 677)[3]

This format brings poetry closer to singing and talking, making it easier to be appreciated, memorized, and spread among the fans. Indeed, the *tan ci* literary genre can be traced all the way back to *bian wen,* a popular form of narrative literature that flourished in the Tang dynasty (618–907), with alternate prose and rhymed parts for the recitation and singing of Buddhist themes. *Tan ci* inherited the rhyme and line-break system of *bian wen* as well as its alternations between telling (prose) and singing (poetry). The combination of singing and talking enhanced the entertainment a great deal. Singing breaks the monotony that may occur in a long narrative, and talking allows the performer to take on the identity of either a character or the narrator. This gives the actress more freedom to seduce the audience into the world of imagination and then pull it back to reality. This tradition has continued since the seventh century. As it has been kept alive in various forms (drama, folk songs, poetic songs, *tan ci,* and its variations) among the people, its rhyming system has become familiar to the masses. *Nu shu* is a good example. When the peasant women of Jiangyong County invented their own secret writing, they automatically adopted this seven-syllable rhyming system for their texts. Like *bian wen* and *tan ci,* it also focuses on storytelling, and the audience can sing along. It is not a coincidence that both Chen Duansheng and the Jiangyong country women used the *bian wen* form for their writing. Redirected from the mainstream of religious teaching, it became the most powerful language and format for women's literature and entertainment.

As a performance art, *tan ci* appeals to an audience that barely knows how to read or write. The language for *tan ci,* therefore, tends to be dialectal, idiomatic, and fresh. It is a language of speech not writing, of everyday life not high literature, of practical, common things not historical or poetic allusions. Even literary *tan ci,* though it has transformed this performance-based art into a female written heritage with a high literary style, has kept many of the oral traditions of *tan ci.* Because it lives and thrives in the mouths of performers, faithful audiences, and enthusiastic readers, the stories and characters often live on beyond the authors. In fact, there is no authorship for any of the performance *tan ci.* And for the literary *tan ci,* only *Destiny of the Next Life* can be definitely attributed to its author, Chen Duansheng.[4] The authorship of most other *tan ci* works remains ambiguous and debatable. Not many people today still remember Chen Duansheng or Tao Zhenhuai (the possible author of *Tian yu hua*) or Wu Yuchang (author of *San xiao yinyuan*), but everyone knows the stories of Meng Lijun taking off her boots, of Zuo Yizhen fighting for her country, and of Tang Bohu's three engagements with the clever maiden Qiu Xiang. As the Chinese folk literature expert Zheng Zhenduo points out,

> Even now, *Tan ci* is still very popular among the people. Women and illiterate men may not know the first emperor of Qin or the first emperor of Han; they may be ignorant of Wei Wei [580–643, Tang politician] and Song Lian [1310–81, a Ming writer]; and they may not have heard of Tu Fu or Li Po. But they all know Fang Qing, Tang Bohu, Zuo Yizhen and Meng Lijun. These characters created by the *tan ci* writers have great influence and have made a deep impression upon the people. (1996, 514)

To write the text or script is only the beginning. The text is usually unavailable to the audience or even the performers. A lot of times, the author is not willing to have it printed, as in Chen Duansheng's case. She stated very clearly in her early chapter that she didn't want to print her play and thereby expose it to vulgar eyes. Her script was not published until years after her death. But *Destiny,* like all other *tan ci* texts, circulated either through *shou chao ben*—handwritten copies—among women, or by word of mouth, among performers and fans. It grew and flowered with each performance, each reading, each repetition. Because of the unavailability and scarcity of the text, because *tan ci* lived and circulated through memory, the performer mixed her own experience and imagination with the stories; during the performance, the experiences and imagination of the author/ performer/characters were further exchanged and mingled with those of the audience. It is like a magic seed. Though it has sprouted many times, it still retains its germinating power. For *tan ci* is like a good story that "does not expend itself. It preserves and concentrates its strength and is capable of releasing it even after a long time" (Benjamin 1978, 90).

There is no record of any actual performance of *Destiny* during Chen's lifetime, though its popularity is not to be doubted. A few years after Chen Duansheng wrote sixty-four chapters of the play, it immediately spread all over the Jiangnan region. When she moved to Yunnan with her father in 1784, the stories went with her and into the province. During the next fourteen years, she was never forgotten, though she didn't write another word. On the contrary, her fans pressed her so hard during those years that she was obliged to pick up her brush again to continue the story. Despite the lack of any record of performances, scenes of *Destiny* can be approximated from the description and records of other plays.

The most spectacular theatrical performances took place on public stages, in the countryside or city, temples or commercial theaters, restaurants or boats, squares or fields. Such a stage was usually high and open and could be viewed from three sides, from land as well as from water. Performances in the countryside took place after the autumn harvests, when peasants had a long period of leisure as well as some cash in their hands. They often hired professional theatrical groups from the city or put together a show themselves. Many peasants were amateur performers. They worked in the fields during the ploughing and harvesting seasons, and when the crops were harvested, they became actors and actresses. Enthusiastic fans often traveled a long distance to watch a play, which could last for days and weeks, and each performance could go on until midnight, even dawn. Such spectacles were shown in Ming paintings such as *Ming nan zhong fan hui tu* and *Ming nan du fan hui tu juan* (figures 16 and 17). A poem, written sometime in the Qing period, describes a stage event in the countryside:

> The temple gathering in the front village is still going on,
> The back village has already started a spring play.
> The village clerk put out a down payment,
> And invited a theatrical troop from the city.
> Men and women in fine clothes come from afar,
> Ten thousands of heads surround the stage.
> Up there the beautiful actresses and actors sing and dance,

Down the stage the applause breaks out like tidal waves.
No one cares whose fields they stand upon,
Let the vegetables be ground into mud.
When the performance stops at sunset,
Women and children return and chat at the village gate:
This year's play is much better than last year's.
At midnight the clerk knocks on the doors to collect money:
Five hundred from the eastern family, a thousand from the west.
Tomorrow morning no smoke will rise from any chimney.

> (Quoted in Zhang Gen and
> Gui Hancheng 1992, 121; my translation)

Tan ci attracted audiences not with its stage props, visual spectacles, colorful costumes, or martial arts but with its music, characters, and stories. Its performance required only one woman with a *pipa* or other stringed instrument to accompany the singing and telling. It could be performed in public places like teahouses or restaurants or *shuchang* (storytelling houses), even private homes. Since elite women and women from rich households were not likely to go to public *tan ci* performances, they often invited female singers to their inner chambers, holding feasts and performances for days. *The Golden Lotus* depicted many scenes where Ximen Qing hired

Figure 16. *Ming nan zhong fan hui tu.* From *Zhongguo xiqu tongshi,* edited by Zhang Gen.

Figure 17. *Ming nan du fan hui tu juan.* From *Zhongguo xiqu tongshi,* edited by Zhang Gen.

theatrical troupes to perform in his house, and his wife invited nuns or singing girls to her chamber to sing and tell Buddhist stories *(bao juan).* The Qing novel *Hong lou meng* (Dreams of the Red Chamber) also describes several scenes of the custom. *Destiny of the Next Life* depicts a women's theater troupe performing at Huangfu Shaohua's wedding (535). A most interesting scene comes from the *tan ci Bi sheng hua,* in which an actual *tan ci* performance by a woman story-singer in the Jiang household is given elaborate treatment:

> The women servants and the maids were excited to madness,
> One by one, they packed the long corridor.
> The mistresses, sisters-in-law, and the concubines,
> Each of them,
> Sitting in the hall, was accompanying (the grand lady).
> The aged lady listened to the story, leaning against a bamboo ottoman,
> The maids waved the fans to invite a cooling breeze.
> The singer slowly plucked the lute strings,
> Her delicate voice was like pearls, making wonderful music.
> She sang an episode in *Xiao jingqian,*
> Which tells about
> Yuechan going to the temple, praying for a son.

> The plum buds were white,
> The chrysanthemums were yellow,
> A series of names of flowers, so long was the list.
>   (Quoted in Hu Siao-Chen 1994, 46–47)

During the Jiajing reign (1522–66), the scholar Tian Rucheng traveled to Hangzhou and recorded in his travelogue that this singing and telling performance was so popular that "most of the blind people in Hangzhou learned how to play *pipa* and sing ancient and contemporary stories as well as *ping hua* [storytelling in a local dialect] as a way to make a living" (*Kang xi yue: shi*; my translation). Apparently, the popularity of *tan ci* continued into the Qing period. In the *tan ci* performance presented in *Bi sheng hua,* it is clear that women of different backgrounds, from the matriarchy to the maids, share the same enthusiasm for this gendered genre (Hu Siao-Chen 1994, 4).

Tan ci attracted women audiences for its content, style of performance, and oral tradition. It appealed to women's feelings, sentiments, suffering, and aspiration and did not require a scholarly background to understand and appreciate the performance. More important, its oral orientation allowed women to participate in the creation of the story. The genre becomes the "literature of women, for women, and by women," as Zheng Zhenduo points out in his *History of Chinese Popular Literature:*

> Women loved *tan ci* most. . . . By and by they started to write the type of *tan ci* they particularly liked. They wove their minds, miseries, and dreams into *tan ci. Shi* [poetry], *ci* [poetry written to certain tunes with strict tonal patterns and rhyme schemes], and *qu* [a type of verse for singing, which emerged in the Southern Song dynasty and became popular in the Yuan dynasty] are men's literary games. Those forms were not suitable for women, and the heavy oppression of tradition made it hard to develop their special talents and express their own ideals. In *tan ci,* they found freedom to release their passions. (1996, 517–18)

Until recently, *tan ci,* together with other types of folk literature, was dismissed by scholars as "blind people's singing and beggars' lies." But it is exactly this "low literature" that gives Chen Duansheng the necessary space and freedom to create her great female characters who are immediately accepted and loved by her female audiences. In the opening poem in the first chapter of her play, she rejects poetry as "awkward and foolish." While she finds it hard "to write a complete line of poetry," she can "compose a whole chapter of plain words *[tan ci]* at ease" (Chen Duansheng 1982, 1). It is not that she doesn't know how to write poetry. On the contrary, being born into a traditional gentry family in Hangzhou and taught classical literature by her parents, Chen Duansheng excelled in crafting poetry. Chen's grandfather Chen Zhaolun opposed the saying that women's virtue lies in their ignorance and believed that they should read and write in their spare time, after they were done with their needlework. Her father, Chen Yudun, a *jinshi* in 1750, took government positions in Shandong and Yunnan. He and his wife taught Chen Duansheng how to read and write poetry when she was young (Zheng Guangyi 1991, 1748). As she recalled at the beginning of volume 17, "Father and Mother explained rhymes and taught me poetry" (Chen Duansheng 1982, 924).

Her poetic skills are self-evident in the poems that begin each chapter. She rejects poetry because it is not her own language but a literary game for men. Instead of joining the mainstream of "high literature" (writing) as a gentry woman poet, she turns to *tan ci* for its oral, performative, and interactive orientation. And since both her father and grandfather are against *tan ci*, she turns to her mother for help and inspiration. Like the seventeenth-century Jiangnan gentry poets and the Jiangyong country women, writing tightens the bonding of mother and daughter, and *tan ci* becomes their secret language.[5] She recalls in the beginning of the seventeenth volume of her play:

> Mother often solves my problems and gives me advice,
> The obsessed daughter talks about her dreams, feeling more attached.
> (924; all translations are mine unless otherwise noted)

With the support of her mother who knew all about *tan ci*, she started writing *Destiny* in 1768 at the age of seventeen and completed sixteen volumes of the rhymed play in 1770. The dialogues about the play between mother and daughter seem extremely intense and crucial to the writing. When Chen Duansheng traveled to Shandong with her father for a government position, she stopped working on the play for three months, perhaps because it was too difficult to hide her writing from her father, but most probably because the intense dialogues and exchange of ideas were no longer possible as she was separated from her mother. Her traveling experiences, however, provided materials for her creation. The story of *Destiny* takes place in Yunnan and Shandong. Traveling also enriched her knowledge of geography, local customs, and the public and private lives of government officials, including the royal family. Her *tan ci* is colored by many elaborate, vivid descriptions. Soon after she completed the sixteenth volume, her mother died. With her emotional and creative tie broken, she stopped writing entirely. Prevailing grieving customs also prevented her from writing *tan ci*: since *tan ci* was considered entertainment literature, it was strictly forbidden to write or perform it during the period of mourning for one's parent. The break lasted fourteen years. It was not until 1784, under pressure from her fans, that she started writing the seventeenth volume of *Destiny*. But this time, she slowed down. Four chapters took her almost a year. Then she stopped completely, though she promised her female audience that she would finish the story when her husband returned from his banishment.[6] Twelve years later, she died, at the age of forty-five, just before her husband was pardoned and was rushing home for their reunion.

The relationship between Chen Duansheng and her mother continued the legacy of female bonding among the Jiangnan women poets and the Jiangyong country women. Just as footbinding became a female "language" that connected women of different backgrounds, writing tied these women together with common ground and space for interactions, dialogues, and networks. For them, writing was no longer the isolated, painstaking activity of an individual wailing at the system (again like footbinding, which was transformed from a feudal code and fetishism to a female heritage), but a group activity among family members, relatives, friends, authors, and fans. Writing in these women's hands resumed many characteristics of speech. By pushing writing onto the stage and making it accessible to women of all backgrounds, by connecting writing to speech and performance, Chen Duansheng expanded writing more deeply and widely than most of the women writers I have discussed earlier. Although her work was not published until long after her death, and the only modern edition did not appear until 1982, her story went beyond the inner chambers and poetry clubs of gentry women poets, beyond the community of sworn sisters and *nu shu* writing, and reached every woman, every household. People may have forgotten or never heard of Ye Xiaoluan, Shen Yixiu, or Shuangqing. They may not understand the secret code of *nu shu* writing without special training. But nearly all Chinese women can tell the story of Meng Lijun, disguising her golden lotuses in black boots. Just as footbinding was transmitted through women's mouths and hands for a millennium, Chen Duansheng's *Destiny of the Next Life* lived, and still lives, as a myth and legend, passed from mouth to mouth.

Inversions and Reversals

The inversion in *Destiny* was profound and complete, starting from its language to the way the protagonists looked, thought, acted, and interacted with one another. Also inverted were the gender and identity roles, the function of the state machine, and the fate that was allotted to women.

The reversal started from the very beginning of writing *Destiny*, when Chen Duansheng refused to write poetry and turned to vernacular forms and *tan ci* instead. Since poetry represents the highest form of writing in China (*shi yan zhi*—poetry speaks about ideals and aspirations), the pinnacle of language and source of all things, it naturally became the most important tool and medium for the patriarchal state. And since this genre forms the very foundation of the Chinese feudal system and represents the psyche of the Chinese male, Chen Duansheng's rejection of poetry already implies a fundamental rebellion against the prevailing political and linguistic system. When she claimed that poetry was "awkward and foolish," she was actually talking about the limitations of poetry, writing, and masculinity, their "lack": their failure to represent language or civilization as a whole, and their inability to interact with so-called lowbrow literature, speech, or femininity.[7]

Rejecting poetry/writing alone is still a kind of escape, a passive denouncement of the patriarchal system, as we saw in the way the Jiangyong women kept themselves inside their secret female writing. Such an escape was apparently not enough for Chen Duansheng. She substituted poetry with *tan ci,* the plain words used by commoners, the oppressed, and women. Although she had to do it secretly at the beginning (she wrote the first sixteen volumes of *Destiny* behind her father's and grandfather's backs), before long her work had spread like wildfire among women, igniting the imaginations and aspirations of her fans. By then, her stories and characters had gained lives of their own, beyond the control of established, traditional literature, even beyond the author. Indeed, the character she created, the transvestite Meng Lijun, becomes the best metaphor for Chen Duansheng's work. The form of *Destiny* is writing (male), but under the mask everything is oral (female), from its content to its language, from its performing style to its audience. In other words, writing itself is a transvestite that sneaks into the opponent's camp, to destroy or subvert the power structure in the name of the opponent. In that sense, Chen Duansheng was a true revolutionary and true feminist ahead of her time, because simply to claim equality between men and women or simply to reject writing does not change a hierarchical relation. In order to dislocate the prevailing system, one must include an inversion or reversal. To use Derrida's words,

> I strongly and repeatedly insist on the necessity of the phase of reversal, which people have perhaps too swiftly attempted to discredit. To neglect this phase of reversal is to forget that the structure of the opposition is one

of conflict and subordination and thus to pass too swiftly, without gaining any purchase against the former opposition, to a *neutralization* which *in practice* leaves things in their former state and deprives one of any way of *intervening* effectively. (1981, 41)

How did Chen Duansheng exactly invert the patriarchal order in *Destiny*? Language is the most basic and fundamental inversion of all. *Bian wen* (changed words, texts, or stories), the genre from which *tan ci* originated, was itself a deviation from mainstream Buddhist teaching. In order to make extremely difficult scriptures more accessible to the masses, Buddhist monks replaced their almost incomprehensible language with the vernacular and used rhymed songs and unrhymed narratives to explain Buddhist literature and tell Buddhist stories. Often, a paragraph of scripture with about twenty words could be expanded into something with thousands of words (see Zheng Zhenduo 1996, chap. 6). Gradually, *bian wen* was no longer restricted to explaining the Buddhist doctrines but was used to tell stories about Buddha and his deeds. It moved further and further away from the teaching until it had little to do with Buddhism. It often bore the name of Buddhist teaching, while its content was substituted with secular stories. Some of them were especially created to appeal to women's emotions and sentiments.

The Golden Lotus features several scenes where women gather together to listen to Buddhist scripture in the *bian wen* form. Chapter 74 describes vividly a typical occasion. When Jinlian intercepts Ximen Qing on his way to Yue Niang's (Ximen's first wife) room, Yue Niang is angry, but she is soothed soon after a nun unrolls the scroll of "Huang shi nu juan" (The Story of Nee Huang) and begins to sing and tell the tale. It is an all-women scene: female audience, female performer, and female story. The tale begins with a Buddhist teaching but is really about a woman who transforms her sex and gender from female to male through incarnation (similar to the transformation through masquerade) simply by chanting sutras (again, the power of speech). The scene of the scripture teaching is followed immediately by prostitutes singing love songs for Ximen Qing's wife and concubines. The religious moral lesson provided by nuns is thus naturally mixed with the secular entertainment provided by prostitutes. The text of "Huang shi nu juan" alternates between narration (unrhymed) and singing (rhymed seven-syllable lines with occasional four-syllable insertions). Its language was the plain words of the vernacular spoken every day by women of the Ming dynasty, comprehensible even to readers in the twentieth century. All these features could be found in Jiangyong women's *nu shu* literature as well as in Chen Duansheng's *tan ci*. The line from *bian wen* to *nu shu* and *tan ci* is clear and continuous. It is perhaps not an exaggeration to say that *bian wen,* derived from written, male-dominated religious teaching, was transformed into a female language and literature rooted deeply in orality and performance, dialogue and interaction.

In that sense, the heritage of these women's writings ran a parallel path to that of footbinding, sharing striking characteristics with each other. Both focused on the oral. Footbinding was transmitted orally, and its euphemisms made the lotus feet edible; *bian wen* and *tan ci* texts were written for oral interaction and transmission. Both deviated from the mainstream as a supplement, appendage, and ornament; in the end, they both became the mainstream of women's culture, surviving longer than much of the male-dominated culture. Many precious written texts and paintings have been lost in wars and natural disasters, yet footbinding, *bian wen,* and *tan ci* remained strong and active through women's hands and mouths for more than a thousand years.

Chen Duansheng's inversion in *Destiny* is profound. She changes the content of the writing from a typical man's story to a woman's tale. On the surface, the work is a continuation of *Destiny of the Jade Bracelet (Yu chuan yuan),* an earlier *tan ci* purportedly written collaboratively between mother and daughter around the end of the Ming dynasty. The narrative focuses on a Song dynasty hero, Xie Yuhui, who has everything a man can dream of: fame, power, wealth, and beautiful women:

> A young man in purple gown,
> With beautiful wives milling around.
> Thrusting his painted halbert, he chases away the Tartars,
> Banners of honor flutter far and near, spreading his magic name.
> He gathers all the fame and wealth on earth,
> With daughters like orchids and sons like trees sitting at his knees.
> After a hundred years of perfect life with many pleasant traces,
> He rises to the immortal world of grace.
>
> (Chen Duansheng 1982, 1)

Yet not all the traces he leaves behind are pleasant. One of his concubines, Zheng Ruzhao, is a gentle, kind, and generous woman. She serves her parents-in-law with care and respect, gets along well with her sisters-in-law and her husband's other concubines. Such a model wife, Chen Duansheng comments, should lead a good life. Yet even she is not to be spared harsh treatment. When she is late for labor, her husband suspects that she is pregnant with another man's child. She is saved only by the baby, who looks exactly like her husband. Although her name is cleared, she feels badly wounded. What if her son did not look like his father? Then she would be wronged for the rest of her life. She turns to religion and becomes a vegetarian. Finally, she is able to become an immortal as a dusting fairy. At a party for the immortals, she encounters Xie Yuhui. As both still remember their past, their emotions are disturbed. She is sad because she is still unable to forget about the unjust fate of being a woman in the other world; he is also sad, but only because he wants to continue his earlier glory and fortune. He asks her in a whisper if she still remembers the husband of her previous life, and his question brings out her sighs. The party's hostess, the Western Goddess, overhears their conversation. Furious that they cannot forget about their past lives of dust, she banishes them back to earth to finish the incomplete affair. Xie Yuhui and Zheng Ruzhao thus become husband and wife with the names of Huangfu Shaohua and Meng Lijun in *Destiny of the Next Life.*

It is not, however, an old story continued and repeated, but a new tale that inverts the relationships in a patriarchal system. In *Destiny of the Next Life,* Huangfu Shaohua suffers endlessly, tormented by his belief in fidelity and loyalty to Meng Lijun. He actually has to go through what his victimized concubine Zheng Ruzhao (and all other women) went through—that is, pining for a love that can never be fulfilled. He still possesses everything a man of privilege can have: an aristocratic title, a high position in government, fame, wealth, and three beautiful women under his name. But all his privileges are blocked, and his power stolen or usurped by Meng Lijun. He marries his third wife, Liu Yanyu, but cannot sleep with her because he has vowed to keep three years of chastity for his first wife. Meng Lijun, however, refuses to be moved by such fidelity. Instead of stepping out of her masquerade, she mocks his chastity and loyalty and keeps him at arm's length by frightening him with her authority as his teacher and boss. At the same time, she keeps his second wife, Su Yingxue, in her own bed. What makes the torment more painful is that Huangfu Shaohua knows that Meng Lijun, the prime minister and his teacher, is his first wife. Yet he can't claim her. To make things worse, he has to bow to her everyday in court. His greatest fear and agony, however, are that no matter how hard he tries, this woman is totally indifferent to him. She does not need him at all. On the contrary, it is his turn to attach his life and death to a woman, to a predestined marriage.

Thus Meng Lijun and other women return to this world to haunt the men in their previous lives with a vengeance, just as the women in *The Golden Lotus, The Carnal Prayer's Mat,* and other writings become the destructive force for their fetishizers or creators. The inversion of *Destiny of the Next Life* takes place, however, not in bloody violence, but through quiet imitation, substitution, and usurpation, which lead to a fundamental transformation. It is not with physical force or military power that Meng Lijun breaks into the men's world and takes over their power as a woman warrior. On the contrary, she first disguises herself as a man, becomes one of them, and then starts to dismantle the hierarchical structure with the most powerful weapon she has stolen from men—their language. Of all the characters in this work, Meng Lijun is the master of speech—as she calls herself, the "three-inch unrottable tongue" *(san cun bu lan zhi she).*

Her ambition to be involved in governing and teaching starts when she is young. As a girl, she dislikes doing embroidery and other needlework, traditional womanly things. Yet her ability in studying and writing surpasses her older brother. Under normal circumstances, she would have followed the path for all women—to marry and bear children. Her opportunity comes when the emperor forces her to give up Huangfu Shaohua and marry Liu Kuibi. She escapes, with the excuse that a good woman does not marry twice. She is not really interested in the traditional role of a chaste woman. When she first plans to escape, she still thinks of avenging her fiancé and his family once she has gained power as a transvestite. The moment she dons a man's robe, however, she thinks of having a wife like her role models Xie Xiang'e and Liu Qingyun. Xie is a character from *Destiny of the Jade Bracelet* and Liu from another *tan ci, The Small Golden Coin (Xiao jin qian).* Both characters disguise themselves as men, become *nu zhuangyuan* (the female champion scholar at the highest imperial examinations), and have beautiful women as their wives. Thinking of the glory in becoming a man and husband, Meng Lijun becomes playful:

> Since I have the beauty that is comparable [to Xie and Liu],
> Why not imitate these ancient heroines when I achieve success?
> If I marry a woman and become her husband,
> My skill to paint her eyebrows will be supreme.

(142)

A traditional woman of chastity is not likely to think or plan like this. She may disguise herself as a man in order to seek help from men to rescue her wronged father or brother, like Wei Yong'e and Liu Yanyu in *Destiny of the Next Life,* but she always resumes her original identity and duties as a woman, like the legendary heroine Hua Mulan. Even the two role models Meng Lijun wants to imitate finally resume their original identities and get married to men. So keeping chaste for her fiancé is just an excuse or, rather, a weapon that Meng Lijun has converted from the patriarchal system to fight against the system. In the name of chastity, she disobeys her parents and the emperor, runs away from the marriage, and gains her freedom by stealing a male identity.

The first thing she does, after she leaves her home, is to change her name from Meng Lijun to Li Junyu, with a style name *(hao)* as Li Mingtang.[8] Thus she discarded her *xing* (father's name) and inverted her *ming* (given name) to the position of a family name, which always comes first. As I discussed in an earlier chapter, naming is not just a personal, private matter but carries social and political meanings.[9] If Meng Lijun had followed the path of the traditional women, she would have been "named" throughout her life: named by the father, by the husband, then by her sons. By discarding her family (or father's) name, she discards her former identity and duty as a woman, a daughter, and a wife-to-be and child bearer. She turns her personal name into a surname, an act that symbolizes her thorough break with her father and the beginning of her freedom as a new person. By turning from being named into naming, she reverses the order of the patriarchal system. Her style name, Li Mingtang, embodies her great dream to lead the country in order and harmony. As Wu Qingyun points out, the name "sparks a historical association with the female emperor Wu Zetian" (1995, 56). When she took the throne in 690, she pulled down the hall of the previous emperor and built Mingtang as her inauguration hall and political center. On top of the hall, she had a sculpture of a golden phoenix flying above nine dragons. The symbolic meaning of a reversed order of the system—yin leads yang instead of yang leading yin—is self-evident. And Mingtang—hall of light or hall of brightness—indicates that this reversed order doesn't have to cause chaos to the system as men have feared. Instead, it will bring harmony, peace, and happiness to society.

Indeed, like the female emperor Wu Zetian, Li Mingtang rules with great wisdom and justice. Her talents to govern and teach surpass the most talented men, including her own father and brother, her fiancé and father-in-law. During her ten days of sick leave, the court is paralyzed. The male ministers (her father and father-in-law) and officials cannot make one single decision and leave all the problems to the emperor. Even the emperor is at the end of his wits in front of the stacks of files and wishes that Li Mingtang would return to run the state soon. Her integrity, uprightness, and justice set a new model for the whole system governed by men, including the emperor. He is liberal, young, and full of the energy of a new dynasty (the successor of the founding emperor of Yuan). Yet like all emperors, he quickly sinks into the luxuries of sex, food, music, and other things, leaving state affairs to Li Mingtang entirely. Soon he becomes a shadow emperor. It is his prime minister Mingtang who gives suggestions, makes decisions, and runs the state. Although she is not an emperor, she is the ruler.

In fact, nearly every woman in *Destiny of the Next Life*, although a subordinate in the family, has quietly or openly usurped the male position and is actually making decisions. They have all, in various degrees, inverted the relationship between men and women. In the Meng family, the father is known to be a henpecked husband. His wife rules in the domain of the inner chamber, and in court she is more daring, outspoken, and aggressive than any man. When the emperor summons her to the palace to confirm the identity of her daughter, she says that the girl Xiang Nanjin, who comes forward during the national search for the real Meng Lijun, is not in fact Meng Lijun, even though her husband and son, having succumbed to the emperor's pressure and the impersonator's sweet tongue, have admitted Xiang Nanjin as their daughter and sister. Only Meng's mother dares to stand up to the emperor. In front of all the male officials, she points to the prime minister, announcing confidently that she is her daughter, Meng Lijun. In front of the emperor and other men, she reprimands Mingtang (Meng Lijun) for abandoning her own parents in order to keep the government position. Even the emperor's anger cannot suppress her voice. The emperor has no choice but to punish the husband instead, suspending his salary for half a year for being unable to control his wife.

The Huangfu family is run by the wife, Yi Liangzhen, the would-be-mother-in-law of Meng Lijun. After many failures to reveal Li Mingtang's former identity, both father and son give up, frightened by the angry prime minister and the emperor. Huangfu Shaohua is bedridden with grief, the usual retreat for a helpless woman. Only Yi Liangzhen dares to disobey the emperor's order and goes to the court to seek help from her empress daughter. With the dowager's help, the empress forces the emperor to agree with her plan of intoxicating Li Mingtang with wine and taking off her boots to testify to her identity.

The Liu family seems to be a traditional family dominated by men. The father, Liu Jie, lives in the capital with his beautiful young concubines, and his old wife lives with her child and the child of her husband's concubine in Yunnan, far away from the capital. Yet it is exactly because he is far away that she is able to establish her own household and exercise power behind her husband's back. She covers for her son after he fails in his attempt to murder Huangfu Shaohua, convinces her husband to plot against the Huangfu family and obtain an imperial order to force Meng Lijun to marry her son. When her stepdaughter runs away from the arranged marriage, she simply replaces her with her niece and reports to her husband that his daughter married the man she had been engaged to and everything is fine. The husband does not know anything about his son's murder or his daughter's escape until he is put in jail. Only then does it dawn on him that his old wife has manipulated him into his own downfall. But it is too late. His regret cannot save him or his clan from an eminent execution.

Finally, there is the emperor, the heavenly prince, the dragon that soars above all the living. But even he can't have everything his way, because of his wife and mother. He hides his passion for his prime minister from the empress. When she finally finds out from her mother's mouth what has been going on in court, she immediately sees through her husband's motives. To protect her own throne and her clan's interest, she is ready to confront him and put up a good fight. The emperor, however, avoids his angry wife, pretending that he is too busy with state affairs while he actually spends his time with his favorite concubine. But his wife outsmarts him by going to his mother and asking her for help. She knows that her emperor husband cannot dodge his mother as he avoids her. Thus she is able to corner him and force him to cooperate with her in her plan to reveal Li Mingtang. She is so determined that she is ready to confront the emperor in court, as she tells the dowager what she might do if she is left with no other choice:

> Why not take over the big golden hall,
> Toll the bell and beat the drum,
> To summon civil and military officials.
> We'll talk about the justice and morality,
> And discuss the emperor's behavior.
> We'll arrest Mingtang and bring him to the court.
> We'll take off his boots and see if he is man or woman on the spot.
> If he is a woman indeed,
> We'll grant her to my brother and finish the business.
>
> (865)

Even though she means it only as a strategy to coerce the dowager to her side, the thought of it is already bold and shocking.

The daughters are even more strong-willed and daring than the mothers. At age sixteen, Meng Lijun runs away from an unwanted marriage, escaping from the inner chamber, from being a daughter and a woman. She enters the men's world disguised as a man and becomes their leader within two years. She breaks all the rules and obligations for women. She abandons her parents and refuses to be united with them. She refuses to be married to Huangfu Shaohua. She resists the emperor's constant advances and rejects his offer of becoming a royal concubine. She defies every obligation the patriarchal system has placed on women: daughter, wife, mother, and sexual object. She turns the yin-yang principle upside-down, proving herself far superior to men at every level.

Other strong daughters are Huangfu Zhanghua (Huangfu Shaohua's twin sister) and the transvestite Wei Yong'e. Together they lead an army of young girls, wipe out the Korean invaders who had been repeatedly defeating the Chinese male army, and rescue their fathers from Korean prison. Even the traditional types like Su Yingxue (Meng Lijun's companion and later her wife under the name of Liang Suhua) and Liu Yanyu show great strength and determination when the occasion comes. Both act boldly when they see their loved one. Su Yingxue engages herself to Huangfu Shaohua in her dream, the man she had only glimpsed from far away. And for this dream love (Shaohua doesn't even know about her feelings until much later), she resists the marriage appointed by the emperor, resists the opportunity of becoming a princess, and tries to assassinate Liu Kuibi at the wedding. When the attempt fails, she throws herself into the river without hesitation.

Liu Yanyu is a shy, obedient princess. But when she receives a message in her dream that she should rescue Huangfu Shaohua, who will become her future husband, she does not hesitate to visit him at midnight, an act equivalent to elopement in old China, and engages herself to him as his concubine. When her stepmother engages her to another man as a gift, she runs away before the wedding and hides in a nunnery. For two years, the princess lives without hope or financial means, earning a meager living by washing, cooking, and making clothes for nuns. What sustains her is her love for Huangfu Shaohua. For love, she turns herself from a princess into a maid and refugee without complaint.

In addition, the four daughters are saviors of their fathers or fiancés. Meng Lijun saves Huangfu Shaohua and his family from total elimination. Wei Yong'e and Huangfu Zhanghua rescue their fathers out of the Korean prison. And Liu Yanyu comes out of hiding in a nunnery when she hears that her family is about to be executed and rushes to the capital to save her parents. She manages to have her whole clan, except for her brother, pardoned by the emperor with the help of her husband's family. On top of all this, these teenage girls actually save their country. The Koreans had been attacking China aggressively. They defeated all the Chinese armies, killing or capturing their commanders. They were threatening to overthrow the Yuan dynasty. It is Meng Lijun who finds the right people to fight the

Koreans, and it is Wei Yong'e and Huangfu Zhanghua who actually defeat the invaders, although they were under the male commander Huangfu Shaohua.

In general, the women in Chen Duansheng's *Destiny of the Next Life* are articulate, determined, and driven. They are emotional but not sentimental, rational but not dogmatic. They never hesitate to lie (especially to men) if needed, yet they are far more upright and just than corrupt men. They put up great fights for their families and themselves and are willing to confront the emperor and disobey his orders at the risk of their lives. They are confined to their inner chambers by their names as daughters, mothers, wives, maids, concubines, yet they find different means by way of their wisdom and language skills to break the boundaries. Under Chen Duansheng's brush, even the maids are much livelier, bolder, and more articulate than men, and all the women are great masqueraders, taking control of their own lives, quietly inverting the relations and orders in the prevailing system.

Many male authors have written books about the reversed roles and relationships between men and women, creating female characters who excel in poetry, painting, scholarship, even the martial arts. The most famous one is perhaps Li Ruzhen's (1763–1830) *Destiny of the Flowers in the Mirror,* a novel centered on women. Set in the reign of the woman emperor Wu Zetian, the book depicts the protagonist Tang Ao's mission to rescue twelve flowers (women) from their exiles in different countries and bring them back to China. These girls, together with eighty-eight other girls, will participate in the imperial examinations especially organized for women by Wu Zetian's decree. His daughter, Tang Xiaoshan, an incarnation of a flower fairy, is banished to earth together with the ninety-nine flowers under her charge because Wu Zetian has once ordered them to bloom in winter and they could not disobey her. Tang Xiaoshan's earthly mission is to lead these women to win all the titles in the imperial exams, demonstrating sisterhood and female superiority.

Unlike Chen Duansheng's women, who are beautiful as well as talented, the women in *Flowers in the Mirror* do not care about appearance or ornament. Some are dressed as hunters or fisherwomen. Some are plain or ugly by convention, like the black-teethed Honghong and Tingting. But according to the author, their intelligence and knowledge make them more beautiful than any ornamented women. All the girls in *Flowers in the Mirror* abandon their needlework and engage in learning, debating, fighting, and traveling—conventional male activities. And they punish men like avenging angels, giving them back exactly what they have gone through because of men. When the merchant Lin Zhiyang is chosen to be a "concubine" for the "king" of the Country of Women, he has to undergo footbinding. The bloody and gruesome description of the binding process is meant to arouse sympathy for women's sufferings:

> [A] black-bearded fellow came in with a bolt of white silk. Kneeling down before him, the fellow said, "I am ordered to bind Your Highness's feet."
>
> Two other maids seized Lin's feet as the black-bearded one sat down on a low stool, and began to rip the silk into ribbons. Seizing Lin's right foot, he set it upon his knee, and sprinkled white alum powder between the toes and grooves of the foot. He squeezed the toes tightly together, bent them down so that the whole foot was shaped like an arch, and took a length of white silk and bound it tightly around it twice. . . .
>
> Merchant Lin felt as though his feet were burning, and wave after wave of pain rose to his heart. When he could stand it no longer, he let out his voice and began to cry. (Lin Tai-Yi 1965, 110–11)

The pain is so unbearable that he tears off the bandages to release his feet when the palace attendant in charge of watching him falls asleep. He is flogged severely as a punishment until blood comes and he is forced to promise never to take off the bandages again. From that time on, he is guarded day and night so that he cannot release himself. Unable to bear the life of endless agony, Lin asks for death, but his request is denied. Soon, the flesh on his toes decays, and his legs gradually wither. Within a fortnight, his feet deteriorate into two stumps, and he loses the ability to walk on his own, hobbling about with the support of two attendants.

A true revenge story, but it is no more than a group of women imitating men's violence and cruelty. Even that is done in a segregated place—the Country of Women. In fact, all their activities are limited to a segregated female world. The imperial examinations are especially designed for women. They go to their own banquets, play their own games, talk and debate among themselves. Their only liaison to the male world is their rescuer, Tang Ao, who soon retires into the Taoist Mountain, Little Penglai. Their scarce interaction with men and the world means that these women, no matter how talented they are, have little social meaning or significance except to display their knowledge or talents. Of a hundred talented women, none of them governs or teaches as a man's equal. Except for the four girls from the Country of Women who later return to their native place to govern, all of them either get married or return to their parental homes after they pass every level of the imperial exams. And their leader, Tang Xiaoshan (she changes her name to Tang Guichen, which has the same sound as the characters meaning "a returning or returned subject") resumes her quest for her father and becomes an immortal at Xiao Penglai. Nothing is changed after all the demonstrations, and nothing reversed after all the struggle and violence.

Compared to these male authors, Chen Duansheng has a much more ambitious plan—to invert the hierarchical order from its very foundation and create a world of justice, order, and harmony. She doesn't want a mere continuation of a man's story with the same violence, corruption, and incompetence. *Destiny of the Next Life* is not a simple, vulgar revenge tale, a story of eye-for-an-eye, blood-for-blood violence, but a true revolutionary manifesto, a monument of feminist utopian literature, in which women become the center, with Meng Lijun/Li Junyu as their head and ideal model. She is a beauty with the most enchanting face and the smallest bound feet, a talented poet and painter, an excellent prime minister, teacher, and doctor. But first and above all, she is a master of speech, an excellent masquerader, an inverter whose sex and identity are ambiguous, volatile, unable to be written or inscribed either by desire or signification. Out of this ambiguity, however, comes the hope and possibility for a new sex, new language, and new order.

The Fabric of Masquerade

"Your Majesty, Li Mingtang has married my daughter and lived with my family for a long time. If he were a woman, how could he not have showed any feminine trace? Not to mention that he championed the three examinations, was in charge of the military department, then became the prime minister. He handles affairs both in the country and abroad, keeping a balance between yin and yang. Nobody in this court can match his talents. How could he be a woman?"

—Chen Duansheng, *Destiny of the Next Life*

Transvestism . . . is probably the best metaphor for what writing really is.

—Severo Sarduy, "Writing/Transvestism"

THIS CHAPTER EXAMINES the two basic groups of masqueraders in *Destiny of the Next Life*. One is represented by the transvestite Meng Lijun/Li Mingtang, who disguises herself as a man and fulfills her dreams as a scholar, teacher, and administrator.[1] The other type is represented by Liu Yanyu, who, deploying femininity as a masquerade, creates a space where she builds a foothold for herself in an environment that is otherwise impossible for women. These female characters use footbinding to fabricate a dazzling mask of femininity. When they cover their lotus feet with another mask, boots, they transform themselves into transvestites. Through their hands and mouths, footbinding becomes a female language, a woman's tale, a masque. Its dazzling and shifting image and language have the power to name and metamorphose, to destroy and reconstruct. And the stage of the masquerade becomes the best metaphor for the stage of the Symbolic, where writing is blurred into speaking and performing, and all the opposites are melted into a universal conglomeration. On this stage, a troop of female masqueraders, veneered and shielded with beautiful images and eloquent sophistry, not only manage to find a place for themselves in the patriarchal system, but also to usurp its language and use it to mimic its ways, mock its values, and dismantle its structures. No longer sacrificing themselves for men, no longer waiting or pining away with endless patience and agony, they use their beauty, talents, virtue, and language skills as masks to enter the world that is forbidden to them, the world of personal dream and political ambition, of self-fulfillment and freedom.

Suspended between man and woman, real and fake, reality and fantasy, origin and simulacrum, they belong to the space of either and neither—androgyny, a space of desire and fear. They bring out the worst anxiety for men: if femininity can be performed and constructed as a masquerade, what about masculinity? They turn men's worst fears into reality: the written is replaced by speech, which can slip so easily into sophistry, and the real is quietly replaced by reproduction and simulacrum. A drama centered on a pair of lotus feet hidden, covered, and masked by a pair of men's boots, *Destiny of the Next Life* enacts a triumph of masquerade, blending classes and genders, high and low, male and female, written and oral, yin and yang. It is not an accident that Chen Duansheng chooses a transvestite as her heroine. Nor is it a coincidence that the tiny-footed prime minister in boots becomes a household name. Chen's masquerade story leads us into the world of footbinding, writing and speech, and the myth around the real and original.

Masquerading as a man gives Meng Lijun the total freedom to move from the inner chamber to the outside world, from one gender to another, and all the way up to the top of the class hierarchy as an examiner, teacher, and prime minister. The effect of such mobility between bodies, genders, and states of being is titillating and threatening, both on a social and individual level. For the individual, masquerade bridges the gap between fantasy and reality, magic and secularity, taboo and order. The magic moment of going beyond the body of the self to enter the other, of blending the two into one, is realized when Meng Lijun puts on a cap, a pair of boots, and a plain robe. She does not try to change her face by wearing a mustache or wig. She does not even take away her makeup. But simply a man's attire is enough to do the trick. In front of the mirror, Meng Lijun watches her own metamorphosis in awe:

> How strange!
> Once in men's clothing, my look completely changed.
> The scholar's cap and robe double my elegance,
> And who could say I'm not an immortal.

(142)

The change of image (the physical body) is followed by a change of mind—attitude and ambition. The moment she puts on the boots, she begins to think of entering the official exams and becoming the champion. Soon she envisions herself marrying a beautiful woman and boasts of her skills as a husband to please a wife.

This transformation goes beyond the individual, beyond the body. As Terry Castle points out, "When the human body escaped its own boundaries, and disobeyed the laws of metaphysics by becoming its own opposite, the body politic, the civil body, was also affected" (1986, 77). Meng Lijun's transvestite masquerade threatens the very foundation of the patriarchal feudal system, which is based on hierarchy, the order of names and things. It is represented by the code of *san gang wu chang*—the three cardinal guides (ruler guides subject, father guides son, and husband guides wife) and the five constant virtues (benevolence, righteousness, propriety, wisdom, and fidelity). In male costume, she no longer needs to submit to the roles of daughter, wife, mother, or concubine. Her father and brother become her subordinates, her husband becomes her student. With the single gesture of masquerade, the boundaries of sex, gender, and class are blurred and crossed, and the logic of ideological polarities as well as categorical opposites, around which the culture is organized, totally collapses. It is no surprise that Chinese imperial law gives the death penalty—often the highest degree, beheading, displaying the corpse to the public, even *ling chi*—to those found guilty of the crime of transvestism, because it disturbs and upsets the order of yin and yang.[2] Meng Lijun constantly cites this law to convince herself and her family to keep the secret of her former identity. When her secret is finally revealed (her boots pulled off and her bound feet exposed), the emperor pays Meng Lijun a private visit. He threatens to behead her unless she agrees to become his concubine:

> Ah, Prime Minister Li, you've made such a big fool of me, the Sovereign!
> . . . .
> How dare you fake your woman's body as a man?
> You mocked your teacher by marrying his daughter.
> You sneaked into the palace to deceive the Majesty.
> You turned yin yang around and became a prime minister. . . .
> If I, the Sovereign, followed the law of Xiao He,
> I am afraid that you wouldn't be able to keep your body whole. . . .
> You could be beheaded and your head hung on the market,
> And your body instantly cut into pieces.

> (964)

It is a heavy price to pay, but the thrill makes it irresistible. The success that Meng Lijun has achieved as a transvestite is impossible for any woman in late imperial China. Even men cannot compete with her. As she looks back at her transvestite career, she summarizes:

> I left my old home in men's clothes,
> Came out of three examinations as a champion, and became an official.
> Soon I was promoted as the head of the military department,
> Then became the prime minister.
> My father and I meet in court but cannot recognize each other,
> My brother, face to face with me every day, is afraid to say anything.
> I treat my father-in-law as my colleague,
> My husband bows to me the way a student bows to his teacher and father.
> I have thousands of students, civil and military officials,
> All regard me with utter respect and awe. . . .
> Hearing my name, aggressive barbarians are scared out of their wits,
> And civilians all smile with happiness when they see my face.
> My reputation is so vast and high that no one can compete,
> Even the heavenly son is awe-inspired by my prestige.
>
> (954)

The other female characters in *Destiny of the Next Life* appear to belong to the feminine tradition: beautiful, frail, obedient, gentle, and virtuous. They wear their femininity, however, as a mask, which is more subtle and in many ways more deceiving than the mask of transvestism. When the occasion arrives, when it comes to defending their own rights and interests, they can put up a good fight, using whatever is available to them as weapons and shields—beauty, virtue, lies, charm, knives, even their own lives. Su Yingxue and Liu Yanyu are good examples of such masqueraders.

Su Yingxue, daughter of Meng Lijun's wet nurse, grew up with Meng Lijun as her playmate and maid. She is gentle, humble, and quiet, and of course, very obedient. Yet she is bold enough not only to fall in love with her mistress's fiancé at first glance but also to engage herself to him as his concubine in her dreams. When her mistress assigns her to marry Liu Kuibi as her substitute, she obeys under the pressure of her mother and her mistress's parents but is determined to assassinate her enemy and keep her chastity for her lover, who doesn't even know of her existence. At the wedding, she pulls out a knife, stabs the bridegroom, then throws herself out the window into the river. These are not the deeds of an obedient woman, but the deeds of a heroine, who deserves an arch built for her, a royal honor.

She does get an honorable title from the emperor, though under the name of her mistress. And she gets even more. She is rescued and adopted by an ex-examiner, then becomes the prime minister's wife. Her acts should not be regarded as a simple sacrifice for the sake of love. Yes, there is love involved. She refuses to marry the empress's brother because she is in love with Huangfu Shaohua, but also because she foresees the inevitable downfall of the Liu family. She is also aware of the fate of being someone's substitute. Once she agrees to become Meng Lijun's simulacrum, her own life as Su Yingxue is over. And once the lie is exposed and the truth revealed, even that shadow life will be over, and she will end in disgrace. So she chooses to die and dies dramatically. Her spectacular death earns her great honor (under the name/masquerade of Meng Lijun) and earns her a new life (another masquerade) as the daughter of Examiner Liang. Her sacrifice has paved her path from a maid to the wife of the prime minister. Her multiple masquerades have given her great personal freedom and class promotion.

Liu Yanyu is a resilient fighter under her mask of femininity. Though growing up as the empress's half-sister, a princess of the royal family, she is in fact an orphan. Her mother, who married her father as a concubine, passed away. Her father lives in the capital with his other concubines. She lives with her surrogate mother, her father's first wife, in a remote province, and is totally neglected. The only person she can talk to and rely on is her wet nurse and maid, Jiangma. She knows her strength is not in her looks or in her talents for poetry or painting, but in her patience and great skill at smooth talking. She knows that her only way out is through a good marriage, and since her surrogate mother will never put out any effort in this matter, she has to act on her own. When she learns about her half-brother's scheme of murdering Huangfu Shaohua, she seizes the opportunity and pays Huangfu a private visit at midnight. She reveals her brother's plot and manages to get his promise to marry her in the future. A genius with words, she, his murderer's sister, wins the trust of someone who is about to be burned to death by her brother—all of this done in a short period of time (probably no more than thirty minutes). When her guardian promises her to one of her relatives as a present, she runs away with her wet nurse to a nunnery and works as a maid for the nuns to support herself. Her patience and endurance help her through two years of hardship. The final blow comes when her father and half-brother's scheme is exposed and the whole clan is locked up in prison, awaiting execution. The humble, fragile daughter stands up for her father. She rushes to the capital and writes a letter to her fiancé. She describes how she suffered to preserve her chastity for his sake. Now that he is so merciless toward her family, she has no choice but to die in place of her parents so that they can be spared being beheaded. At the same time, she returns him his fan and demands her handkerchief back, keepsakes from their engagement three years before. Touched by her fidelity to him and her parents, Huangfu Shaohua petitions the emperor to spare the lives of the Liu clan by having them exiled instead of executed. The letter helps her not only to save her family but also to become Huangfu Shaohua's third wife. In her new home, her skill in talking and comforting eases her awkward and difficult situation (she is the daughter of her husband's enemy, sister of her husband's attempted murderer). Her feminine masquerade wins the trust of her parents-in-law and the respect of her reluctant husband. Soon, she becomes the family diplomat, smoothing conflicts and fights among family members and servants. After her husband writes to the emperor demanding that Li Mingtang is his wife, the relation between them becomes tense. The prime minister refuses to accept his apology. At the end of his wits, he begs his wife Liu Yanyu to pay a visit to his teacher and ask for his forgiveness. Her gentle manner and diplomatic rhetoric of apology win sympathy from the prime minister, who finally agrees to be reconciled with Huangfu Shaohua.

When the two women meet face to face, one representing masculinity, the other femininity, they immediately recognize and acknowledge each other's great capacity for masquerade. What makes it more interesting is their genuine admiration for the authenticity of each other's mask. Liu Yanyu is in awe of the prime minister's golden crown and purple robe, his white skin and red lips, particularly the way he clicks his boots and clears his throat before he enters the room. Li Mingtang, on the other hand, admires her colorful clothing, her fragile waist, and of course, her lotus feet. What really impresses Li Mingtang, however, is Liu Yanyu's smooth speech. Her apology in the name of her husband, passionate with sincerity, humble with dignity, wins Li Mingtang's admiration and respect. She sizes her up and says to herself: "No wonder Zhitian [Huangfu Shaohua] sent her over to persuade me. / This Liu Yanyu is indeed a clever woman" (702). For the word *woman*, she uses a metonymic metaphor *qun chai*—skirt and hairpin. Just as Liu Yanyu sees Li Mingtang's crown, robe, and black boots as the symbol/mask of masculinity, Li Mingtang takes Liu Yanyu's skirt and hairpin for her femininity. Masquerade does not need a complete, inside-out transformation or a total cover-up. A few props—a pair of boots, a hairpin—can do the trick.

Yet the masqueraders do pay a heavy price for their performances. Each has gone through a symbolic death as well as many physical hardships. Meng Lijun's parents cry when they discover her escape, assuming that she will die in poverty, hunger, coldness, and shame. In fact, she is soon trapped in an inn a few days later, her maid badly ill. She would have been in serious trouble if she hadn't been rescued by an old, kind country gentleman and become his adopted son. Su Yinxue is able to create a totally new identity as Liang Suhua only by drowning herself in the river, then being revived by the former examiner and his wife. As for Liu Yanyu, the moment she runs away, her surrogate mother simply erases her existence by covering her disappearance in the family and sending a relative's daughter to marry the man Liu Yanyu is supposed to marry. Liu Yanyu's father doesn't even know of her escape until she appears in the capital and saves the family from execution. Her two years in the nunnery are marked by the total erasure of her former identity and the slow consumption of her physical being. When she leaves the nunnery, she is no longer pretty. The washing and mending in the heat and cold have coarsened her skin and enlarged her lotus feet, and malnutrition has made her skinny and weak.

They suffer and endure many ordeals. Unlike the traditional *jiaren*— beautiful women—recorded in history and represented in literature, whose pain and death become the object of fetishistic consumption, women in the *Destiny of the Next Life* are able to erase their old selves, then reconstruct new identities, new genders, new masks. They rise above their ordeals and are resurrected from their symbolic deaths. Once out of her parents' house, Meng Lijun is no longer a daughter or a high-priced bride. She turns herself into a sex that is a combination of masculine and feminine— a woman in boots, a man with golden lotuses—renaming herself as Li Junyu/Li Mingtang. After Su Yinxue survives the suicide, she is no longer a maid or a substitute of her mistress, but an examiner's daughter and the prime minister's wife. And Liu Yanyu leaves her father's home as the humble, insignificant daughter of a dead concubine and returns to her father as the family savior, a heroic daughter, and a duke's wife.

What the masqueraders in this scenario have revealed is both terrifying and titillating: gender, identity, sexuality, and class have little to do with origin, blood, inheritance, but can be stripped, erased, and rebuilt at one's will. In other words, a person's gender and identity are no longer the work of nature or the divine, but that of culture, the efforts of each individual. And not only femininity but also masculinity can be constructed through masquerade, through language and performance. If genuine womanliness and the masquerade are indeed the "same thing," as stated by Joan Riviere in her essay "Womanliness as a Masquerade" (1989), the theory can be also applied to manliness and its mask. One can slip in and out of these man-made artifices like stage props. Through effort and endurance, one can create a new set of masks, which then lead to further transformation. The merging of self and other, the combining of opposites, and the dream of metamorphosis are no longer merely magic but become a reality.

As the leader of the masquerade troop, Li Mingtang stages a full performance of self-concealment and self-representation by pushing the masquerade to excess. She uses substitutes and simulacra of herself to hold and flaunt the male gaze, making a mockery of masculinity, patriarchy, and the binary system on which civilization has been founded. Households and the royal court become the testing grounds where her gender and sex are constantly questioned and challenged. At the same time, they are a stage for her great performance, a place to see and be seen, to display and be displayed, to represent and be represented.

The masquerade theater is formed out of two major elements: image and language. First is image. To masquerade is to seduce and deceive, to fortify and gratify. It is "the masquerader's duty to be beautiful or uncanny" (Castle 1986, 75). Either as a woman or man, Meng Lijun/Li Mingtang is the symbol of ultimate beauty. No one can compete with her/him. All the beautiful girls and handsome men become pale in front of her/him. Her most celebrated body parts are her face and feet. The stunning, breathtaking face, open to the public, has multiplied itself into numerous substitutes and simulacra. The feet, wrapped in layers of bandages and hidden in boots, become the center of the drama, the final point of the gaze, the key to all the mysteries.

The first simulacrum Li Mingtang leaves behind is the self-portrait she draws before her escape from her home. For Chinese readers, this act itself immediately resonates with the famous self-portrait of Du Liniang from Tang Xianzu's *The Peony Pavilion (Mudan Ting)*, written in 1598 and one of the most influential plays in the history of Chinese drama. The portrait Du Liniang draws before she dies makes it possible for her dream lover (the man she saw in her dream, fell in love with, and died for) to discover and retrieve her from the netherworld. Meng Lijun draws the portrait for her parents to ease the pain of her disappearance, as she tells them in her letter:

> No one knows what will happen to me during the journey.
> I now leave my little shadow to accompany my parents morning and dusk.
> Please take care of yourselves and do not weep for me,
> Seeing the portrait is as good as seeing Lijun.
>
> (138)

It is a difficult, almost impossible, task to paint the "true appearance"— *zhen rong*—of oneself. Every time Meng Lijun looks at herself in the mirror, she is so startled by her own beauty that she has to question her maid to confirm that this is really she. The first portrait fails because it is not nearly as beautiful as the original, the *zhen rong*. The second comes out well, but as soon as Meng Lijun sees the lovely face on paper, she weeps for her own fate and her tears destroy the work. She has to wait for the next day to start painting all over again. When it is done, she hangs the picture and looks at herself:

> Face of peony sparkling with dewdrops,
> Eyebrows of willow leaves tremble in spring breeze.
> Rouge of plum and shadow of rose,
> Her cherry mouth and pearl teeth embrace silent words.
> Almond eyes at gaze ripple with autumn water,
> Tender pink on her snow-white cheeks.
>
> (135)

As she gazes at the painting, she sighs with admiration at the figure on the wall. "I've seen hundreds of beauties in my life / None of them can match the one on paper" (135). Once again, she calls her maid to confirm that the portrait resembles the real person, that it is not overdone. And the maid assures her that the portrait is perfect, that it resembles the "true appearance" exactly.

Yet Meng Lijun still refers to this portrait as "little shadow" or "fragments of shadow" in her departure letter to her parents. The figure on paper is like the skin a snake sheds after it outgrows its own body. The shell left behind among the grass is real, but real only in the manner of a ghost. The shedding is a painful and alienating process. Each stroke, each line of the portrait, is accompanied by tears, as if Meng Lijun were mourning the death of her old self and the alienation she feels while seeing herself in the mirror and on paper were too shocking. When Meng Lijun goes off to live a life as a totally new person, the self-portrait—her cast masque, the empty shell, fragments of shadow—continues living as old Miss Meng Lijun, a substitute, a simulation of the original.

Whoever sees the portrait is always shocked. Their first reaction is disbelief: such an ideal of feminine beauty is impossible in real life; if the painter didn't exaggerate herself, how much more beautiful can the original be? The second response is recognition: the girl in the portrait looks exactly like the Prime Minister Li Mingtang. Then comes the speculation: if the original looks so astoundingly breathtaking in boots, she will look even more beautiful in lotus shoes. The speculation is followed by a fiery desire and obsession to see and possess the original. When Huangfu Shaohua sees the portrait, he demands it, claiming that he, Meng Lijun's husband, is more entitled to keep it than the mother. He hangs it in the chamber that he has been keeping for Meng Lijun as his first wife, burns some incense, and gazes at the picture from different angles all night long until his desire fires and "his spirit and soul float out of his body" (471). During countless tormented days and nights, he talks to her, gazes at her, and begs her to come out of her disguise, as if the portrait were alive. He even takes the painting to bed during his sleep. He tricks Li Mingtang into viewing the portrait, to show her how he has been keeping his chastity for her, hoping that his sincerity and loyalty as well as his illness will touch her. But all his worshiping, praying, begging, and demanding can't bring his wife back. Instead, she mocks him, advising him to get as many concubines as possible, and threatens to punish him when he tries to force her to reveal her identity.

The beauty even shocks the emperor. Before he sees the portrait, he promises Huangfu Shaohua that if the prime minister is Meng Lijun, he will not only pardon her crime of upsetting the yin-yang principle, but also will make sure that she marries Huangfu Shaohua. As soon as the scroll opens, revealing the "peach face" and "lotus shoes," the smiling emperor jumps off his throne and stands in front of the painting in shock. Meng Lijun's beauty is beyond words. Even goddesses cannot compete with her. The emperor forgets that Huangfu Shaohua is waiting for his response. He gazes at the "shadow" of the portrait, "his heart shakes, his spirit stampedes, and his soul flies away" (672). Like Huangfu Shaohua, he also becomes obsessed with the prime minister and tries all kinds of schemes to lure her into his bed.

The second simulacrum Li Mingtang creates is Su Yingxue. As her playmate and maid, Su has been a symbolic shadow of her mistress. During the shooting contest between bridegroom candidates in the beginning of the play, Su Yingxue stands on the balcony to watch and is mistaken for Meng Lijun by one of the suitors, Liu Kuibi, who falls in love with her at first glance. He is so obsessed with the shadow, the simulacrum of Meng Lijun, that he plunges himself into the abyss of desire, bringing his whole clan down with him. In a sense, the entire play is about this obsession with the shadow, the substitute, the simulacrum. He dies without knowing that he has never set eyes on the real Meng Lijun. When Meng runs away from home, she instructs her parents to adopt Su Yingxue as their daughter so that they can marry her to Liu Kuibi as her substitute. Thus Su is doubly masked, substituting both as a daughter and bride for Meng Lijun.

The most interesting simulacra are perhaps the two girls who answer the call of the national search for Meng Lijun and travel to the capital to claim Meng's identity and her title as the first wife of Huangfu Shaohua. The first arrival is Piao Luyun from Wu Chang County, Huguang Province (now Hubei). Orphaned as a child, she lives with her adopted brother and works as the family maid. She seizes the opportunity to masquerade as Meng Lijun as a way out of her unhappy situation. She knows nothing about Meng Lijun, nor does she resemble her. But she has beauty and that alone, according to her adopted brother, is enough for the masquerade. She almost succeeds. Her beauty and her talent for poetry, her sweet talking and her tears win the sympathy of the emperor, who urges Huangfu Shaohua and Meng's father to acknowledge the simulacrum as the real. Though Mr. Meng knows that the girl is not his daughter, he is so touched by her pleading and her pitiful (that is, lovable) look that he actually considers claiming her as his daughter. Huangfu Shaohua, however, rejects her, mostly because she has degraded herself by living with a grocery owner for three years. If he married this girl, then the low merchant would become his brother-in-law. And that would be unacceptable to him.

The second girl, Xiang Nanjin, is a much more successful masquerader. She resembles Meng Lijun in appearance and learns all the private details of Meng Lijun and her family from their former maid. Her best weapon, however, is her ability to talk and make up stories according to her circumstances. She has Meng Lijun's quick wit and sharp tongue. The process of simulation has started before Xiang Nanjin travels to the capital. After her maid tells her Meng Lijun's story, she sheds tears for her talent and ambition and begins to imitate Meng's fashion and manner and recite her poems from time to time. She adopts her father's plan to masquerade as Meng Lijun but feels guilty, knowing that her own talent and looks can't possibly match the original. Still, she prepares herself diligently during the journey, reading history books and practicing poetry for the coming tests. Once inside the palace, face to face with the emperor, Huangfu Shaohua, and Meng Lijun's father and brother, she is transformed into an excellent performer. Determined to get the handsome Huangfu Shaohua and the glamorous title of Duke Piety and Loyalty's first wife, she tells the story of Meng Lijun's engagement, Liu Kuibi's revenge and murder plot, Huangfu Shaohua's exile, and Meng's escape from home, with vivid details and passion, as if she had genuinely gone through each ordeal. Having finished the true story, she makes up the second half, the story of how she wanders in disguise, how she becomes a teacher and how her disguise is discovered by her students when they take off her boots in her drunken sleep. She weeps, sighs, and stops from time to time for dramatic effect, causing the listeners, especially Meng Lijun's father and Huangfu Shaohua, to weep and sigh with her. The real Meng Lijun, Prime Minister Li Mingtang, is totally awed and amused by such a tale of mixed truths and lies. When the masquerader first enters the court, Li Mingtang is already amazed by such a coincidence. "How strange! Doesn't she resemble the picture? Now even I begin to doubt myself. . . . Perhaps she is the real Meng Lijun from Yunnan? . . . Perhaps she is a gift from heaven to be my simulacrum?" (735). When the emperor orders her to point out the father and brother from hundreds of officials in court, the first person she recognizes is Huangfu Shaohua, although she has never met him. The two start to flirt with their eyes. Li Mingtang, so impressed by this cleverness, secretly wishes that she could help her out, as she talks to her substitute and herself quietly in a playful tone:

> Hey, you pretender, if you can recognize my father and brother, I'm willing to hand my Duke Zhongxiao to you. . . . Hey, I, Li Mingtang, wish I could point them out for you. . . .
> So that I can keep my position.
> And you get your wish to marry Huangfu.
>
> (739)[3]

By the time Xiang Nanjin points out the father and brother and once again starts to tell the family secrets with sobs and tears, Li Mingtang begins to wonder if this is a work of magic or the gods:

> I thought I, Li Mingtang, excelled in speech, and have never expected a girl with such a tongue of sword and lips of gun.
> She just opens her mouth and turns lies into truth,
> Gripping with her teeth as if she had all the justice.
>
> (750)

The most attractive image, of course, is the transvestite Li Mingtang. She dazzles and mesmerizes everyone who sees her. Her husband can barely look at him/her for too long because every time he sees the face, his heart and spirit start shaking. He ends up gazing at and sleeping with a portrait. Women are equally mesmerized. Xiang Nanjin is shocked to see a beauty in a purple robe among the officials in court. He wears a black cap decorated with gold and jade. On his purple robe flies a dragon above green waves. A white jade belt circles his waist, and he wears black boots with pink soles. Under the man's attire, however, is a face that the most beautiful women and most handsome men in history cannot match (742). The emperor treats his prime minister like "jewels and treasure." He can never have enough of his/her lovely face. For this face, he is willing to risk his *jiangshan*—rivers and mountains, a symbol for his state—and steal Li Mingtang from his subject, his brother-in-law. He lures Li Mingtang into his garden, planning to spend the night with her. He deliberately shakes a tree to spray dew-drops over Li's face. The effect makes him nearly lose his soul. He writes a poem on the spot to test and flirt with Li Mingtang:

> The admirable *[feng liu]* prime minister wears his hat aslant,
> Dewdrops from the willow tree splash on his face of cloud.
> Today the spring in the royal garden loses its color,
> Only one flower remains to reveal the riddle.

> (717)

Feng liu has three layers of meaning in Chinese: (1) distinguished and ad-mirable; (2) talented in letters and unconventional in lifestyle; (3) dissolute and loose. Li Mingtang represents all three meanings in the eyes of the em-peror and her other admirers. Even the author Chen Duansheng calls Li *feng liu zai xiang* from time to time in her narration. If one looks at *feng liu* separately and literally, an additional layer comes in. *Feng* is wind; *liu* is flow, a movement from place to place; the verb form means to drift and wander, and to go into exile. In the play, the identity and origin of the transvestite Li Mingtang cannot be fixed. They shift and metamorphose from one face to another, one masque to another, and one simulacrum to another, just as the wind and flowing water. The viewer is forever mesmer-ized but can never put his or her finger on it.

The masqueraders' language is as dazzling and shifting as their images. Since their words and stories always oscillate between the real and the fan-tastic, or blend half-truths with half-lies, the listeners can no longer tell which is real and which is not. In the end, all lies become truth and all the fantastic occurrences turn into reality.[4] The masqueraders only need to mask parts of their bodies to pass for the whole. Meng Lijun passes as Li Mingtang with a cap, robe, and pair of boots, keeping her face as it is, which happens to be the most feminine, the most beautiful part. No mat-ter how much her beauty shocks people, they don't question her gender, because of the male attire, until Huangfu Shaohua raises the issue. Similarly, her simulacrum Xiang Nanjin only partially resembles Meng Lijun. But the viewers are so willing to believe her that they keep giving her excuses and accept her attempts to fill in the gaps in her stories. They all as-sume that the self-portrait has exaggerated her own beauty, that three years of exile has somewhat coarsened her look. When she starts talking, her words, her seamless stories and performance make up for the doubt created by her appearance. Language is a powerful weapon for masqueraders. It covers up whatever the image cannot.

Li Mingtang uses this weapon well. She curses, teases, scolds, mocks, threatens, and consoles according to the circumstances. She never hesitates to twist truth or make up stories to build a new identity. When her masquerade is questioned, she puts on a show to silence those who suspect her. She scolds and threatens Huangfu Shaohua as a teacher to scare him away and suppress his suspicion. She quotes the ancient teachings and uses the feudal ethical codes to fend off the emperor's advances. She ignores her parents' pleadings. In order to keep up her masquerade, she makes sure that all her opponents are silenced, and she alone has the narrative. When she realizes that she is surrounded by people who are ready to reveal her old identity, she boasts that she has nothing to fear because she has a three-inch tongue that does not wear out.

Her linguistic gift and freedom come out only after she transforms herself into a transvestite. As Meng Lijun in her father's house, she is silent (here silence also works as a masquerade, which marks her as a good, virtuous girl). In that *prison* (a term she uses over and over again for her parents' and her husband Huangfu Shaohua's homes as well as the emperor's palace), silence is her only weapon. When it can no longer protect her, she escapes. A few pieces of men's clothing turn her into the most eloquent and cunning speaker. Traveling alone with a young maid, her only weapon to defend herself is her smooth talking. After she becomes the prime minister, her tongue, her three-inch unrottable tongue *(san cun bu lan zhi she)*, becomes her most convenient, resilient, and powerful weapon. It helps her get away from her entangling husband and parents and fend off the emperor's pestering. Apart from the three-part male disguise, her entire identity and gender are built and guarded with words. As long as she speaks, nothing and nobody can destroy her masquerade, which is woven seamlessly into her narrative.

Spoken words protect Li Mingtang's transvestite masquerade while writing only brings her trouble. Before she disappears from her parents' home, she also leaves them a poem written at the bottom of the self-portrait. When it falls into Huangfu Shaohua's hands, it is not the portrait but the writing that stirs his suspicion. He argues that people may look exactly alike, but having the same handwriting is quite unlikely. He then concludes that the prime minister is actually a woman, who is his wife Meng Lijun, and he starts the whole drama of revealing the masquerade.

The writing thus becomes an unmasking tool, just as her spoken words maintain Li Mingtang's masquerade. Once she realizes this, she restricts her writing to office use only, signing official documents, marking examination papers, and making comments. In other words, she uses writing only when she functions as a man in the male system. Other than that, she never leaves a trace of her writing anywhere, on any occasion, be it at home, at parties, in private or public. It is spoken words that she depends on totally—for self-defense, self-representation, self-concealment, and counterattacking.

Thus, the court becomes a theater in which Li Mingtang's gender and identity are questioned, tested, and destroyed over and over again, where she sharpens her tongue and plays the game of self-presentation and self-concealment. One of the most exciting and fearful moments occurs when she realizes the serious mistake she has made before she enters the examination hall as the chief examiner. She has just been forced to admit her former identity as Meng Lijun to her mother, who fakes a dying scene in her bed. Though she has made her family promise not to reveal the secret to anyone outside the family, she knows that while she is in seclusion, the news has leaked out and her husband, Huangfu Shaohua, has taken actions to reveal her masquerade to the emperor, using her own parents as witnesses. Since she is not allowed to speak or be spoken to, to see or to be seen during the examination days, she can't do anything to prevent their maneuvering. But she reassures herself that she has nothing to fear as long as she denies everything:

> Since I was born with gifts from heaven,
> I lack no talents or artifice.
> No need to fear my parents' scheme with their son-in-law,
> Or my husband writing a plea to the emperor.
> Let them confront me with their accusation,
> Let us battle face to face at court.
> I have Su Qin's[5] three-inch tongue,
> And I'll convince all the dukes with a single word.
>
> (676)

And so she does. When the emperor shows her the secret memorial from Huangfu Shaohua, she bursts with anger, tearing the memorial into pieces. She denies that she is a woman. Yes, she did say she was Meng Lijun to the Mengs, only because she wanted to save the poor old woman's life—just a doctor's kind deed. Then she turns around and accuses Huangfu Shaohua of playing pranks on his teacher and cheating the emperor with lies. Her denial and accusations make her husband tremble with anger and fear and send her own father into total confusion. The poor father feels dizzy, as if he were in a dream world. The prime minister looks exactly like his daughter Meng Lijun, who has held his wife's hands and called him "father" a few days before. But now, he no longer knows. Pressed by his in-laws to speak up, he turns to the emperor and begs forgiveness for being old and poor-sighted. The battle ends with Li Mingtang's victory. The emperor denies Huangfu Shaohua's plea and orders him to drop the case and show proper respect to his teacher. Anyone who dares to talk about the prime minister as a transvestite will be punished.

The power of speech to twist the mind and perception is such that a father no longer knows his daughter, brother no longer knows his sister, and husband no longer knows his wife. The border between truth and lies, real and fake is blurred and crossed. The two simulacra of Meng Lijun are able to fool people's eyes because they both know that the visual masquerade (face and bound feet) alone is not enough: their success depends on their speech, the linguistic masquerade. Piao Luyun bears no resemblance to Meng Lijun at all. Her skill in writing poetry is helpful; the poem she wrote in court touches everyone's heart. But she only begins to win the battle when she clings to Mr. Meng's sleeve and starts talking to him about her suffering. Her words are so convincing that Meng actually starts considering her as his daughter, even though he knows she is only a substitute. The second simulacrum resembles Meng Lijun in looks *and* language skill. She knows Meng Lijun's history inside out, knows how to act according to circumstances, and she is a great performer. Although her visual masquerade is exposed when Meng Lijun's mother suddenly lifts her skirt to reveal her feet and begins to mock the simulacrum's fat, badly bound feet, she is able to counter the doubt with a quick story. All these make her so real that even the genuine Meng Lijun becomes confused and begins to question her own identity. Huangfu Shaohua gazes at her with much love, already silently calling her his wife. Between the real and unreal, Mr. Meng chooses the latter, who acts more like a daughter than the real one. She is all smiles, clinging to him and calling him "Daddy" in her sweet, singing voice. He convinces himself that the past three years of exile and suffering must have changed a silent, severe girl into a sweetheart. Xiang Nanjin's great masquerade performance has called authenticity and reality into serious question.

Whoever has the image (the visual masquerade that is mostly realized through footbinding) and the narrative (the linguistic masquerade) has the power to name and transform. Liu Yanyu smooth-talks her way up to the position of Lady Jiexiao, the wife of Duke Piety and Loyalty, transforming her harsh, hostile circumstances into a livable environment. Her skill in soothing and diplomatic conversation helps her survive her hostile surrogate mother, the greedy nuns, and the snobbish servants in her husband's house. When her husband offends Li Mingtang, he sends her to apologize in his name and get Li's forgiveness. She has become his diplomat and spokesperson.

Meng Lijun's mother, Han Suxin, is perhaps the most outspoken and boldest of all in the play. At home, she has the final say in all family matters; her husband will not make any decision before talking to her first. When Meng Lijun's second simulacrum Xiang Nanjin appears in court and convinces everyone that she is the real Meng Lijun, Mr. Meng is also persuaded and acknowledges her as his daughter. But although he is mesmerized by her charm, he still dares not take her home without having his wife's confirmation. He would rather bear the emperor's mocking reprimand for being a henpecked husband than make his wife angry. Finally, the emperor gives in and summons Han Suxin to the court. With one look at her face, hands, and feet, she praises the girl mockingly:

> Round, plump wrists and long nails,
> Jade and gold rings on many fingers.
> A spoiled brat, unable to bear pain,
> A pair of high heels to pass for lotuses.
> Big and tall, a face full,
> From which family is this girl?
>
> (752)

The simulator trembles and blushes, knowing that she is face to face with an equal, that she must fight with all her might to win this battle. Between sobs, she starts telling the story again from the very beginning, hoping her narrative will also work miracles on the mother. But the mother is not as willing to be fooled as everyone else in court. She raises one question after another, until her husband, fearing that his wife's stubbornness may anger the emperor, interrupts. He reminds her that this girl has already been approved by the emperor, that she should accept the majesty's gift with graciousness. Li Mingtang also steps out to give another push. The prime minister apologizes for passing herself off as Meng Lijun, causing the real daughter to be rejected. She tells Mrs. Meng to accept the girl as her daughter, to stop taking the fake for the real, the real for the fake. Already annoyed by her husband's interference, Han Suxin gets furious at Li Mingtang's advice. Look at this rascal, she says to herself:

Black cap and purple robe,
Boots clanking and belt tingling.
Where is that girl wearing rouge and powder in her chamber?
She is the country's column sustaining the sun and sky.
So majestic, so glamorous,
Of course, she brushes her parents to the side.
. . . .

Today I'll speak up in the golden palace,
To curse you until you shut your mouth and have nothing to say.

(755)

She turns to the emperor, telling him that the girl is not her daughter but a fake. Then she points to the prime minister, announcing that Li Mingtang is her real daughter. She accuses her of abandoning her parents for fame and official rank. Li Mingtang is forced to make her last move—to take off her cap and robe and resign—until the emperor interferes, persuading his favorite minister to ignore "the dogs' barking and cows' mooing" and put her clothes back on.

Han Suxin is the only one in court who cannot be silenced by the power of the prime minister or the order of the emperor. Although the father is misled by images and words, the mother cannot be fooled. In order to cover up her transvestite masquerade, Li Mingtang has no other choice but to threaten to resign. And the emperor, unable to silence Han Suxin with his order, has to punish the husband for his inability to control his wife and family business, an impotence that reflects his ineptness in state affairs.

Throughout *Destiny of the Next Life,* the most beautiful women and the best story weavers are the best masqueraders: the transvestites Li Mingtang and Wei Yong'e; the persuasive talker Liu Yanyu; the charming simulators Piao Luyun and Xiang Nanjin; the sharp-tongued shrews Han Suxin, Yi Liangzhen (Mrs. Huangfu), the empress dowager, and the woman general Huangfu Zhanghua who later becomes the empress. As long as they talk, whether it is sweet or sharp, true or false, they have absolute control. Their masquerade fails only when they are silenced by force and deceit.

Xiang Nanjin gives a perfect account of Meng Lijun's history before and after her escape from home, except for one small error: she presents a wrong maid. Mrs. Meng breaks her facade by weakening that hole, pointing out if one link rots, the whole chain falls apart. She then takes over the court scene and starts a riot by accusing the prime minister of abandoning her parents. Unable to stop her, the emperor advises Li Mingtang to ignore her words and finally has to throw her out of the palace.

Li Mingtang, armed with eloquence and sophistry, is impenetrable and indecipherable. It is her words against the whole system of patriarchy, against the code of gender, sex, and family (or blood) ties. And her words alone are enough to beat them all, including her own parents, her husband, and the heavenly son. She is defeated only when she loses her speech when she is drugged by her sister-in-law with herbal wine and her boots are taken off, her tiny lotus shoes stripped as evidence—a double castration indeed. When the emperor visits her home, he mocks,

> Ha ha, Mr. Li, where are your severe look and sharp tongue?
> In the royal garden of Heavenly Fragrance,
> Your speech was hard like steel and sharp like a drill.
> I, the Majesty, was terrified of you as if seeing a tiger.
>
> (964)

Speechless and maskless, Li Mingtang can only bow and remain silent. The emperor now has power over all the narrative. He makes up a story for her and orders Li Mingtang to tell it to the public so that he can keep her in his palace as a concubine. He wants her to say that she is not Meng Lijun, has never been engaged to Huangfu Shaohua, but a girl from some rich family who wanted to imitate the ancient female transvestite heroes to fulfill her ambition. He reminds her of how he has saved her from the empress, how he will treasure her above all other royal concubines. If she disobeys him, he threatens, she will be beheaded and her whole clan exiled. Li Mingtang, without her boots or lotus shoes, can only remain silent.

Language has the ambivalent power to create or destroy a masquerade, just like its dual force that initiates its user into the phallic power or leads him to castration. For Li Mingtang, silence means the end of masquerade and the completion of castration. Words, images, and masquerade are so intertwined and dependent on one another that one loss inevitably leads to that of the rest. Her outermost layer is the boots—the symbol of masculinity, power, and written words. When these are taken away, everything else collapses. She can no longer go back to court as a prime minister to conduct state affairs or as a teacher to mark papers, but is ordered to stay home to recover from her "coma" and await the emperor's further instructions. The exposure of the first layer leads to the revelation of the second and third layers of the masquerade. Beneath her thick socks and silk bandages, the maids reveal a pair of red lotus shoes that measure only 2.7 inches. When they take them off, they are shocked to discover a third layer: a pair of bed slippers that measure only 2.6 inches. The royal maids exclaim with genuine admiration: "The number-one bound feet on earth belong to

Prime Minister Li!" (922). On their way to the palace to report the discovery to the empress, the emperor intercepts them and confiscates the red lotus shoes, the emblem of ultimate femininity and the iron proof of Li Mingtang's sex. If stripping the outer mask means the loss of her official position and her access to written words, the loss of her inner mask cuts off the root to her very being—her speech and body. Words, written or oral, are no longer available to her. Instead, she is forced to swallow the emperor's proposal, which is designed to reduce her to a mere sex object. Silence is once again her only means of resistance, as it was when she was a girl. But even that is denied to her. When the emperor demands an immediate answer from her, she bows and asks for immediate death, the highest punishment of a thousand cuts. When she opens her mouth, blood instead of words spurts out and splashes all over the emperor's robe. Once the masks (boots and lotus shoes) are stripped and words are taken away, the body falls apart from the inside.

In the hands of masqueraders, language becomes a game, a glamorous display, and an artful prop for a fantastic performance. For masqueraders, words acquire meaning only through their opposition to each other, not through their link to the original, the substance of things. In fact, they have so little to do with the real that everything they point to is a mere simulacrum, reproduction, representation, and artifice, easily destroyed or substituted. Nothing is sacred, natural, divine, or permanent. Confucius, writing two thousand years ago, was already aware of the void between language and substance, of the alienation between the subject and signification. He called for the *zheng ming*—straightening of names—as a remedy. Everyone has his or her own name and position and must act accordingly. Thus, a prince must act as a prince, a subject as a subject, a father as a father, a son as a son. If names are not straightened or corrected constantly, he warned, speech will not follow its logic, and society will end in total chaos. Confucius's nightmare seems to come true in Chen Duansheng's world of the masquerade. Names, sexes, genders are made up at will. Personal identities and class hierarchies are invented and performed like stories. Families are not necessarily tied by blood (nature), but more often constructed according to personal needs and social circumstances. In the world of masquerade, the categories of male and female, high and low, true and false, reality and fantasy, on which civilization and society are founded, are constantly blurred, crossed, challenged, and violated until the whole system collapses into a language game, a mocking fit of laughter.

The transvestite Li Mingtang, the master of speech and masquerade, is the biggest teaser of all. Outside the feudal ethical codes, she laughs at her father, her husband, and the system of patriarchy without mercy. Outside her own frame of gender and identity, she is able to mock herself, or selves, her old identity, her substitute, and her simulators. She laughs when she sees the emperor's order to search for the missing Meng Lijun as if she were a criminal. She amusingly watches her former self coming back to life in the faces and words of her simulators. She admires her talent for imitating and simulating performance, her ability to fool even her father, brother, and husband. Her admiration is such that she gives a hand to her simulacrum to make her more convincing, more real.

Li Mingtang is a simulator herself. Instead of passing as another woman, she simulates men's clothes and words. She is so successful that her father does not know her anymore, even when he is face to face with her, and even though she looks exactly like his daughter. She has mastered the language so well, the language that has always belonged to the master, always been male, that she is not only accepted as one of them but becomes their leader and destroyer. By manipulating their perception and language, she steals their capacity to see and talk. She is, as she tells her husband, every man's ill star: whoever sees her and wants her becomes sick, miserable, or obsessed. Her husband loses his power to speak in front of her. He either sends his concubine to speak for him or takes to his bed and weeps like a deserted woman. He has no desire for anyone except Li Mingtang. And his desire makes him impotent. Her father and father-in-law used to be excellent ministers in the royal court. But once Li Mingtang takes over the administration, they suddenly become senile, unable to make a single decision without her. The emperor loses interest in his wife and concubines as well as in his affairs of state. All he can think about day and night is how to get her into his bed. Throughout the play, men share one common symptom: the loss of the capacity to tell the real from the false.

This is man's worst nightmare: someone alien (woman) sneaks into their base camp in masquerade, steals their language—their most potent symbol and tool—and uses it to castrate the masters and destroy their house. Li Mingtang makes the nightmare come true, as Guo Moruo, the icon of China's modern literature and culture, points out in his essay on Chen Duansheng's play:

> [Meng Lijun] fights the hierarchy of feudalism with the feudal ethical codes, subverts the order that puts women beneath men with the official rank she usurps, casts her own parents through the emperor's hands, rejects her husband in the name of a teacher, and disobeys the order from the imperial court in the name of chastity and fidelity. (Guo Moruo 1961)

To make the scenario worse, Li Mingtang simulates the masters' language so well that though they know something is seriously wrong, they cannot pinpoint what it is. Their fear makes them unwilling to know who and what she is. For simulation is much more dangerous than open defiance. It suggests that law and order, gender and sex, class and hierarchy could be constructed as simulation as well. And if women can construct their own sex as well as men's, the logical next question is: Is man likewise not fact but artifact, himself constructed and simulated with detachable parts? Transvestites and masqueraders put not only sexuality and hierarchy but also the categories themselves in flux. Such anxiety over the crisis is best expressed through the mouth of a royal concubine, to whom the emperor confides his obsession for Li Mingtang and his scheme to steal her from his wife's brother. She warns him about the danger and impossibility of possessing the transvestite. First of all, Li Mingtang will never submit herself to the emperor's will. Even if she did, the consequences would be disastrous. The empress would cause a riot. With her background as a former general and martial art master, the empress could seize the throne as easily as she defeated the most aggressive invaders from Korea. And no one would be able to save the emperor, not even Li Mingtang, because she would be stripped of her power. The emperor knows this danger, but his desire for Li Mingtang has rendered him powerless, just as the same desire has done to all other men. The only thing they can do is to seek out the less successful simulators like Piao Luyun and Xiang Nanjin in order to hang onto the shadow of Li Mingtang, the so-called original and real, who is in fact a simulation herself, the master masquerader.

The problem is no longer that of imitation or reduplication. It is about the fear (and fascination) of the body being usurped by simulators and simulacra, the fear that one can no longer tell the real from the fake, the original from the reproduction. This theme has appeared repeatedly in different cultures through all kinds of literary and entertainment genres: myth, folklore, drama, science fiction, and horror movies. In the Chinese classics, there is the Monkey King from *Xi you ji (The Journey to the West)*, who often creates thousands of simulacra of himself to confuse his enemy in their battles. Pu Songling's tales feature ghosts and fox spirits that always simulate the shape of beautiful girls in order to seduce men. The Japanese novel *The Face of Another* (1964) by Kobo Abe is a dark journey about the protagonist's loss of face (disfigured by scars) and the thrill, power, and destruction his new face brings him. Hollywood has produced classics like *The Thing (from Another World)* (directed by Christian Nybyo, 1951), *Invasion of the Body Snatchers* (directed by Don Siegel, 1956), *Blade Runner* (directed by Ridley Scott, 1982), all of which were based on works of science fiction. And new ones keep mushrooming out of pop culture. There is John Woo's *Face Off* (1997), which dramatizes a cop and a criminal who swap faces (the criminal wakes up from his coma and takes advantage of his new identity and rights, including the right to sleep with the cop's wife). And the popular television series *The X-Files* has featured many episodes on this subject. One such story line revolves around a man who can transform his face into any shape. He goes into different houses masquerading as the husband and impregnating the wives. As a result, these women give birth to children with tails, a genetic mark of the simulator. The stage for the simulators and simulacra has apparently moved from the public sphere to the private space of the bedchamber.[6]

Fear, however, is not the root of the problem. The problem lies in the fact that what one fears most is what one desires most. The simulations in *Destiny of the Next Life* are more glamorous, more authentic, more appealing than the real thing. Men constantly ponder over why they have not eliminated the transvestite Li Mingtang. They make a long list of reasons why they should forget about her, hate her, or even execute her. Yet the longer the list gets, the more fiery their desire becomes. They are trapped by their longing. They long for her glamour and her freedom to oscillate between male and female, real and false, original and reproduced, and all other binary oppositions. She is neutral—both male and female and neither male nor female—a genuine androgyne.

Such an androgynous body represents an ideal that can be traced back to "the Yellow Emperor's body" (Furth 1999, 19). As one of the mythical sage founders of civilization in China and the inventor of acupuncture, the Yellow Emperor acquired the secrets of health and longevity through his dialogues with a commoner physician named Qibo. As demonstrated by Charlotte Furth in her analysis of the classic on Chinese medicine *The Yellow Emperor's Inner Cannon (Huangdi neijing)*, the sage's body is "more truly androgynous, balancing yin and yang functions in everyone," and it "has no morphological sex, but only gender" (1999, 46). This medical imagination of the androgynous body opens the door for the blurring and crossing of gender boundaries, and it conflicts with the values of a strictly gendered social hierarchy. It is through this tension of blurred boundaries, however, that an androgyne (hermaphrodite) achieves a protean eroticism. As Chu Feng states in *Bequeathed Writings of Master Chu (Chu shi yi shu)*, a treatise attributed to him, in the bodies of hermaphrodites who are "neither male nor female *[fei nan fei nu]*, when influenced/stirred by a woman the male pulse beats in response; and when stimulated by a man, the female pulse is felt responding in compliance" (quoted in Furth 1991, 53).[7] Hermaphrodites have the power to balance yin and yang in one body, to transgress gender boundaries, to oscillate between sexes, to reverse and transform the order of yin and yang, connecting them to the cosmos's creative power of transformation. Such transforming power is often feared and desired at the same time. In each dynasty, historical annals recorded and interpreted incidents of spontaneous changes of sex in humans and animals as good or evil omens according to the circumstances. Meng Lijun, in her transvestite attire, embodies the ideal of androgyny, whose power, beauty, and talent, like the banished immortal Shuangqing, are beyond human imagination, beyond linguistic capacity.

As an androgyne, Meng Lijun/Li Mingtang is everything and neutral at the same time. But being *everything* can also mean nothing, and *neutral* can mean neutered. The price of entering the realm of immortality is annihilation. Li Mingtang has represented herself as a man so successfully that the masque has become her own skin. She is stuck to the image and the language she has usurped from the male world and can no longer go back to her old self. The masque can be peeled off only by force, by killing the masquerader first; Li Mingtang is drugged by the herbal wine, which is so strong that it puts her into a coma-like stupor—a symbolic death. Once exposed, she is silenced. And silence means another kind of death. In fact, the emperor orders the maids to send a fictitious report to the empress that Li Mingtang is spitting blood and her face is turning blue. She may never wake up again from her coma. His story turns into reality. As soon as Li Mingtang wakes up and discovers her peeled feet, blood comes out of her mouth, and she is no longer the eloquent, glamorous Prime Minister Li Mingtang. The transvestite, once stripped of her mask, is now silenced.

No one can finish the story of Li Mingtang once the mask is lifted. Chen Duansheng, the master storyteller, laid down her brush when Li Mingtang, intoxicated with the drugged wine, fell into a deep coma and was about to be unbooted by the empress's maids. She would have preferred to have her heroine in an eternal sleep, to preserve her as a transvestite, as a riddle, as an ambivalence forever, in order to preserve herself. It is only because of pressure from her fans, or possibly because of economic necessity, that she woke up Li Mingtang twelve years later and finished one more chapter. A decade later, she herself died spitting up blood, leaving the story unfinished (or impossible to finish), leaving the transvestite Li Mingtang suspended, unmasked, also dying spitting up blood.

According to the account of Chen Duansheng's nephew, she was waiting for her husband's return to complete the story (Zheng Guangyi 1991, 1750). This might have been her excuse to soothe her anxious audience who wanted to know the end of the story. They expected a happy ending, a tradition in Chinese fiction and drama. Li Mingtang would either resume her former sexual gender and become an obedient wife, filial daughter-in-law, and good mother, or accept the emperor's proposal to become his concubine. But such endings would betray the logic of Chen's narrative, the spirit of the drama, and the development of the heroine's character. Once she escapes the imprisonment of being a woman and tastes the freedom of masquerade, Li Mingtang can no longer go back to her origins. The other choice is also impossible: that Li Mingtang would reject the emperor's proposal and be executed. That would be the end of the utopia, the end of female imagination and narrative. Chen Duansheng could not possibly have destroyed the world she created for herself and her fans. Her predicament is that between writing and speech, male and female, the logic of the patriarchy and the logic of all the oppressed. Above all, it is the matter of language, its violence and revenge. No matter how much control Chen Duansheng and Li Mingtang have over the narration, in the end they cannot avoid being overwhelmed and swallowed by their own words. In Chen Duansheng's last chapter, it is no longer Li Mingtang who speaks with eloquence, but language that finally speaks Li Mingtang and her creator, and speaks through them. It tears them apart from the inside out. They have no way to escape. Even silence cannot save them. The only way out is the death of the author, together with her heroine.

With or without an ending, Chen Duansheng's *Destiny of the Next Life* continues to live on. Meng Lijun has been and will continue to be remembered as Li Mingtang, a transvestite with shiny black boots masking a pair of golden lotus, forever beautiful and desirable, forever dangling in between, forever on the verge of being unmasked. Return is not possible since there is no departure. An ending is not possible either, since there has never been a beginning.

Masquerade charms and conquers through what Jacques Lacan calls the third term: "seeming" or "appearing" instead of "having" or "being" the phallus. It replaces the "to have" with the "to seem" in order to "protect it on the one side, and mask its lack in the other" (1977, 289). This is exactly the language of footbinding, exactly what lotus feet have achieved in the end, despite all the earlier intentions and motivations from men or women. Both masqueraders and footbinders simulate, cross, and eliminate opposites— male and female, high and low, nature and artifice, genuine and substitute, and so forth. Both have substituted the real with perfect simulacra that try to conquer death. Both become objects of desire that are forever unreachable, forever fascinating. By pretending to have what she lacks, Li Mingtang, the master masquerader and footbinder, makes the fake one even better, more glamorous, more authentic, more desirable than the real. By eliminating the boundaries of all opposites, she enters a third space, the space of androgyny. A perfect simulacrum, she is purged of death, forever radiating with its own fascination, forever beyond reach. In Li Mingtang's transvestite performance, her feet, the three-inch golden lotuses as an image of beauty and femininity, are linked to her mouth, the "three-inch unrottable tongue" as a symbol of language—spoken words, euphemisms, sophistry, and violence. Bound feet, once interwoven with language, become the indispensable fabric of her masquerade and her most powerful weapon. As the best footbinder, speaker, and masquerader all at once, Li Mingtang in her transvestitism allows us to glimpse the mystery of footbinding, writing, and speaking and reveals their innate connections with one another.

Conclusion:
Aching for Beauty and Beyond

Who would take us to be women? Why, women.
They alone were not fooled.
— Colette, *Pure and Impure*

The first word, *Ah,* blossomed into all others.
Each of them is true.
— Kukai, "Singing Image of Fire"

FOOTBINDING IS THE CODE OF THE FEUDAL SYSTEM, the symbol of the patriarchal oppression of women. But it goes beyond the exotic and curious custom of some Chinese women deforming their bodies to please men. As feet are bound and rebound, the body part (nature) is turned into a work of artifice, then transformed back into nature as the only proof of true femininity, true gender and sex. Thus footbinding brings out a series of critical issues of the quest for beauty that always goes hand in hand with violence, the making of culture, of hierarchy, of gender and sex, and finally, the making and remaking of nature. It reopens the long-standing questions of masquerade and representation, of language and desire. Using footbinding as masquerade, Chinese women display themselves as artifacts, as theatrical creatures who can be dismantled and put back together according to circumstance. Footbinding then leads to this inevitable question: if femininity is the work of culture, artifice, and simulation, what does it say about the making of masculinity? What makes a man a man? If genuine womanliness and the masquerade are indeed the "same thing," as Joan Riviere (1989) says, the theory can be also applied to manliness. Masculinity, like femininity, can also be constructed through masquerade.

For a thousand years of Chinese history, footbinding branded a person's gender, sex, beauty, and class. Yes, biological anatomy of the body still counted, as breasts and vagina made a woman and a penis made a man. But ultimately it was the bound feet that determined the line between genders. A woman with her feet unbound was not really a woman, no matter how pretty her face, how slim and willowy her body. An ugly woman with bound feet could pass for a beauty, and a good-looking woman with perfectly bound feet was the ideal of femininity (figure 18). Binding their feet, women turned their bodies into artifice, art, poetry, writing, culture. Through pain and mutilation, they became the codes of beauty, femininity, and eroticism. While footbinding entered language and literature as a gendered construction and an objectification, the firm layers of bandages and the tightly fitting shoes became masks through which women writers achieved literary productivity and linguistic liberation. Under the banner of footbinding, women were recruited into the theater of masquerade, the stage of the Symbolic, of language, where they were directors, performers, and audience all at once. Over the thousand years, Chinese women transformed footbinding and writing—the two most oppressive patriarchal codes—into a female culture. They turned the binding into a bonding among women family members, relatives, and friends. And they inverted male writing that fetishized the female body into a female writing that was rooted in speech and interaction among a female community. Footbinding allowed Chinese women to usurp the power and language from the master through imitation, simulation, and inversion and to turn it into their own—female language, female writing, female culture.

Footbinding may have started as an aesthetic impulse between a talented royal dancer and a decadent emperor. Its widespread practice throughout late imperial China as a cultural fetish and a moral restriction for women, however, shows that footbinding reflected an anguished response to the shifting and eroding boundaries of gender, sex, and hierarchy, and the indulgence in spending. Chinese intellectuals encouraged footbinding as a way to consolidate these eroding boundaries and straighten the deteriorating sense of morality. Although it helped, to some degree, to confine women to their inner chambers and tighten the moral rein on them, it caused a further boundary crossing and a combination of many opposites. The dual nature and the ambivalent force of footbinding were manifested in the ambivalence of language, the vehement clashes between the written and the spoken within the system of Chinese language. It was through lin-

Figure 18. Hong Kong "China Girl." Courtesy Peabody Essex Museum, Salem, Massachusetts.

guistic violence that the physical violence involved in footbinding obtained its full social and moral standing. And the fetishization of the female body was possible and complete only through a linguistic fetishization. Through the violent and magic work of remainders, metaphors, and euphemisms, language not only made possible the interplay of footbinding between surface and inside, immortality and death, beauty and violence, flesh and spirit, expenditure and reason, but also allowed the constant flow between foot and mouth, sex and food, transcendence and descent, nature and culture.

Through the furnace of language, footbinding cooked the raw, wild female body into cultural artifice, introducing it into erotic games and economic cycles.

Footbinding opened a wide door for masquerade, especially transvestism. When Chinese men masqueraded as women, the most important, most convincing mask was bound feet. As for women transvestites, as long as they covered their three-inch lotuses with boots, they could easily simulate masculinity. The tension thus moves not only from the whole to the part, but also from the inside to the surface, from a pair of lotus shoes as the locus of erotic imagination to a pair of black boots shining as the symbol of masculine power. The drama now focuses on the process of lifting the surface, the tension that something is about to be revealed, rather than on what is actually inside the boot. We all know what's inside. In myth and folklore, in stories and real life, we have seen over and over again that when the boots are taken off, there is nothing except for cotton and bandages wrapped around the tiny appendage. But that is not the point. The point is that on the stage of the masquerade the enigma is not about who or what is hiding under the outward appearance. When the mask falls, it reveals nothing but the very fact of the masquerade itself. All the value and meaning of the mask reside on the surface alone: it is the coexistence of masculine and feminine, the original and reproduction, the real and simulacrum, all in one single body, the body that is neither male nor female, the body that belongs to the space of desire. One must take it at face value. One must accept that beauty/femininity is only skin deep, and so is masculinity. The peeling of the mask, therefore, means the end of the masquerade, the end of performance, the end of narrative, the end of writing/speech. Unmasking leads to the death of the author/heroine (as it happened to Chen Duansheng and Li Mingtang), and the death of eroticism.

When the lotus foot is covered with another layer of mask—a boot or another piece of male clothing—it becomes a more desirable object, desirable because it initiates every viewer into the game of masquerade. Li Mingtang is a typical case. The famous Ming courtesan Liu Rushi (1618–64), who often dressed up as a transvestite to entice men, always made sure that their gaze would finally fall and fix on her tiny feet. In myth, folklore, and stories of the late imperial period, the exposure of the transvestite's tiny feet often leads to the protagonists' deaths.[1]

The emperor in *Destiny of the Next Life* tries all he can to prevent the unmasking of Li Mingtang. He knows from very early on that his prime minister is a transvestite. He helps her to keep the mask, not only because he wants her, both as his minister and as his object of desire, but also because he knows that once the transvestite is unmasked, the game is over. He objects to his wife's plan to intoxicate Li Mingtang and examine her feet. When he is forced to accept it, and when he sees his beloved transvestite drugged and taken away for the examination, he walks away in great agitation. Once the red lotus shoe falls into his hand, he immediately takes all the necessary steps to conceal the news, to keep the transvestism intact. Even when he pays Li Mingtang a private visit at her home, he still calls her "Mr. Li," threatening to execute her if she reveals her original identity. What makes it most interesting, however, is that the emperor himself is now part of the masquerade. He sneaks out of his palace disguised as a eunuch, a sex that is neither male nor female. On the one hand, he does so out of necessity; as the emperor the only way he can move around without stirring up a scene is to mask himself as something other, and the only choice for his masquerade is a eunuch, since there is no other man in the palace and since a woman is not allowed to wander out of the palace. On the other hand, his masquerading as something that is neutral, between genders and sexes, makes a lot of sense. This space in between, the space of desire and sheer representation, the space of androgyny, is exactly what transvestism represents and strives for. Since Li Mingtang is unmasked and is no longer able to occupy that liminal space, the emperor takes it over. And since the emperor loses all hope of ever reaching and possessing the transvestite, he becomes one himself.

Footbinding, by the paradoxical way of concealment and representation, allows us to glimpse the myth around the real and original. It reveals that the so-called reality and origin can also be a masque, veneered with power, money, politics, and the written word; in other words, truth and origin are also a matter of representation. It proves how fragile and destructible they are, and how easy it is to replace them with simulacra and reproductions. Chen Duansheng's story about the tiny-footed transvestite shows us how the reality of gender and sex can be subverted or inverted, and how no one can represent the origin or truth, just as no one can pin down who Li Mingtang is. Huangfu Shaohua possesses Meng Lijun's self-portrait before she turns into Li Mingtang. The father has only her words that were spoken in the heat of passion, words that confirmed to the father that she was his daughter Meng Lijun. But those words are soon denied and erased, vanished like a ghost. Even the emperor, who himself is supposed to be the signifier of power, runs after Li Mingtang's shiny boots relentlessly, using all the faculties of his power and wit. And all he ends up with is a red lotus shoe that he intercepts from the maids. The other Li Mingtang, the Li Mingtang of the clicking boots and the three-inch tongue, is forever illusive, like a phantom. All we can do is to hold onto simulacra and simulators—a hall of mirrors. All are only parts; all are artifice. Yet all represent and substitute the whole, and all are true.

Footbinding thus leads us into the maze of language, its violence and ambivalence that especially characterized literature, sexuality, aesthetics, morality, and other aspects of culture in late imperial China. Male writers showed a tendency to fetishize language in its written form and narrative by categorizing and fetishizing bound feet. Their obsession reflected the anxiety and need to control language, to gain power through the manipulation of the female body, be it textual or sexual. Such efforts, however, always backfired. The fetishists often ended up being fetishized. The authors lost control of their narratives and the actions of their male characters, who started out as womanizers and sex hunters but ended as the sex objects of their prey. As their narration moved on, the women characters, who were categorized and dissected into parts as a fetish, grew more alive and powerful, until they became masters of both the authors and male protagonists. It was a complete and profound inversion. Instead of the author speaking the language or telling the story, it was now the language speaking the author, and the narrative took on a life of its own.

Just as women inverted footbinding, the code of oppression that worked by fetishizing the female body, into a language and heritage of their own, women writers treated writing as something performative and interactive, woven together with their handiwork, conversation, and lifestyle. Although footbinding was not the object of their own erotic gaze or fetishistic obsession, it appeared everywhere in their texts as a natural part of the whole organic body. Footbinding and writing played an extremely important role in Chinese women's self-identity. Both practices provided a public and private space for women to get together, to read and share their work—literary or craft-based—and to form female liaisons. Writing for them was not threatening like a beast of prey, but was a collective act and a public performance within the female community. Their writing was so interlocked with the contents of their daily routines—weaving, embroidering, footbinding—and so deeply rooted in talking that they were all woven into the fabric of female language. It was a living language that brought the written word and speech as close as possible and defied the textualization and fetishization of the female body that appeared in many men's writing. This language gathered all women in the roaring undercurrents of the female heritage that had been quietly and significantly affecting mainstream history of late imperial China, written mostly by men. This female heritage, rooted firmly in speech, performance, and interaction, grew and was passed on among Chinese women from hand to hand, foot to foot, and mouth to mouth.

An examination of footbinding also opens doors to many other issues. One of them is the homoeroticism that evolved out of footbinding. Lesbian relationships among tiny-footed women can be traced in the works of the seventeenth-century Jiangnan gentry women poets, in the texts of *nu shu,* as well as in the bonding of *lao tong* and sworn sisterhoods of the *nu shu* authors and their fans. In *Destiny of the Next Life,* Li Mingtang's marriage to her former maid is an obvious example. For such relationships, bound feet serve as a main attraction to catch another woman's eye, to draw admiration, sympathy, and passion, or to serve as a tool and metaphor to express amorous feelings. The most effective prop for male transvestites was a pair of small feet. Some had real bound feet, and some, especially actors, wore shoes that made their feet look small and bound. Such actors played female roles on stage, and off stage they often provided sexual entertainment for their male patrons, a bit similar to the relationship between a master (scholars, poets, or students who prepared for official exams) and his *shu tong* (its literal translation is "book boy," who serves as his servant, secretary, and sex object). *The Golden Lotus, The Carnal Prayer Mat, Liaozhai's Records of the Strange,* and *The Three-Inch Golden Lotus* all feature vivid stories and descriptions of such homoerotic relationships and male transvestism. Even in *Destiny of the Next Life,* the secret of Meng Lijun's magical allure is that she dresses, talks, and acts as a man, not as a woman. But at the same time, her entire body, from her face to her masked bound feet, radiates with feminine charm. In other words, she embodies the qualities of both masculinity and femininity—the body of androgyny. Thus, what she stirs up in her admirers, from the emperor to her own husband, is not just the passion of homoeroticism, but also the longing for the ideal of an androgynous body that embraces both yin and yang, feminine and masculine. Footbinding has come close to such an ideal body through its dual nature in physicality, aesthetics, and ethics.

Records of Gathering Fragrance (Cai fei lu) contains numerous cases of male footbinding and foot compressing in history, dating back to the Song dynasty (1:220). As more and more women practiced footbinding, men also preferred to have small feet for themselves. At the beginning of the twentieth century, it became a fashion among upper-class families in Beijing to compress boys' feet with binding cloths so that they could fit into the narrow shoes in vogue (in Levy 1992, 192). Men in Tianjin, a city close to the capital, also wrapped their feet tightly with a square piece of cloth and wore socks so tight and unyielding that their feet became narrow, flat, and pointed at the tip. They wore special shoes marked by Beijing and Shanghai styles (Levy 1992, 195). Is this a mere matter of fashion, or a few men's impulsive imitation of a female practice? Or is it something larger, something that is once again like women's footbinding, linked to language, desire, body, and violence, something that blends and crosses the borders of gender, sex, and hierarchy? And how does this male impulse or desire to bind their own feet relate to the questions of fetishism, masquerade, transvestism, homoeroticism, and finally, androgyny? If female footbinding was encouraged as a way to mark the difference between men and women, then male footbinding and foot compressing seem only to have the opposite goal—that is, to make men more feminine. This is even more interesting if one considers the fact that while Chinese women bound their feet to make themselves more feminine, more beautiful, and more different from men, they bound their breasts tightly to prevent them from protruding, as large, prominent breasts were considered unfeminine, uncivilized. Once again, the phenomenon can be explained by the common desire of both sexes for a more androgynous body, balanced evenly between yin and yang forces. It is a vision that, when realized in an individual's body, can lead to health, longevity, even immortality, and when achieved by a state, an empire, or a dynasty, can lead to its legitimacy, stability, and prosperity. A future close study of such a custom of eliminating bodily differences would surely illuminate the long-standing issues of body, gender, desire, politics, language, and representation.

In *The Vagina Monologues,* Eve Ensler interviewed hundreds of women with this question: "If your vagina got dressed, what would it wear?" The replies include the following:

> A leather jacket.
> Silk stockings.
> Mink.
> A pink boa.
> A male tuxedo.
> Jeans.
> Something formfitting.
> Emeralds.
> An evening gown.
> Sequins.
> Armani only.
> A tutu.
> See-through black underwear.
> A taffeta ball gown.

Something machine washable.
Costume eye mask.
Purple velvet pajamas.
Angora.
A red bow.
Ermine and pearls.
A large hat full of flowers.
A leopard hat.
A silk kimono.
A beret.
Sweatpants.
A tattoo.
An electrical shock device to keep unwanted strangers away.
High heels.
Lace and combat boots.
Purple feathers and twigs and shells.
Cotton.
A pinafore.
A bikini.
A slicker.

(1998, 15–17)

What contemporary American women imagine or practice had already been translated into reality in China a thousand years ago. For a millennium, Chinese women bound their feet (their symbolic vaginas) and dressed them in all manners (binding, covering, piercing) and in all styles (transvestites, animals, plants, objects), just as twentieth-century Americans imagine in their vagina monologues. Across time, space, and culture, the currents of Eastern and Western female imaginations have finally merged.

When I, a girl of nine, bound my own feet secretly with elastic bands, I was not only trying to create beauty, but also to write/inscribe my personal, political, and cultural signature upon my body. Beauty and pain, twin sisters, are the only passage through which I could be initiated from a girl into the family and society, into the women's camp in the jungle of culture. There I'd be taught the art of seducing, usurping and subverting, breaking and mixing all the established boundaries in order to make new boundaries, new orders, and a new language. I'd be trained how to inherit the great female heritage and how to pass it on to the next generation.

In this secret camp, I was not, and will not be, alone.

Notes

Preface

1. Dorothy Ko is currently completing her book on the history of footbinding. Most Chinese and Western scholars have approached the subject from the perspectives of history, feminism, or cultural studies. Since the May Fourth Movement of 1919, footbinding abolitionists and scholars have considered footbinding as the symbol of women's suppression and victimization of the patriarchal feudal system, the symbol of China's backwardness, and the cause of the nation's humiliation in the world. Howard Levy's *The Lotus Lovers: The Complete History of the Curious Erotic Custom of Footbinding in China,* first published in 1966, is a fairly well-documented book on the origin, development, and end of footbinding. It also has a good amount of translations from the essays and books by bound-foot advocates and abolitionists, including his interviews with tiny-footed women. His choice of materials and his comments reinforce the notion of footbinding as the sheer victimization and fetishization of women. And, just as the title indicates, the book remains on the whole a Westerner's curious gaze on the Chinese female's eroticized body. Since the 1970s, historians and anthropologists have been looking into the subject and its impact on the status of women and gender constructions in various regional and historical periods (Ropp 1976; Rawski 1985; Ebrey 1990; Blake 1994; Ko 1994, 1997a, 1997b).

Patricia Ebrey tries to explain the phenomenon of footbinding as a means to gender reconstruction during the Song dynasty. The footbinding of women not only allowed Chinese men to become refined themselves without being too feminized, but it also set them apart from their northern rivals. Fred Blake adopted Nancy Scheper-Hughes and Margaret Lock's (1987) three-dimensional model of the "mindful body" to look into this Chinese practice. Footbinding embroiled a mother and daughter in a painful process of physical discipline on the body. It also ensured the connection between the predefined natural body (woman's fate) and her control over such a fate by overcoming intense pain. Finally, footbinding "masked the work of women by defining incubation more as 'nature' than as 'labor' and by defining foot-bound women's labor as worthless"(Blake 1994, 705–6).

In *Teachers of the Inner Chambers: Women and Culture in Seventeenth-Century China* (1994), Dorothy Ko points out that such characterization of footbinding as female restriction and suppression "leaves out the complex motives and feelings of the mothers and daughters involved" (148). She demonstrates, with rich historical and literary materials, how educated women in the seventeenth century viewed their own bodies and their feet with pride and even a secret delight, and how footbinding became a means of socialization for these women. She also points out later that the practice can be seen as a female expression of *wen* culture, a form of female writing on the body (1997b, 96).

2. My primary materials include poetry by men and women of the late imperial period in China; the Qing writers Li Yu and Fang Xun's essays (*Xian qing ou ji* and *Xiang lian pin zao*); oral accounts and collected essays about footbinding edited at the turn of the twentieth century by Yao Lingxi *(Cai fei lu)*, Ming and Qing erotic novels by Lanlin Xiao Xiao Sheng (*Jin ping mei cihua,* translated by Clement Egerton as *The Golden Lotus* and by David Roy as *Plum in Golden Vase*) and Li Yu (*Rou pu tuan,* translated by Patrick Hanan as *The Carnal Prayer Mat*); a novel by the Qing writer Li Ruzhen (*Jing hua yuan,* translated as *Flowers in the Mirror*); a contemporary novel by Feng Jicai (*San cun jin lian,* translated as *The Three-Inch Golden Lotus*); the short stories by the Qing writer Pu Songling (*Liao zhai zhi yi,* translated as *Liao zhai's Records of the Strange*); the Qing scholar Shi Zhenlin's memoir and travelogue *Xiqing sanji* (translated as *Random Notes of West-Green*); and finally, the Qing woman playwright Chen Duansheng's monumental play *Zai sheng yuan* (translated as *Destiny of the Next Life*).

Except for Fang Xun's and Yao Lingxi's work, the materials I use for the analysis do not directly deal with footbinding. In any case, most of the existing data we have were recorded (mostly by men) at the end of the nineteenth century and the beginning of the twentieth century. Such information was heavily tinted not only by the writers' nostalgia for the practice on the verge of its doom but also by the general belief among intellectuals that footbinding symbolized nothing but China's backwardness, barbarism, and the victimization of women. The materials that go back to the earlier period concern more the social elite and gentry women than ordinary laboring women. Since footbinding affected people across the country in all walks of life, a comprehensive and "accurate understanding of foot-binding must include the ordinary people" (Blake 1994, 699). And since the lives of ordinary working people were passed down mostly through oral history, myth, folklore, folksongs, drama, and novels, I attempt to extract the trace of footbinding from the sources I mention above. They depict in subtle detail the emotional, psychological, and cultural life in the Ming and Qing periods, during which footbinding reached its peak and became a cultural fixation.

The novels can actually be read as a storehouse of Ming and Qing social and cultural history that was marked by the rapid growth of commerce, agriculture, technology, population, publishing, Neo-Confucian ethics, and indulgence in sensual pleasures. Through these works, I examine how footbinding gave rise to a whole language of its own in literature and daily life, how male authors fetishized women in their writing through textualizing bound feet, and how the fetishized objects (female characters and language) inverted the relationship and began to haunt the authors. My discussion focuses on how women writers from different periods and backgrounds tried to defy the male textual fetishization with their own writing, by borrowing the male poetic form and language to write about their own lives. They formed women's writing clubs and created their own secret language. They bonded through their handiwork and literary communities. They questioned and challenged the imposed hierarchy, gender, and sex roles. And finally, they inverted male poetic writing into a dialogic female language (close to the oral) and turned footbinding into a masquerade performance.

1. Three-Inch Golden Lotuses

1. This list is based on Howard Levy's illustration in *The Lotus Lovers* (1992, 24–25).

2. The Chinese classical medicine text *Inner Cannon (Su wen)* describes the development of a girl's body as the following: "At seven years of age *[sui]* a girl's Kidney *qi* is flourishing; her adult teeth come in and her hair grows long. At fourteen she comes into her reproductive capacities *[tiangui zhi]*; her Conception pulse moves and her Highway pulse is abundant; her menses flow regularly and she can bear young. At twenty-one her Kidney *qi* is stabilized, and so her wisdom teeth come in and her growth has reached its apogee" (quoted in Furth 1999, 45).

3. One of the standards for a perfect pair of lotus feet is that one can insert a silver coin into the crease.

4. *Cai fei lu* features the following newspaper story titled "The Red Chestnut Soaked by White Juice": "There were a certain male actor and an actress in a Tientsin troupe. The actor admired the actress for her tiny and beautiful feet and wanted to become intimate with her, but he was rejected. He therefore stole her shoes, discharged semen into them, and put them back in their original place. The actress discovered this only when she was about to go on the stage and was extremely embarrassed and annoyed, but she had to maintain silence. The actors circulated the story, and it was published in several newspapers" (*Cai fei lu*, quoted in Levy 1992, 139–40).

5. Many lotus lovers believed that footbinding naturally broadened a woman's hips and increased the vaginal folds, therefore enhancing her feminine charm both in bed and in appearance. Gu Hongming (1857–1928), a conservative Chinese writer and intellectual, commented on one of the advantages of footbinding: "The smaller the woman's foot, the more wondrous become the folds of the vagina.

(There was the saying: the smaller the feet, the more intense the sex urge.) . . . Women in other districts can produce these folds artificially, but the only way is by footbinding, which concentrates development in this one place. There consequently develop layer after layer [of folds within the vagina]; those who have personally experienced this [in sexual intercourse] feel a supernatural exaltation" (*Cai fei lu,* quoted in Levy 1992, 141). Gu's theory was backed up by Dr. Zhang Jingsheng, who also believed that footbinding made the vagina more developed: "From the viewpoint of sex, footbinding was very profitable" (in Levy 1992, 141). But Zhang withdrew his remark after he returned from abroad for postgraduate study, saying that footbinding actually destroyed sexual desire.

6. Howard Levy translated some of the accounts in *The Lotus Lovers*: "There was an old woman who had only one daughter, famed for her beauty. The girl drew shoe patterns for neighbors and showed them how to embroider flowers on the shoes. She had tiny bowed feet and walked with elegance. She was admired for a long time by several shiftless youths, who found her bowed shoes most lovable. But they had no chance to touch her feet, as she was zealously guarded by the widow. One day she attended a village play with a few girl friends. It was a dark night in winter, and the weather was so cold that her lower limbs became numbed. When the play ended, she discovered the loss of one shoe. She had to endure the pain of walking home leaning on walls for support. She said nothing to her mother and went to sleep beside her. Suddenly, something was thrown through the paper window in the bedroom. The widow awoke in fright and noticed the object, her daughter's missing shoe. It had been lewdly saturated with semen. The girl wept with shame, but the understanding mother comforted her without a word of scolding. Culprits spread the news around until it became public gossip" (*White Dew Immersing the Red Chestnut,* in *Cai fei lu,* quoted in Levy 1992, 139).

7. See Huang Huajie's "Nao Xinfang" for more details (1991, 154–73).

8. The text within the brackets is in Latin in Clement Egerton's version (1955), and I have translated it into English from the original in Chinese. Except where a translator is noted, all translations from Chinese sources are mine.

2. A Brief History of Footbinding

1. From *Lang huai ji,* 3 vols. (quoted in Gao Hongxin 1995, 21; translation is mine). Some believe it was written by the Yuan writer Yi Shizhen, while others believe it was composed by a Ming writer.

2. Zhang Bangji is cited in Tao Zongyi's *Chuo geng lu* (quoted in Gao Hongxin 1995, 21). The theory that footbinding began in the court of Li Yu with Yao Niang is accepted by many scholars, such as R. H. van Gulik, who states in his *Sexual Life in Ancient China,* "All literary evidence points to the custom having begun in or about her time, that is in the interval of ca. 50 years between the T'ang and Sung dynasties" (1961, 216).

3. *Yi jian zhi,* fiction in the style of notes and journals, was written and com-

piled by Hong Mai (1123–1202). Only 206 volumes (some in parts) out of 420 volumes have been passed down to the present. Apart from telling ghost and fairy tales, it also recorded the life of the commoners of his time.

4. Yu Zhenxie states in *Shu "jiu Tang shu: yu fu zhi" hou*: "Wu Zimu says in *Meng liang lu*: 'a tiny-foot boat is specialized in carrying merchants, young prostitutes, wandering singers, and female pilgrims.'. . . By the end of the Song, the term has become a synonym for women" (quoted in Gao Hongxin 1995, 17).

5. Liang Qichao published this essay in 1896 in the *xinmin chongbao,* when he was a member of the Society for Outlawing Bound Feet.

6. Women often helped in the fields during ploughing and harvesting seasons and during wars and natural disasters when every hand was needed. Except for some areas where customs made women the major laborers in and outside homes, however, Chinese women normally worked at home, as weaving and embroidery were part of the agricultural economy, while men worked in the fields.

7. It is never confirmed that Zhu Xi actually introduced footbinding to Fujian women. See the discussion in *Cai fei lu xu bian* (351) in which the possibility is raised that these remarks were attributed to Zhu Xi by later generations. However, the northern Fujian area, especially Zhangzhou and Xiamen, was known for its tiny-footed women.

8. Guanyin, the symbol of female benevolence and beauty, has natural feet. It is possible that the belief in footbinding went so deeply into the Chinese psyche that they wishfully forgot about the natural feet of Guanyin.

9. At the end of the Qing dynasty, it was a fashion among young men from royal and upper-class families as well as male prostitutes to compress their feet with binding cloth to the size of two inches wide and six inches long (*Cai fei lu di san bian* 22–23).

3. Footbinding and the Cult of the Exemplary Woman

1. See Bray 1997, especially the chapter on "Power of Fabrics"; and Blake 1994.

2. For more detail, see Ko 1994, 115–42.

3. The bracketed text is my translation.

4. The account is told by Hu's former maid and recorded by San You in *Cai fei lu* (266–68).

5. *Gujin tushu jicheng* (Collection of the ancient and contemporary books), also titled *Gu jin tu shu hui bian,* was compiled by Chen Menlei, Jiang Tingxi, and others during the Qing dynasty, featuring ten thousand volumes. For more details on martyred women, see Dong Jiazun's "Lidai jiefu lienu de tongji" (1990, 110–16).

6. Keith McMahon's work focuses on the men and women represented in the Qing erotic fictions, but the phenomenon of shrews, henpecked husbands, and misers has existed before and throughout the late imperial China.

7. In chapter 10, he is exiled after he tries to kill Ximen Qing to avenge his murdered brother, but he kills Ximen's friend by mistake.

8. When Qin Shihuang became the first emperor of China, he unified the law, measurements, and Chinese characters to consolidate his new empire. He simplified the extremely complicated and difficult *zhuan shu,* the ideographic scripts that had been used by different states, and named the simplified writing *li shu,* which became the standard written language for the Qin empire and has been used as the only standard writing since then, with more simplified versions coming with each dynasty.

9. The original in Chinese is "If you have the heart [for me]."

4. Edible Beauty

1. *Zongzi* are sweet rice dumplings with bamboo wrappings and various kinds of fillings that are featured as a sacrificial food for the *duanwu* festival, celebrating the memory of the Warrior State poet Qu Yuan.

2. Since Clement Egerton's translation (1955) omitted the food details, I use Frederick W. Mote's paraphrase of the earlier *Cihua* text of *The Golden Lotus* that appears in K. C. Chang's anthology *Food in Chinese Culture* (1977).

3. There has been a lot of research and studies on the authorship of the novel. Practically no one believes that Wang Shizhen wrote it, although he is listed as the author in most library card catalogs. The story that the novel was written in poison and used to kill his enemy was passed down until the present day as hearsay from a long time ago, probably from the early seventeenth century. What matters is the power of words, or the rumor that people believe in or want to believe in. In that sense, historical accuracy is less important.

5. Silken Slippers

1. I have so far concentrated on the obsession that appeared in literature. The large variety of ancient Chinese medicine for virility that has been passed on to the present and the various sex manuals for that purpose reflect that this obsession is not a mere fantasy of Chinese intellectuals but is rooted in the reality of late imperial China and is still affecting Chinese people today. Journalist Jan Wong wrote in her *Red China Blues* (1996) that she once interviewed Dr. Long, an expert on penis extension, who had a long waiting list of patients for his operations. The doctor strongly believed that "The longer the penis, the greater the sexual satisfaction for the woman." He also confirmed that the difference in penis sizes among Africans, Caucasians, and Asians is not a myth but a truth (358–62).

2. Human flesh and blood were believed to be the most potent *yao ying* for treating incurable diseases.

3. Wu Hong talks about how a number of late Ming and early Qing texts reveal a collective effort to compile a written iconography of a typical Beauty: "As a consequence, women's world (as well as women themselves) dissolves into frag-

mented features—dwellings, furnishings, adornment, physique, gestures and movements, maidservants, style, literacy, activities, and so on—all catalogued in the manner of a (male) connoisseur's handbook. . . . It condenses persons and events into 'bare bones' themes *(gu)*, only to be fleshed out again in poetry, novel, and painting" (Wu Hong 1997, 359–60).

4. Pu Songling passed the exam as a *gongsheng*—the lowest rank of the official titles for intellectuals—at the age of seventy-one.

5. The "weaving girl" alludes to the most popular Chinese myth "Niulang Zhinu" (The Cowboy and the Weaving Girl). Zhinu, the goddess's weaving girl, fell in love with Niulang and eloped to the earth. They got married and had two children together. When the goddess found out, she abducted Zhinu back to heaven. Niulang ran after them, carrying their children in baskets on each side of the yoke. Seeing that he was about to catch up, the goddess pulled out her hairpin and scratched a line on the sky, which turned into Yin He (the silver river, equivalent to the Milky Way). Niulang and Zhinu were thus separated forever, each turning into a star across the Milky Way. Only on the seventh day of the seventh lunar month are they allowed to meet. On that day, magpies build a bridge with their bodies so that the husband, wife, and children can cross the river to be reunited. The myth is another good example of how mortal men can reach immortality (becoming stars in the sky is equivalent to becoming gods) through the female body. It is no coincidence that Pu Songling used the weaving girl for his story. In the next chapter, I will discuss how weaving and writing are interlocked with women's literacy and literature.

6. See also Hu Shi (1971) and Kang Zhengguo (1988), who have raised the same issue.

7. This dramatic episode raises the question that remains problematic throughout Shi's text: how did Shi Zhenlin, an elite who belonged to a totally different class, get to see what happened inside a peasant's household and hear what was supposedly Shuangqing's conversation with her neighbor and even her monologues?

8. Shuangqing appears for the last time in *Random Notes* in chapter 4. Shi Zhenlin reports in the spring of 1735 that Shuangqing had endured worse abuse from her husband and mother-in-law with greater patience, recorded her last two song lyrics, and had her ask her neighbor why she tasted bitterness even when she was eating sweets.

9. Shi Zhenlin mentioned Shuangqing two more times later, one as a didactic story to warn two young women to avoid Shuangqing's ill fortune (4:68–71), and the other to praise Shuangqing's capacity to maintain lifelong virtue, sensitivity, and accomplishment (4:75). To quote Grace Fong, she "has been the object of his gaze, idealized, exploited, fetishized, and then forgotten" (1997, 281).

10. It is too tempting not to link this phenomenon with the Bill Clinton–Monica Lewinsky scandal, a typical case in which a woman's body becomes a site for political power battles. It also reminds one of Marv Albert, the sportscaster, whose right and power to speak were taken away because of his "abnormal" sexual conduct with women.

11. In the sixteenth century, wars coupled with natural calamities in Shandong, Henan, Nanjing, and Shaanxi Provinces forced many peasants into bankruptcy. Faced with poverty, some of these peasants castrated themselves and/or their children in order to make a living as eunuchs in the palace. In 1507, one village alone produced several hundred self-castrated men (*Zhengde Veritable Record,* cited in Tsai 1996, 24). See Shih-shan Henry Tsai's *The Eunuchs in the Ming Dynasty* (1996) for more details on the social and economical environment that caused the rise of self-castrated men. Examples include Zhang Zhong, who cut himself because he was detested and rejected by his father. Later, he became one of the three most powerful eunuchs during the Zhengde reign (1506–21). And Wei Zhongxian (1568–1627) castrated himself after his wife married someone else because of his poverty. He entered the court through connections and became the most powerful and cruelest eunuch in Ming history.

12. A good example is found in Liu Ruoyu. He had been studying for the civil service examinations until the age of fourteen. In 1589, he had himself castrated and quickly found work as a scribe in the palace, becoming a well-respected and informed palace eunuch (Liu Ruoyu 1935, 201–7).

13. Because of all these benefits and power, many men in the Ming dynasty castrated themselves and waited in the capital for an opportunity to serve in the palace. By mid-dynasty, the number of self-castrated men surpassed the need for eunuchs from the palace market. In 1424, Ming Emperor Chengzu passed a law banning self-castration. After that, even more laws and heavier punishments, including fines, beatings, exile, hard labor, and the death penalty, were passed to outlaw self-castration, with little effect. When Li Zicheng, the peasant rebel, barged into Beijing in 1644, he dismissed seventy thousand eunuchs who served in the palace, plus another thirty thousand outside the court waiting to be hired (Wang Yongkuan 1991, 146, 147).

14. As noted, Zhang Wenling was the supervisor of Liu Jin's execution. The person who recorded Zhen Man's execution, though not mentioned in the article, seemed to be present, judging from the tone and style of the writing.

15. As he confessed at the end of *The Tears of Eros,* "This photograph had a decisive role in my life. I have never stopped being obsessed by this image of pain, at once ecstatic (?) and intolerable" (1991). Perhaps the connection that Bataille is making between horror and eroticism, agony and ecstasy, is not such a far-fetched conclusion. After all, according to Zhang Wenlin's eyewitness account of Liu Jin's execution, the condemned did stop bleeding after the first few cuts when his blood reversed its flow due to the shock and pain.

6. Binding, Weaving, Chatting

1. See this source (Waltner and Pi-ching Hsu 1997) for a more comprehensive background of the two poets and detailed analysis of their writing.

2. There of course were exceptions to this rule. For example, in Shen Fu's *Fu*

sheng liu ji (Six Records of a Floating Life) his wife Yun did needlework to pay for her brother's tuition.

3. The most famous embroiderers were the women of the Gu family in the sixteenth century. Han Ximen, the wife of Gu Mingshi's second grandson, brought Gu embroidery art to its peak. Most of her work was modeled on famous paintings of the Song and Yuan dynasties. See Ko 1994 (173–75) for more details.

4. See Kang-i Sun Chang 1990 and Ko 1994 for details on the cult of *qing*.

5. The seventh evening of the seventh moon is the night the Cowboy *(Niulang)* and the Weaving Girl *(Zhinu)* meet in Heaven once a year, according to the legend. It is one of the most important festivals for women, who pray and offer food and incense while making their wishes.

6. In *Xiqing sanji* (Random Records of West-Green), in which her life stories and poems were recorded by Shi Zhenlin, she was called merely Shuangqing, and the surname *He* appeared only later in anthologies of poetry. It seemed that Shi was reluctant to attach such a *jiaren* (embodying beauty, virtue, and especially talent, whether true or partly fabricated by the author) to an illiterate brute woodchopper, Zhou, to whom Shuangqing was married. On the other hand, such an omission of the surname indicates Shi's intention of creating an ideal woman through his writing. Without a surname, Shuangqing belongs to everyone who appreciates her talent and virtue, especially to Shi Zhenlin, who records her life, collects her poems, and spreads her name. In that sense, he is her creator. (See Ropp n.d.)

7. Shuangqing's life and poetry, as pointed out by Grace Fong (1997), were "unquestionably constructed and framed as an ideal in a male vision" (265). Many scholars, including Paul Ropp, suspect that Shuangqing is entirely created by Shi Zhenlin, including her life and work. (See my earlier discussion in chapter 5.) Through a careful reading of the work, I agree with the speculations of Grace Fong and Zhou Wanyao (a Chinese scholar mentioned in Fong's 1997 essay). Behind the aestheticized and partly fictionalized veil of Shuangqing's persona in the *Random Records,* there was a talented rural woman poet who sings to us "across cultural and temporal boundaries" with a voice that belongs unquestionably to Shuangqing and to her alone (Fong 1997, 281).

8. Shuangqing's lyric song "Moyu'r" implies that her girlfriend Han Xi has fragrant shoes and pointed prints: "Beyond the lonely mountain haze, sky light blue / Where strips of moss are dry, fragrant shoes can tread. / Sharp [pointed] prints left on the purplish mud still soft" (in Ropp n.d.).

9. All the translations of Shuangqing's lyric songs here are modified from Grace Fong's version (1994). Much of my analysis of Shuangqing's lyrics is indebted to Fong's essay.

10. All translations of *nu shu* are mine unless otherwise noted.

11. The Chinese word for embroidery is *xiu.* Its original meaning is painting with colors. Embroidery patterns are denoted by the term *wen.*

12. There was no private mail service at that time. All *nu shu* letters were hand delivered by women friends or relatives.

13. In the *nu shu* text, Zhu Yingtai travels from Sichuan to Hangzhou to seek education. The road is extremely hard and long. The poet Li Po wrote the famous poem on the path: "How steep the road of Shu [Sichuan]! / Steeper than the road to heaven." But Zhu Yingtai shows no difficulty traveling alone on her bound feet. (Since all Jiangyong women in the old days bound their feet, and references to lotus feet appear everywhere in their texts, we could assume that the heroine is also tiny-footed, although it is not mentioned in this text.) On the way to the city, she meets Liang and initiates a conversation with him. They become sworn brothers, sharing the same studies and bed. At night, when she goes to bed in her clothing, Liang begins to suspect her. She agrees to take them off, but only if she can place four bowls of water around her. If the water spills, she will have to be whipped forty times. She tells him that it was a promise she made to her parents to show her determination to study hard and not to fool around with other students. The method prevents Liang from touching her body.

Later, when Shanbo sees Yingtai go to bathroom sitting down, he begins to doubt again. She replies that those who stand to urinate are animals, and those who sit down are gods. In the morning, when she washes up, she exposes her breasts. To answer Shanbo's question, she makes up the story that men who have big breasts have good fortunes. They are destined to pass the exams and rise to high positions. Men with flat chests, however, are ill fortuned. Again, her stories are so convincing that Liang Shanbo swallows everything with wide eyes. After three years, Yingtai decides to go home. She throws a bunch of riddles at Shanbo, giving him hints that she is a woman, that she has loved him and wants him to send a matchmaker to her parents. When Shanbo finally discovers Yingtai's identity and gender and sends his mother to ask for the match, he is three days too late. Yingtai's father has already engaged her to the Ma family. Yingtai predicts that Shanbo will die soon and tells his mother to bury him at a specific spot so that she can visit the grave later. On her way to her future husband's family, she stops at the tomb, orders it opened, and unites with her lover as a pair of mandarin ducks. Throughout the story, the young girl makes her way in the world utilizing her quick wit and sharp tongue.

7. From Golden Lotus to Prime Minister

1. Chen Duansheng had planned to write the play in one hundred chapters, twenty volumes, but stopped at the seventeenth volume. After Chen's death, Liang Chusheng (in late Qing period) completed the play.

2. Nancy Hodes (1990) divides *tan ci* into three categories: performance (no text involved), performance-related texts (prompting books for performers), and simulated *tan ci* (texts created purely for reading). Hu Siao-Chen (1994, 3) puts *Zai sheng yuan* into the category of the simulated *tan ci* or Zhao Jingshen's *wenci*. It is true that there is no record of *Zai sheng yuan* being performed during Chen's lifetime. But considering that the text was published much later after the author's

death, it is hard to imagine that it could have reached its popularity and widespread visibility only as a hand-copied script among elite women of the inner chambers. It is quite possible that parts of the text were performed in private households.

3. This and all other translations of Chen's text are mine.

4. In *Lun Zai sheng yuan* (1980) Chen Yingke has traced and located the author through her verses that open each chapter of *Zai sheng yuan,* in which she embeds her autobiographical details as well as the time of the writing. Like many of the male vernacular *xiaoshuo* (novel) writers, women *tan ci* writers remain anonymous, mostly due to the controversy over women's writing. But many of them also incorporate their personal information in the prefaces and anecdotes as well as in the opening verses for each chapter. For them, *tan ci* becomes a vehicle and space for their imagination and ambition. See Hu Siao-Chen (1994, chap. 2) for more analysis.

5. *Yu chuan yuan,* a *tan ci* for which Chen Duansheng wrote the sequel *Zai sheng yuan,* was believed to be a collaboration between mother and daughter. See Hu Siao-Chen (1994, chap. 2) for more details.

6. Chen Duansheng was married to Fan Tan, an intellectual in Shaoxing (in the Jiangnan area), and she gave birth to a daughter and a son. When she turned thirty, her husband was caught hiring someone to take the exam in his name and was exiled to Yili in Xinjiang to grow vegetables for soldiers as a slave. Alone, she raised the two children and took care of her husband's mother.

7. Jean-Jacques Rousseau's notion of writing as supplement and speech as origin is reversed here: poetry/writing becomes the origin of Chinese civilization whereas speech (dialects, folk literature) is regarded as something added on, as supplemental. But Jacques Derrida's theory about writing and speech (1981, 76) is still applicable (though the names need to be reversed) to Chen Duansheng's case. *Tan ci,* which represents oral, illiterate, low, and female, can be compensatory, a supplement to writing, only because poetry (meaning writing, knowledge, essence, male) has always already suffered from an innate absence. Supplementation is possible only because of an original lack.

8. A style (or poetic) name *(hao),* which symbolizes something about the person, is sometimes adopted by a person in adulthood. The given name *(ming)* is chosen at birth; a courtesy name *(zi)* would be chosen in adolescence or at the onset of adulthood, often by the father, to reflect something about the person.

9. As Judith Butler points out, "To have a name is to be positioned within the Symbolic, the idealized domain of kinship, a set of relationships structured through sanction and taboo which is governed by the law of the father and the prohibition against incest. For Lacan, names, which are emblematic and institute this paternal law, sustain the integrity of the body. What constitutes the integral body is not a natural boundary or organic telos, but the law of kinship that works through the name. . . . To be named is thus to be included into that law and to be formed, bodily, in accordance with that law" (1993, 72).

8. The Fabric of Masquerade

1. To avoid confusion for the names and genders of Meng Lijun/Li Mingtang in this chapter, I use the name *Meng Lijun* when I describe and analyze the character before she becomes a transvestite and the name *Li Mingtang* when I talk about the transvestite. Throughout this chapter, I will use *she* for both for the sake of convenience and clarity.

2. It seems that phobia of female transvestism is not restricted to China. On October 13, 1998, the *Star Tribune,* the Minneapolis daily newspaper, quoted the following news from the Associated Press after college student Matthew Shepard was found beaten to death in Wyoming for being gay: "In December 1993, Teena Brandon, a 21-year-old woman who often dressed as a man, was shot to death in her Nebraska home by John Lotter and Marvin Thomas Nissen. One week before the killing, the duo raped her as punishment for convincing friends she was a man."

3. The original was written in prose to indicate that the protagonist is speaking in dialogue.

4. It is similar to the trick played by Living Sufferer in Feng Jicai's novel *The Three-Inch Golden Lotus* (1986). He peels off the lower halves of his master's antique paintings and replaces them with the fake. He is able to fool his master, an expert at identifying forgeries, because the master only unrolls half of the painting whenever he checks his collections. Living Sufferer then switches the other real parts for the fake and sells them as the originals. Living Sufferer's success partly depends on his skill of mixing the real with the forgery, and partly on his master's habit of seeing a part as the whole.

5. Active in the Warring States Period (475–221 B.C.), Su Qin was known for his speech skills. He was sent by Lord Yan to the state of Qi as a spy, where he rose to the position of prime minister. When he was exposed, he was given the *chelie* death sentence—torn asunder by five horse carts.

6. Face changing is no longer limited to the fantasies of science fiction and cinema. Advances in technology have already made it a possibility. The *Minneapolis Star Tribune* printed the following brief news item on October 7, 1998: "Just days after the world's first arm transplant, a group of U.S. surgeons said the medical achievement could lead to another type of transplant: a face transplant. Jon Barker and plastic surgeons at the University of Louisville in Kentucky said recently in *New Scientist* that improvements in anti-rejection drug therapy make a full-face transplant possible. Such transplants could benefit people whose faces are damaged by fire, traffic accidents, animal attacks or disease, he said. He dismissed fears that the operation would allow the wealthy to get the face of their choice from a dead person. "That type of thing is more from science-fiction movies," he said.

7. Chu's text explains how to tell the homologous patterns of yin-yang gender opposition through the pulse: "The male's yang pulse movement follows an ascending path in compliance [with cosmic direction], and the Vital Gate [is felt] at

the foot position of the right hand. . . . The female's yin pulse movement follows a descending path against the direction [of cosmic influences], so that the nadir and the Gate of Life [are felt] at the inch position of the left hand" (quoted in Furth 1991, 53).

Conclusion

1. The oldest and most popular story is that of Liang Shanbo and Zhu Yingtai. Zhu Yingtai kept giving Liang Shanbo hints about her transvestite masquerade. As long as he didn't realize it, he was fine; once he knew that the person with whom he had been sleeping in the same bed and sharing the same table at school was a woman, who was now forever out of his reach (she was now engaged to another man), he died of despair. His death led to her suicide at his grave. The Qing novelist Pu Songling also wrote numerous transvestite tales in his *Strange Records from the Chatting Studies.* One tale, which he later expanded into a play, describes a young woman, Shang Sanguan, who masquerades as a male entertainer to avenge her father's murder. She seduces a village bully, her father's murderer, who takes her to his home for the night. In the morning, servants discover the bully dead in his bed, his head cut off, and the young "boy" hanging from the ceiling. While moving the body, the servants feel the emptiness of the boy's boots and pull them off. To their surprise, they find a pair of white shoes as tiny as hooks. The boy is in fact a girl.

Bibliography

Primary Works

Cai fei lu. 1936. Ed. Yao Lingxi. Tianjin: Shidai gongsi. Reprint.

Cai fei lu di san bian. 1936. Ed. Yao Lingxi. Tianjin: Tianjin shuju.

Cai fei lu xu bian. 1936. Ed. Yao Lingxi. Tianjin: Shidai gongsi.

Cai fei lu di si bian. 1938. Ed. Yao Lingxi. Tianjin: Tianjin shuju.

Chen Duansheng. 1982. *Zai sheng yuan*, ed. Zhao Jingsheng. Henan: Zhongzhou shuhuashe.

Feng Jicai. 1986. *San cun jin lian*. Tianjin: Baihua chubanshe.

———. 1994. *The Three-Inch Golden Lotus*, trans. David Wakefield. Honolulu: University of Hawaii Press.

Gao Yinxian and Yi Nianhua. 1991. *Nu shu*, ed. Gong Zhebin. Taipei: Funu xinzhi jijinhui chubanshe.

He Shuangqing. 1935. Tune: "Shi lo yi." In *Xi qing san ji*, Shi Zhenlin. *Zhongguo wenxue zhenben congshu*, series 1, vol. 5. Shanghai: Shanghai zazhi gongsi.

Lanlin Xiao Xiao Sheng. 1982. *Jin ping mei cihua*, 6th ed. Hong Kong: Hong Kong Taiping chubanshe.

———. 1955. *The Golden Lotus*, trans. Clement Egerton. 4 vols. London: Routledge & Kegan Paul.

Li Ruzhen. 1957. *Jing hua yuan* (Flowers in the Mirror). Taipei: Shijie chuban gongsi.

Li Yu (Mr. Qing Yin). 1657. *Yu pu tuan* (*Rou pu tuan* or *Jue hou chan*). Reprint of Ming edition. Taipei: Risheng chuban youxian gongsi.

———. 1990. *The Carnal Prayer Mat*, trans. Patrick Hanan. New York: Ballantine Books.

———. 1996. *Xian qing ou ji*, Qing edition. Beijing: Zuojia chubanshe.

Pu Songling. 1990. *Liao zhai zhi yi*, 3 vols. The *Quan zhu xue zhai liao zhai zhi yi* edition. Beijing: Zhongguo funu chubanshe. First appeared in 1751 as a hand-written copy.

Shi Zhenlin. 1987. *Xiqing sanji*. Beijing: Zhongguo shudian. Reprint.

Secondary Works

Abe, Kobo. 1980 [1964]. *The Face of Another,* trans. E. Dale Saunders. New York: Perigree Books.

Abel, Elizabeth, ed. 1982. *Writing and Sexual Difference.* Chicago: University of Chicago Press.

Apter, Emily. 1991. *Feminizing the Fetish: Psychoanalysis and Narrative Obsession in Turn-of-the-Century France.* Ithaca, N.Y.: Cornell University Press.

Apter, Emily, and William Pietz, eds. 1993. *Fetishism as Cultural Discourse.* Ithaca, N.Y.: Cornell University Press.

Bao Jialin, ed. 1991. *Zhongguo funu shi lunji xuji* (Collected Essays on the History of Chinese Women). Taiwan: Daoxiang chubanshe.

Bataille, Georges. 1991. "The Big Toe." In *Visions of Excess: Selected Writings, 1927–1939,* ed. and trans. Allan Stoekle. Minneapolis: University of Minnesota Press.

———. 1986. *Erotism: Death and Sensuality,* trans. Mary Dalwood. San Francisco: City Lights Books.

———. 1989. *Tears of Eros,* trans. Peter Connor. San Francisco: City Lights Books.

Baudrillard, Jean. 1988. "For a Critique of the Political Economy of the Sign." In *Selected Writings,* ed. Mark Poster. Stanford, Calif.: Stanford University Press.

———. 1983. *Simulations,* trans. Paul Foss, Paul Patton, and Philip Beitchman. New York: Columbia University Press.

Beal, Samuel, ed. and trans. 1906. *Buddhist Records of the Western World.* London.

Benjamin, Walter. 1978. "The Storyteller." In *Illuminations.* New York: Schocken Books.

Blake, Fred C. 1994. "Foot-Binding in Neo-Confucian China and the Appropriation of Female Labor." *Signs: Journal of Women and Society* 19, no. 3: 676–712.

Bray, Francesca. 1997. *Technology and Gender: Fabrics of Power in Late Imperial China.* Berkeley and Los Angeles: University of California Press.

Butler, Judith. 1993. *Bodies That Matter: On the Discursive Limits of "Sex."* New York: Routledge.

Cahill, Suzanne E. 1993. *Transcendence and Divine Passion: The Queen Mother of the West in Medieval China.* Stanford, Calif.: Stanford University Press.

Cao Xueqin. 1973. *The Story of the Stone: The Golden Days,* trans. David Hawkes. Harmondsworth: Penguin.

Carlitz, Katherine. 1994. "Desire, Danger, and the Body: Stories of Women's Virtue in Late Ming China." In *Engendering China: Women, Culture and the State,* ed. Christina K. Gilmartin, Gail Hershatter, Lisa Rofel, and Tyrene White. Cambridge: Harvard University Press.

Castle, Terry. 1986. *Masquerade and Civilization: The Carnivalesque in Eighteenth-Century English Culture and Fiction*. Stanford, Calif.: Stanford University Press.

Cha, Theresa Hak Kyung. 1995. *Dictee*. Berkeley, Calif.: Third Woman Press.

Chang, K. C., ed. 1977. *Food in Chinese Culture*. New Haven, Conn.: Yale University Press.

Chang, Kang-i Sun. 1980. *The Evolution of Chinese Tzu'u Poetry: From Late T'ang to Northern Sung*. Princeton, N.J.: Princeton University Press.

———. 1992. "A Guide to Ming-Ch'ing Anthologies of Female Poetry and Their Selection Strategies." *Gest Library Journal* 5, no. 2 (winter): 119–60.

———. 1990. *The Late Ming Poet Ch'en Tzu-lung: Crises of Love and Loyalism*. New Haven, Conn.: Yale University Press.

———. 1997. "Ming and Qing Anthologies of Women's Poetry." In *Writing Women in Late Imperial China,* ed. Ellen Widmer and Kang-i Sun Chang. Stanford, Calif.: Stanford University Press.

Chen Dongyuan. (1937) 1990. *Zhongguo funu shenghuo shi* (History of Chinese Women). Shanghai: Shanghai Wenyi Press.

Chen Yinke. 1980. "Lun *Zai sheng yuan*." In *Hanliu tang ji.* Shanghai: Shanghai guji.

Chow, Ray. 1991. *Woman and Chinese Modernity: The Politics of Reading between West and East*. Minneapolis: University of Minnesota Press.

Colette. 1967. *The Pure and the Impure,* trans. Herma Briffault. New York: Farrar, Straus, and Giroux.

Culler, Jonathan. 1982. *On Deconstruction: Theory and Criticism after Structuralism*. Ithaca, N.Y.: Cornell University Press.

Deleuze, Gilles. 1990. *Logique du sens,* trans. Mark Lester with Charles Stivale. New York: Columbia University Press.

Derrida, Jacques. 1981. *Positions*. Chicago: University of Chicago Press.

———. 1976. *Of Grammatology.* Baltimore: Johns Hopkins University Press.

Dong Jiazun. 1990. "Lidai jiefu lienu de tongji." In *Shoujie zaijia chanzu ji qita.* Shanxi: Shanxi renmin chubanshe.

Du Fangqin, ed. 1988. *Nuxing guannian de yanbian* (The Evolution of the Definitions about Womanhood). Henan: Henan renmin chubanshe.

———. 1993. *He Shuangqing ji.* Zhengzhou: Zhongzhou guji chubanshe.

Ebrey, Patricia Buckley. 1990. "Women, Marriage, and the Family in Chinese History." In *Heritage of China: Contemporary Perspectives on Chinese Civilization,* ed. Paul S. Ropp, 197–223. Berkeley and Los Angeles: University of California Press.

Ebrey, Patricia Buckley, and James L. Watson, eds. 1986. *Kinship Organization in Late Imperial China, 1000–1940*. Berkeley and Los Angeles: University of California Press.

Ensler, Eve. 1998. *The Vagina Monologues*. New York: Villard.

Erotic Art of China: A Unique Collection of Chinese Prints and Poems Devoted to the Art of Love. 1977. New York: Crown Publishers.

Feng Menglong. 1986. *Qingshi* (Anatomy of Love). Changsha: Yuelu shushe. Reprint.

Field, Adele M. 1887. *Pagoda Shadows.* London.

Fielding, William J. 1956. *Strange Customs of Courtship and Marriage.* New York.

Fong, Grace. 1994. "Engendering the Lyric." In *Voices of the Song Lyric in China,* ed. Pauline Yu. Berkeley and Los Angeles: University of California Press.

————. 1997. "De/Constructing a Feminine Ideal in the Eighteenth Century: *Random Records of West-Green* and the Story of Shuangqing." In *Writing Women in Late Imperial China,* ed. Ellen Widmer and Kang-i Sun Chang. Stanford, Calif.: Stanford University Press.

Forman, Werner, and Cottie A. Burland. 1970. *The Travels of Marco Polo.* New York: McGraw-Hill.

Foucault, Michel. 1978. *The History of Sexuality: An Introduction. Vol. 1,* trans. Robert Hurley. New York: Vintage Books.

Freeman, Michael. 1977. "Sung." In K. C. Chang 1977.

Freud, Sigmund. 1953–74. *The Standard Edition of the Complete Psychological Works of Sigmund Freud,* trans. James Strachey. 24 vols. London: Hogarth Press.

————. 1931. "Female Sexuality." In *Standard Edition,* 22:225–43.

————. 1933. "Femininity." In *Standard Edition,* 22:112–35.

————. 1927. "Fetishism." In *Standard Edition,* 22:152–57.

————. 1989. *The Pleasure Principle.* In *Standard Edition.*

Fu Xihua. 1959. *Mingdai chuanqi quanmu* (Complete Catalog of Ming Southern-Style Dramas). Shanghai: Renmin wenxue chubanshe.

————, ed. 1981. *Zhongguo gudian wenxue banhua xuanji* (Selected Wood Engravings from Classical Chinese Literature). 2 vols. Shanghai: Shanghai Renmin meishu chubanshe.

Furth, Charlotte. 1988. "Androgynous Males and Deficient Females: Biology and Gender Boundaries in Sixteenth- and Seventeenth-Century China." *Late Imperial China* 9, no. 2: 1–31.

————. 1986. "Blood, Body, and Gender: Medical Images of the Female Condition in China." *Chinese Science* 7:43–46.

————. 1994. "Rethinking van Gulik: Sexuality and Reproduction in Traditional Chinese Medicine." In Gilmartin and Hershatter 1994.

————. 1999. *A Flourishing Yin: Gender in China's Medical History, 960–1665.* Berkeley and Los Angeles: University of California Press.

Gamble, Sidney D. 1943. "The Disappearance of Footbinding in Tinghsien." *American Journal of Sociology* (September): 181–85.

Gao Dalun and Fan Yong, eds. 1987. *Zhongguo nuxing shi: 1851–1958* (History of Chinese Women: 1851–1958). Chendu: Sichuan daxue chubanshe.

Gao Hongxin. 1995. *Chan zu shi* (History of Footbinding). Shanghai: Shanghai Wenyi chubanshe.

Gao Yinxian and Yi Nianhua. 1991. *Nu shu* (Female Writing), ed. Gong Zhebing. Taipei: Funu xinzhi chubanshe.

Garber, Marjorie. 1993. *Vested Interests: Cross-Dressing and Cultural Anxiety.* New York: Harper Perennial.

Gates, Hill. 1989. "The Commoditization of Chinese Women." *Signs: Journal of Women in Culture and Society* 14, no. 4: 799–832.

Gilmartin, Christina K., and Gail Hershatter, eds. 1994. *Engendering China: Women, Culture and the State.* Cambridge: Harvard University Press.

Girard, René. 1979. *Violence and the Sacred,* trans. Patrick Gregory. Baltimore: Johns Hopkins University Press.

Grosz, Elizabeth. 1994. *Volatile Bodies: Toward a Corporeal Feminism.* Bloomington: Indiana University Press.

Gubar, Susan. 1982. "'The Blank Page' and the Issues of Female Creativity." In Abel 1982.

Guo Moruo. 1961. "On the First Seventeen Chapters of *Destiny of the Next Life* and Its Author Chen Duansheng." *Guangming Daily,* 5 May.

Hanan, Patrick. 1988. *The Invention of Li Yu.* Cambridge: Harvard University Press.

Hawkes, David, trans. 1959. *Ch'u Tz'u, The Songs of the South.* Oxford: Clarendon Press.

Hersey, George L. 1996. *The Evolution of Allure: Sexual Selection from the Medici Venus to the Incredible Hulk.* Cambridge: MIT Press.

Hinsch, Bret. 1990. *Passions of the Cut Sleeve: The Male Homosexual Tradition in China.* Berkeley, Calif.: University of California Press.

Hodes, Nancy. 1990. "Singing and Drumming the 'Three Smiles Romance': A Study of the Tanci Text." Ph.D. diss., Harvard University.

Hu Shi. 1971. "He Shuangqing kao" (Investigations on He Shuangqing). In *Hu Shi wencun* (Collected essays of Hu Shi), 3rd. ed. Taibei: Yuangdong tushu gongsi, 3:683–85.

Hu Siao-Chen. 1994. "Literary Tanci: A Woman's Tradition of Narrative in Verse." Ph.D. diss., Harvard University.

Huang Huajie. 1991. "Nao xinfang." In *Funu fengshu kao,* ed. Gao Hongxin and Xu Jiangjun. Shanghai: Shanghai wenyi chubanshe.

Irigaray, Luce. 1980. "When Our Lips Speak Together," trans. Carolyn Burke. *Signs* 6, no. 1 (autumn): 69–79.

Jia Shen. 1990 [1929]. "Zhonghua funu chanzu kao." In *Shoujie zaijia chanzu ji qita.* Shanxi: Shanxi renmin chubanshe.

Jia Yi, ed. 1937. *Xin shu.* Shanghai: Shangwu yinshuguan.

Jiang Xiaoyuan. 1989a. *Xing zai gudai zhongguo—dui yizhong wenhua de tansuo* (Sex in Ancient China—Research on a Cultural Phenomenon). Zhejiang: Zhejiang renmin chubanshe.

———. 1989b. *Zhongguoren de xing shengmi* (The Mystery of Sex in China). Beijing: Keji chubanshe.

Kang Zhengguo. 1988. *Fengsao yu yanqing* (A Study of Chinese Classical Poetry by Women and on Women). Zhengzhou: Henan renmin chubanshe.

———. 1994. "Bianyuan wenren de cainu qingjie jiqi suo chuanda de shiyi: *Xiqing sanji* chutan" (The "Talented Woman Complex" of the Marginalized Literatus and Its Poetic Flavor: The Case of *Xiqing sanji*). *Jiuzhou xuekan* (Chinese Culture Quarterly) 6, no. 2 (summer): 87–104.

Ko, Dorothy. 1994. *Teachers of the Inner Chambers: Women and Culture in Seventeenth-Century China.* Stanford, Calif.: Stanford University Press.

———. 1997a. "The Body as Attire: The Shifting Meanings of Footbinding in Seventeenth-Century China." *Journal of Women's History* 8, no. 4: 9–27.

———. 1997b. "The Written Word and the Bound Foot." In *Writing Women in Late Imperial China,* ed. Ellen Widmer and Kang-i Sun Chang. Stanford, Calif.: Stanford University Press.

Kroll, Eric, ed. 1995. *Bizarre.* 26 vols. Cologne and New York: Taschen.

Kukai. 1990. "Singing Image of Fire." In *The Ink Dark Moon: Love Poems by Oro Komachi and Izumi Shikibu, Women of the Ancient Court of Japan,* trans. Jane Hirshfield with Mariko Aratani. New York: Vintage.

Lacan, Jacques. 1977. *Ecrits: A Selection,* trans. Alan Sheridan. New York: Norton.

Lacan, Jacques, and Wladimir Granoff. 1956. "Fetishism: The Symbolic, the Imaginary and the Real." In *Perversions, Psychodynamics, and Therapy,* ed. Sandor Lorand. London: Tavistock.

Laing, Ellen Johnston. 1988. "Wives, Daughters, and Lovers: Three Ming Dynasty Women Painters." In *Views from Jade Terrace,* ed. Marsha Smith Weidner et al. Indianapolis: Indianapolis Museum of Art/Rizzoli International Publications.

———. 1990. "Women Painters in Traditional China." In Weidner 1990.

Lecercle, Jean-Jacques. 1990. *The Violence of Language.* London: Routledge.

Leclerc, Annie. 1982. "La Parole de femme." In Abel 1982.

Legge, James, trans. 1967. *Li Chi: Book of Rites,* ed. F. Max Muller. New York: University Books.

———, trans. 1983. *Confucian Analects (Lun Yi).* In *The Chinese Classics,* vol. 1. Oxford: Clarendon Press.

Lévi-Strauss, Claude. 1983. *The Raw and the Cooked,* vol. 1, trans. John and Doreen Weightman. Chicago: University of Chicago Press.

Levy, Howard S. 1992 [1966]. *The Lotus Lovers: The Complete History of the Curious Erotic Custom of Footbinding in China.* Buffalo, N.Y.: Prometheus.

Li Yanshou. n.d. *Nanshi.* 80 volumes. Taipei: Yiwen yinshu guan (photolithography edition).

Lin Tai-Yi, trans. 1965. *Flowers in the Mirror.* Berkeley and Los Angeles: University of California Press.

Lin Yutang. 1995. *My Country and My People.* Beijing: Zuojia chubanshe.

Little, Mrs. Archibald. 1899. *Intimate China.* London.

Liu Qingan. 1971. *Geyao yu funu* (Folk songs and women). Taipei: Orient Cultural Service.

Liu Ruoyu. 1935. *Zhuozhongzhi*. Shanghai: Commercial Press. Reprint.

Liu Xiang. 1988. *Gu lienu zhuan* (Biographies of Ancient Exemplary Women). Henan: Henan renmin chubanshe.

Lu Tonglin. 1991. *Rose and Lotus: Narrative of Desire in France and China*. Albany, N.Y.: SUNY Press.

Luo Chongqi. 1990. *Zhongguo xieshi* (History of Chinese Shoes). Shanghai: Shanghai keji chubanshe.

Mann, Susan. 1991. "Grooming a Daughter for Marriage: Brides and Wives in the Mid-Ch'ing Period." In *Marriage and Inequality in Chinese Society*, ed. R. S. Watson and P. B. Ebrey. Berkeley and Los Angeles: University of California Press.

———. 1994. "The Education of Daughters in the Mid-Ch'ing Period." In *Education and Society in Late Imperial China, 1600–1900*, ed. Benjamin Elman and Alexander Woodside. Berkeley and Los Angeles: University of California Press.

McMahon, Keith. 1995. *Miser, Shrews, and Polygamists*. Durham, N.C.: Duke University Press.

Meng Yuanlao, ed. 1957. *Dongjing meng hua lu*. Shanghai: Gudian wenxue chuban she.

"Ming Zhang Ruiyan gong (Wenling) nian pu" (Chronicles of Mr. Zhang Ruiyan's [Zhang Wenling's] life in the Ming). n.d. In *Xinbian Zhongguo minren nianpu jichen* (New Edition of Collected Chronicles of Chinese Who's Who).

Mote, Frederick W. 1977. "Yüan and Ming." In K. C. Chang 1977.

Nan shi (History of the Southern Song). n.d. Taipei: *Yiwen yinshuguan* (photo-lithography edition).

Polo, Marco. 1938. *The Description of the World*, 2 vols., trans. A. C. Moule and Paul Pelliot. London.

Rawski, Evelyn S. 1985. "Economic and Social Foundations of Late Imperial Culture." In *Popular Culture in Late Imperial China*, ed. David G. Johnson, Andrew J. Nathan, and Evelyn S. Rawski, 3–33. Berkeley and Los Angeles: University of California Press.

Rich, Adrienne. 1976. *Of Woman Born: Motherhood as Experience and Institution*. New York: Norton.

Riviere, Joan. 1989. "Womanliness as a Masquerade." In *Formations of Fantasy*, ed. Victor Burgin, James Donal, and Cora Kaplan. London and New York: Routledge.

Ropp, Paul S. 1993. "Love, Literacy, and Laments: Themes of Women Writers in Late Imperial China. *Women's History Review* 2: 107–41.

———. 1992. "Voicing the Feminine: Constructions of the Gendered Subject in Lyric Poetry by Women of Medieval and Late Imperial China." *Late Imperial China* 13 (June): 63–110.

———. 1994. "Women in Late Imperial China: A Review of Recent English-Language Scholarship." *Women's History* 3:12.

———. 1976. "The Seeds of Change: Reflections on the Condition of Women in the Early and Mid Ch'ing." *Signs* 2, no. 1: 5–23.

———. n.d. "Search for a Banished Immortal: China's Peasant Woman Poet Shuangqing." Unpublished manuscript.

Ropp, Paul S., ed. 1990. *Heritage of China: Contemporary Perspectives on Chinese Civilization.* Berkeley and Los Angeles: University of California Press.

Scarry, Elaine. 1985. *The Body in Pain: The Making and Unmaking of the World.* New York: Oxford University Press.

Scheper-Hughes, Nancy, and Margaret Lock. 1987. "The Mindful Body: A Prolegomenon to Future Work in Medical Anthropology." *Medical Anthropology Quarterly* 1, no. 1: 6–41.

Shen Defu. 1827. *Wanli yehuo bian.* Guangzhou: Fuli shangang.

Shen Fu. 1960. *Chapters from a Floating Life: The Autobiography of Chinese Artist,* trans. Shirley M. Black. London: Oxford University Press.

Shen Yixiu. 1935. *Lichui ji* (Oriole tunes). In *Wumengtang quanji, shang* (Complete Works from the Hall of Meridian Dreams), ed. Ye Shaoyuan. Shanghai: Beiye Shanfang.

Shen Yixiu, ed. 1935 [1636]. *Yirensi (Her meditations).* In *Wumengtang quanji, shang* (Complete Works from the Hall of Meridian Dreams), ed. Ye Shaoyuan. Shanghai: Beiye Shanfang.

Silber, Cathy. 1991. "From Daughter to Daughter-in-Law in the Women's Script *(Nushu)* of Southern Hunan." Unpublished manuscript, Asian Language and Cultures, University of Michigan, Ann Arbor.

Stratton, John. 1996. *The Desirable Body: Cultural Fetishism and Erotics of Consumption.* Manchester: Manchester University Press.

T'ein, Ju-kang. 1988. *Male Anxiety and Female Chastity: A Comparative Study of Chinese Ethical Values in Ming-Ch'ing Times.* Leiden: E. J. Brill.

Tsai, Shih-shan Henry. 1996. *The Eunuchs in the Ming Dynasty.* Albany: SUNY Press.

Van Gulik, R. H. 1961. *Sexual Life in Ancient China.* Leiden.

Veblen, Thorstein. 1992 [1899]. *The Theory of the Leisure Class.* New Brunswick, N.J.: Transaction Publishers.

Waltner, Ann, and Pi-ching Hsu. 1997. "Lingering Fragrance: the Poetry of Tu Yaose and Shen Tiansun." *Journal of Women's History* 8, no. 4:28–51.

Wang Renxiang. 1994. *Yinshi yu Zhongguo wenhua* (Food and Chinese Culture). Beijing: Renmin chubanshe.

Wang Yongkuan. 1991. *Zhongguo gudai kuxing* (Torture in Ancient China). Taipei: Yunlong Press.

Watt, James C. Y. 1987. "The Literati Environment." In *The Chinese Scholar's Studio: Artistic Life in the Late Ming Period,* ed. Chu-tsing Li and James C. Y. Watt. New York: Asia Society Galleries.

Weidner, Marsha Smith, ed. 1990. *Flowering in the Shadows: Women in the History of Chinese and Japanese Painting.* Honolulu: University of Hawaii Press.

West, Stephen H. 1972. "Studies in Chin Dynasty (1115–1234) Literature." Ph.D. diss., University of Michigan.

Widmer, Ellen. 1992. "Xiaoqing's Literary Legacy and the Place of the Woman Writer in Late Imperial China." *Late Imperial china* 13, no. 1: 1–31.

Wong, Jan. 1996. *Red China Blues.* Toronto: Doubleday.

Wu Hong. 1997. "Beyond Stereotypes." In *Writing Women in Late Imperial China,* ed. Ellen Widmer and Kang-I Sun Chang. Stanford, Calif.: Stanford University Press.

Wu Qingyun. 1995. *Female Rule in Chinese and English Literary Utopias.* New York: Syracuse University Press.

Wu Yenna. 1988. "The Inversion of Marital Hierarchy: Shrewish Wives and Henpecked Husbands in Seventeenth-Century Chinese Literature." *Harvard Journal of Asiatic Studies* 48: 363–82.

Xiang yan cong shu (Collection of the Fragrant and the Beautiful). 1914. 20 vols. Shanghai: Guoxue fulunshe.

Xie Zhaozhe. 1959. *Wu za zu* (Five Miscellanies). Ming edition. Shanghai: Zhonghua shuju.

Xu Song, ed. 1957 [1809]. *Song hui yao zhi gao.* Beijing: Zhonghua shuju.

Ye Shaoyuan, ed. 1935. "Bairi ji shen anren wen." In *Wumengtang quanji, shang* (Complete works from the Hall of Meridian Dreams), ed. Ye Shaoyuan. Shanghai: Beiye Shanfang.

Ye Xiaoluan. 1935. *Fanshen xiang* (Fragrance Reborn). In *Wumengtang quanji, shang* (Complete works from the Hall of Meridian Dreams), ed. Ye Shaoyuan. Shanghai: Beiye Shanfang.

Yu qiao hua Zhen Man ben muo: Gu xue hui kan (Zhen Man's Story). In Wang Yongkuan 1991.

Yuan Mei. 1943. *Du wai yu yan: Eminent Chinese of the Ch'ing Period,* trans. Arthur W. Hummel. Washington, D. C.

Zeitlin, Judith T. 1993. *Historian of the Strange: Pu Songling and the Chinese Classical Tale.* Stanford, Calif.: Stanford University Press.

Zhang Gen and Guo Hancheng, eds. 1992. *Zhongguo xiqu tong shi* (History of Chinese Drama). Beijing: Zhongguo xiju chubanshe.

Zhao Jingshen. 1960. *Tanci kaozheng.* Taipei: Commercial.

Zhao Xingqin. 1986. "Cai yu mei: Mingmo Qingchu xiaoshuo chutan" (Talent and Beauty: A Preliminary Investigation from Novels in the Late Ming–Early Qing Period). In *Ming-Qing xiaoshuo luncong* (Studies in Ming-Qing Fiction), vol. 4. Shengyang: Chunfang wenyi chubanshe.

Zheng Guangyi, ed. 1991 [1750]. *Zhongguo lidai cainu shige jianshang cidian.* Beijing: Zhongguo gongren chubanshe.

Zheng Zhenduo. 1996. *Zhongguo suwenxue shi.* Beijing: Dongfang chubanshe.

Zhou Mi., ed. 1957. *Wuln jiushi.* Shanghai: Gudian wenxue chubanshe.

Zhu Peichu. 1987. *Zhongguo de cixiu* (Chinese Embroidery). Beijing: Renmin chubanshe.

Index

Created by Eileen Quam

WANG PING is assistant professor of English at Macalester College. Her publications include a collection of short stories, *American Visa*; a novel, *Foreign Devil*; and a book of poetry, *Of Flesh and Spirit*. She is also the editor and cotranslator of *New Generation: Poetry from China Today*.